THE BEDFORD SERIES IN HISTORY AND CULTURE

The Nuremberg
War Crimes Trial 1945–46
A Brief History with Documents

SECOND EDITION

Michael R. Marrus

University of Toronto

bedford/st.martin's
Macmillan Learning
Boston | New York

For Bedford/St. Martin's

Vice President, Editorial, Macmillan Learning Humanities: Edwin Hill
Program Director for History: Michael Rosenberg
Senior Program Manager for History: Laura Arcari
History Marketing Manager: Melissa Rodriguez
Director of Content Development: Jane Knetzger
Assistant Editor: Melanie McFadyen
Associate Editor: Mary Posman Starowicz
Content Project Manager: Lidia MacDonald-Carr
Workflow Manager: Lisa McDowell
Production Supervisor: Robert Cherry
Media Project Manager: Michelle Camisa
Manager of Publishing Services: Andrea Cava
Project Management: Lumina Datamatics, Inc.
Composition: Lumina Datamatics, Inc.
Director of Rights and Permissions: Hilary Newman
Permissions Manager: Kalina Inghman
Senior Art Director: Anna Palchik
Cover Design: William Boardman
Cover Photo: Herman Goering (1893–1946), Rudolf Hess (1894–1987), Joachim von
    Ribentrop (1893–1946) and Wilhelm Kietel (1882–1946) at the Nuremberg Trials,
    1945–46 (photo)/ American Photographer, (20th century)/Private Collection/
    Bridgeman Images
Printing and Binding: LSC Communications

2 1 0 9 8 7
f   e   d   c   b   a

For information, write: Bedford/St. Martin's, 75 Arlington Street, Boston, MA 02116

ISBN 978-1-319-09484-3

Acknowledgments
*Text acknowledgments and copyrights appear at the back of the book on pages 279–80,
which constitute an extension of the copyright page. Art acknowledgments and copyrights
appear on the same page as the art selections they cover.*

    At the time of publication all Internet URLs published in this text were found to
accurately link to their intended Web site. If you do find a broken link, please forward the
information to history@macmillan.com so that it can be corrected for the next printing.

*For Randi, and for Jeremy, Naomi, and Adam,
and Alan, Noah, Aaron, and Judah*

Foreword

The Bedford Series in History and Culture is designed so that readers can study the past as historians do.

The historian's first task is finding the evidence. Documents, letters, memoirs, interviews, pictures, movies, novels, or poems can provide facts and clues. Then the historian questions and compares the sources. There is more to do than in a courtroom, for hearsay evidence is welcome, and the historian is usually looking for answers beyond act and motive. Different views of an event may be as important as a single verdict. How a story is told may yield as much information as what it says.

Along the way the historian seeks help from other historians and perhaps from specialists in other disciplines. Finally, it is time to write, to decide on an interpretation and how to arrange the evidence for readers.

Each book in this series contains an important historical document or group of documents, each document a witness from the past and open to interpretation in different ways. The documents are combined with some element of historical narrative—an introduction or a biographical essay, for example—that provides students with an analysis of the primary source material and important background information about the world in which it was produced.

Each book in the series focuses on a specific topic within a specific historical period. Each provides a basis for lively thought and discussion about several aspects of the topic and the historian's role. Each is short enough (and inexpensive enough) to be a reasonable one-week assignment in a college course. Whether as classroom or personal reading, each book in the series provides firsthand experience of the challenge—and fun—of discovering, recreating, and interpreting the past.

Lynn Hunt
David W. Blight
Bonnie G. Smith

Preface

"The greatest trial in history" was how the distinguished English jurist Sir Norman Birkett described the Nuremberg War Crimes Trial, the trial of twenty-two high-ranking Nazi defendants before the International Military Tribunal, made up of American, British, French, and Soviet judges meeting in Nuremberg between November 1945 and October 1946. A prodigious undertaking, conducted in four languages, the Nuremberg War Crimes Trial involved 403 open sessions over the course of a year. The tribunal heard 94 witnesses in court (33 for the prosecution and 61 for the defense) and received written responses to interrogatories of an additional 143. To deal with accused organizations—including the Reich Cabinet, the SS, the Gestapo, and the German Armed Forces High Command—the tribunal heard 22 witnesses and received tens of thousands of affidavits from across Germany. The Nuremberg tribunal scrutinized thousands of pages of documents, largely gleaned from the huge hoard of Nazi material captured by the Allied armies at the end of the war. Lawyers for both sides submitted document collections—prosecution document books, defense document books, rebuttal books compiled by the prosecution to contest defense document collections—plus briefs and motions having to do with the conduct of the trial.

What was this celebrated trial actually like? At times, it was grave and solemn—one of the awesome chapters in the history of our terrible century, providing ample evidence for Birkett's assessment. But it was also imperfect—hastily improvised, tainted with politics, and inadequate to the great expectations of many that it would be a turning point in world history.

Seeking a balanced view, this book looks at the Nuremberg Trial historically, examining both the high and the low, the memorable and the quotidian, the positive and the negative. It sets the trial in its historical context, understanding Nuremberg as an event framed in the intellectual and material circumstances of the immediate post–World War II period—when the wounds of the war were still fresh, when the Cold

War had not yet begun, and when the ravages of Nazism were not yet fully understood. This new edition, prepared twenty years after its progenitor, adapts the text to the format used in more recent volumes in the Bedford Series in History and Culture, and also introduces some new documents and ideas, drawing upon considerable research on the topic conducted in recent decades.

In keeping with the aims of the Bedford Series in History and Culture, this book samples the trial material, keeping the volume of reading within the span of one or two weekly assignments in a college course. For the most part, this volume draws on records of the trial itself. In Part One, the Introduction surveys the subject as a whole. Its chapters outline the antecedents and background to the trial; trace the specific preparations made by representatives of the victorious powers and introduce the principal actors in the courtroom drama; and considers how the prosecution, the defense, and the judges dealt with the various counts against the accused. Part Two presents a selection of key documents from the period, many of which come from the trial's proceedings. These documents are, of course, only a sample. For a more complete sense of the rhythm and atmosphere of the trial as well as detail on specific issues, students may turn to the Nuremberg volumes themselves, guided by the chronological and subject index in volume 23. In addition, the Chronology, Questions for Consideration, and Selected Bibliography, revised for this edition, provide further pedagogical aids at the end of this volume.

ACKNOWLEDGMENTS

I offer special thanks to Natalie Zemon Davis, co-editor of the first edition, who invited me to prepare a quite different volume for this collection and who supported the project enthusiastically once my course was set. It is a pleasure as well to acknowledge the help of colleagues and friends who provided assistance at various points along the way: Jean-Marc Béraud, Doris Bergen, Michael Burns, Vicki Caron, Lawrence Douglas, David Dyzenhaus, Roger Errera, David Fraser, Martin Friedland, Dominique Gros, Peter Hayes, Natalia Lebedeva, Wendy Lower, Randi Marrus, Michael Phayer, Ron Pruessen, Beverley Slopen, Denis Smyth, Peter Solomon, Richard Weisberg, and Rebecca Wittmann. Jonathan Bush, one of the most distinguished interpreters of the Nuremberg proceedings, has been especially helpful in my understanding of recent developments in Nuremberg scholarship, and I am happy to acknowledge his generous assistance here. I am grateful as well for the help of the following people from Bedford/St. Martin's: Program Director for History Michael Rosenberg; Senior Program Manager Laura Arcari; History Marketing Manager Melissa Rodriguez; Assistant Editor Melanie McFadyen; Associate Editor Mary Posman Starowicz; Content Project Manager Lidia MacDonald-Carr; Cover Designer William Boardman; Project Manager Sumathy Kumaran of Lumina Datamatics.

Michael R. Marrus

Contents

Illustrations

PART ONE

Introduction:
Introduction to the
Nuremberg Trial

*The wrongs which we seek to condemn and punish have been so calcu-
lated, so malignant, and so devastating, that civilization cannot tolerate their being ignored, because it cannot survive their being repeated.
That four great nations, flushed with victory and stung with injury stay
the hand of vengeance and voluntarily submit their captive enemies to
the judgment of the law is one of the most significant tributes that Power
has ever paid to reason.*
— Robert H. Jackson, Chief Prosecutor for the United States,
Opening Address before the International Military Tribunal,
Nuremberg, November 21, 1945

HISTORICAL PRECEDENTS

The Nuremberg War Crimes trial reflected the widespread sense among
the anti-Nazi Allies in the Second World War that the terrible conflict
against Germany, the most destructive war in history, should not end
like other wars: It was not a calamity to be overcome, but an unprecedented crime to be punished. To the victors, Nazi war making appeared
indistinguishable from organized plunder, gratuitous destruction, and
unrestrained killing. From the beginning of the conflict, horrifying evidence of systematic atrocities on an unprecedented scale poured out of

occupied Europe. Reports referred to the uprooting and enslavement of entire populations, the slaughter of political opponents, prisoners of war, and ordinary people persecuted for reasons of race, religion, and nationality—all on a scale hitherto unimaginable. At the war's close, liberating troops encountered pitiful survivors from concentration and death camps, their wasted, skeletal appearance a sign of the terrible suffering and tortures they had endured. The number of these victims, it was learned, extended into many millions of men, women, and children.

In response to such horrors, Allied leaders promised that justice would be done when the guns went silent. Beginning in 1942, when news of wartime atrocities flooded Western news media, the leaders began several years of negotiations in order to formulate a common policy. Discussions intensified in 1944 when victory seemed near. These were still under way a year later, when the Allied troops broke into Germany itself and when the ferocious Allied aerial bombardment devastated German towns and cities, reducing them to rubble. Eventually the Allies decided on an international trial, to be held under the auspices of the four principal Allied powers—the Americans, British, French, and Soviets. After much discussion, they decided to hold the trial in the ruined Bavarian city of Nuremberg, in the American-occupied zone. Chosen partly for its symbolic significance—Nuremberg had in the early years been the heart of the Nazi movement—and also for practical reasons—the city had one of the few courthouses still standing in a heavily bombed Germany—Nuremberg became the site of the Allied judgment of the leaders of Nazi Germany. This year-long trial of the "major war criminals" became known as the Nuremberg Trial or the Nuremberg War Crimes Trial.[1]

How did the Allied leaders arrive at the idea of an international trial in Nuremberg? Seeking direction, policymakers consulted the historical record and pondered how they could do better than some of their predecessors after other wars. One of their prime references was the treatment of Napoleon Bonaparte in 1815. Particularly when justifying their decision to launch an elaborate judicial proceeding, Allied representatives contrasted their decision with that taken to deal with the defeated French emperor. Following the latter's escape from exile on the island of Elba, the victorious European powers issued a Declaration at Vienna, declaring Napoleon an international outlaw. Captured by the British after his defeat at Waterloo several months later, the emperor was dispatched to the remote island of St. Helena, where his incarceration was overseen by the European partners in the coalition against France. This arrangement, one authority noted, had some resemblance to the American, British, French, and Soviet control over the German war criminals eventually convicted at Nuremberg.[2] Napoleon was never tried, however. Allied representatives simply decided among themselves what they wanted to do with him. The disposition of his case represented one option for dealing with Nazi Germany by what came to be called "executive action"—dispensing with a trial altogether. In the mid-twentieth century, much harsher in its treatment of political foes than the early nineteenth, this meant summary execution.

Even more relevant to the planners of the Nuremberg Trial were the war crimes trials that occurred after the First World War, known as the Leipzig Trials of 1921. No one disputed that a repetition of this experience was to be avoided at all costs. Allied wartime propaganda promoted the idea that the First World War was an Allied crusade against a criminal coalition led by the German Empire. Some campaigners, particularly in England and France, issued fervent calls for retribution, spurred by colossal wartime devastation and staggering numbers of casualties. Responding to these pressures, London and Paris argued energetically for the prosecution of enemy war criminals. In practice, however, the task proved difficult and the Allies were deeply divided on the subject. The Americans were ambivalent, with President Woodrow Wilson fearful that a trial would generate resentment among the German people and might trigger a Communist revolution. "Had you rather have the Kaiser or the Bolsheviks?" he asked, in response to a campaign to bring the German kaiser, Wilhelm II, to the bar of justice. French leader Georges Clemenceau, for his part, wanted to try Wilhelm II and his son the crown prince, but not "great soldiers, who had merely obeyed orders." And the Italians differed among themselves, with Premier Vittorio Orlando wanting to see the kaiser hauled before an international court while his foreign minister, Sidney Sonino, opposed the idea of "making a scape-goat."[3] Allied disagreement thereafter hung over the war crimes issue like a dark cloud.

Timing was an additional problem. In what proved to be a major tactical error, Allied negotiators failed to determine a mechanism for the punishment of war criminals at the time of the armistice of 1918. Instead, they raised the issue only during the peace negotiations that began the following year and spent additional time negotiating among themselves about how to proceed. The 1919 peace conference at Paris consigned the problem of war crimes to an auspicious-sounding Commission of Responsibilities of the Authors of the War and the Enforcement of Penalties, sometimes known as the Commission of Fifteen, chaired by the U.S. secretary of state, Robert Lansing. Composed of fifteen distinguished international lawyers, two from each of the five major Allies — the United States, England, France, Italy, and Japan — and one each from five lesser powers, the commission met in Paris for several months. On the question of war crimes, debate was fierce and agreement proved impossible. At the root of the conflict was the Americans' opposition to international adjudication proposed by the British and French. As historian James Willis, the leading authority on this issue, notes,

> Lansing . . . opposed international punishment of war crimes, believing observance of the laws of war should be left to the discretion of military authorities of each state. Understandably, he did not generally articulate this viewpoint in public. Rather, he stressed the lack of precedent, opposed all innovations, and rejected virtually every important proposal offered by the Europeans.[4]

Finally, at the end of March 1919, the commission released its report, extending personal responsibility for war crimes even to heads of state. The report argued against the constitution of an international tribunal to try offenses related to the launching of a war of aggression but felt that an international "High Tribunal" was appropriate to try certain "violations of the laws and customs of war and of the laws of humanity." The report was not unanimously accepted, however: Spirited reservations were appended by the Americans, and further objection was added by the Japanese. The result was a remarkable display of Allied disunity, which was soon to have important consequences in undermining international war crimes prosecution (Document 1).

Strikingly, in view of the American promotion of an international trial twenty-five years later, the U.S. representatives in Paris in 1919 openly dissented from the majority report, showing real reluctance to join an international effort to prosecute German war criminals. Secretary of State Lansing and his colleague at the conference James Brown Scott argued for a restrictive approach, not only with respect to the role of an international tribunal and to the determination of who could properly be tried but also with respect to the idea of charging people with violating "the laws of humanity." The Paris peace conference, the dissenters reminded the others, had asked the Commission of Responsibilities to "report upon 'the facts as to breaches of the laws and customs of war committed by the forces of the German Empire and their Allies, on land, on sea and in the air, during the present war.'" Highly conservative in their legal reasoning, the U.S. representatives denounced the proposed international tribunal for the adjudication of war crimes (Document 2).

Notwithstanding American dissent, the representatives at the Paris peace conference agreed in the end to include four articles on war crimes in the Versailles treaty with Germany, signed in May 1919. These set the stage for a trial of the defeated kaiser before a specially constituted international court and for the appearance of other accused war criminals before military tribunals in individual Allied countries (Document 3). The trials contemplated in these articles never materialized, however. The government of the Netherlands, to which Wilhelm II had fled at the end of the war, refused to extradite the former German kaiser in 1920, despite the appeals of the Allies—a refusal undoubtedly facilitated by the Allies' own divisions over the matter. In addition, a new obstacle appeared when the German government refused to cooperate, despite having signed the treaty. Moved by a great wave of popular feeling against the idea of Allied military tribunals, the German political leadership denounced these articles as an unconscionable humiliation, a denunciation that fed Allied fears of a monarchical restoration or a Communist upheaval in Germany. Reluctantly, the Allies agreed to a compromise, worried over the stability of a German democratic regime defending itself against the allegation that its supporters had "stabbed Germany in the back" at the end of the world war.

The compromise agreement was that the Germans would try their own war criminals before their *Reichsgericht*, or supreme court, sitting in Leipzig. But from almost every standpoint, the results were unsatisfactory. Originally, the Allies proposed that the Germans deal with nearly nine hundred accused criminals. The Germans agreed to try forty-five, and only twelve were ever brought to court. Six were convicted. Of these, one was immediately released, while the others received very light sentences. And finally, of those convicted, several managed to escape from their German prisons. This outcome was, in the opinion of the *London Times*, a "scandalous failure of justice"—or, as Peter Calvocoressi, later a junior official at Nuremberg, put it, an "unjust and injudicial farce."[5] At the summer 1945 London planning conference for the Nuremberg Trial, the British negotiator and future prosecutor Sir David Maxwell-Fyfe took up the charge that the earlier proceedings were "a farce." British Foreign Minister Anthony Eden referred to them as an "ill-starred enterprise," and the chairman of the wartime United Nations War Crimes Commission branded them a "fiasco."[6] In his opening address to the Nuremberg Tribunal, the American prosecutor Robert Jackson mentioned that the trials after the First World War taught the victorious powers the "futility" of leaving adjudication to the vanquished.[7] As precedent, in the opinion of almost every Allied leader who remembered these events, the experience of the Leipzig trials was something strenuously to be avoided.

In the decade that followed, the catastrophic effects of warfare were never far from the thoughts of statesmen and jurists. Many of them sought by means of international agreements to relieve the great burden that the Great War (First World War) pressed upon the conscience of humanity. As in the half century before 1914, when the landmark Hague conventions of 1899 and 1907 had codified the "laws and customs of war," there were some efforts after First World War to humanize the impact of armed conflict: Several international accords built upon the Hague conventions, extending the range and enlarging the provisions of the earlier agreements. But opinion seemed far less keen on these achievements in the wake of the unprecedented carnage of the First World War than it had been before. For what was so terrible about that war, world leaders increasingly realized, was not so much the violation of established agreements on the conduct of warfare as the very launching of a world war by modern industrial societies. The scale of modern war far exceeded anything the world had previously known. Many agreed, therefore, with the declaration of an Inter-Parliamentary Union in 1931 that the "real policy of peace should be to prevent war, not to humanize it."[8] Translated into diplomatic terms, the result was a series of agreements addressing what were thought to be the causes of war and seeking to curb aggression. These efforts, part of the postwar drive for collective security, were frequently mentioned at Nuremberg.

Much of the effort to prevent aggression took place within the framework of the League of Nations, an international body established in the wake of the war, with a covenant that urged its signatories "to respect and preserve as against external aggression the territorial integrity and existing political independence of all Members of the League."[9] In 1924, the Assembly of the League unanimously approved a "Protocol for the Peaceful Settlement of International Disputes" that, among other things, condemned wars of aggression as international crimes. Unfortunately, this agreement was linked to disarmament negotiations that proved unsuccessful. As a result, the resolution remained an expression of opinion rather than a fully effective treaty. Not least of the problems with these and other diplomatic efforts was the absence at the table of the United States, whose government had rejected membership in the League of Nations after a bitter ratification fight.

The most comprehensive effort to legislate peace outside the League framework occurred in 1928, the final outcome of a grassroots campaign to outlaw war that was launched in the midwestern United States some five years before. Fired by religious idealism, the movement to achieve this laudable objective won the support of prominent American diplomats, politicians, and academics. "The essence of its appeal," notes a historian of the League, "was that war was not just an ordinary social abuse or crime to be repressed or prevented; it was *the* abuse, *the* crime, *the* evil *par excellence*. It was *the* great canker in modern civilization which must be eradicated at all costs." [10] Eventually the cause was taken up by U.S. Secretary of State Frank Kellogg and sold to the idealistic French premier Aristide Briand. The result was the Pact of Paris, or the Kellogg-Briand Pact, as it came to be called, which seemed to herald the dawn of a peaceful era.

Drafted with a view to what was widely believed to be the distaste of the American public for excessive diplomatic subtleties, the treaty was short and direct (Document 4). Signed by the representatives of fifteen governments including Germany, Italy, and Japan, the pact bound some sixty-five states by the time Hitler came to power. Much was made of the Kellogg-Briand Pact by the prosecution at Nuremberg, which held it to be the principal juridical basis by which Nazi aggression could be condemned. The pact was, in the words of the British attorney general and chief British prosecutor Sir Hartley Shawcross, a "great constitutional instrument of an international society awakened to the deadly dangers of another Armageddon"; or, as his French counterpart François de Menthon contended, it was "the fundamental charter of the law of war."[11] Highly idealistic, the Pact of Paris was nevertheless taken very seriously at the time by some statesmen, who believed it to be a landmark of international law. One of the most prominent of these was Henry L. Stimson who, as U.S. secretary of war, was the driving American force behind the idea of an international trial in 1945 and who, as secretary of state addressing the Council on Foreign Relations in 1932, had unwittingly prescribed the basis for the American charge against Germany thirteen years later (Document 5).

BACKGROUND

In the United States, the surprise attack on Pearl Harbor in December 1941 mobilized public opinion against the Japanese as the great source of Axis treachery and villainy. It thus took a considerable time for Nazi Germany to be stigmatized as a *criminal* enemy—an opponent whose conduct was outside the bounds of civilized behavior and the international rule of law. According to historian Bradley Smith, Americans remained aloof from the savagery of Nazi war making and occupation policy almost until the end of the war. Only the shock of the Battle of the Bulge, he argues, between December 1944 and January 1945, brought Americans face to face with the ruthless, inhuman cruelty of the Third Reich. Specifically, the massacre of some seventy helpless American prisoners by members of an SS panzer regiment near the Belgian village of Malmédy—a rather modest atrocity as Nazi crimes went, Smith says — turned Americans' feelings sharply against Nazism as an incorrigibly criminal enterprise.[12]

Europeans, of course, came sooner to that point because of their experience of Nazism and the ravages of war. Meeting at St. James's Palace in London in January 1942, the Czechs, Poles, Norwegians, Belgians, Dutch, Luxembourgers, French, Greeks, and Yugoslavs issued a joint declaration that denounced an occupation "regime of terror characterized amongst other things by imprisonments, mass expulsions, the execution of hostages and massacres." Declaring these atrocities to be in violation of "the laws and customs of land warfare," particularly the Hague convention of 1907, the signatories—referring to themselves as the Inter-Allied Conference on war crimes—committed themselves to "the punishment, through the channel of organized justice, of those guilty of or responsible for these crimes, whether they have ordered them, perpetrated them, or participated in them."[13] That spring and summer, terrible reports poured into Western capitals, detailing unimaginable horrors in Nazi-occupied Europe. Accounts documented the systematic murder of European Jews, then said to have involved hundreds of thousands killed and many more subjected to inhuman treatment. Desperate, the Inter-Allied Conference and many others appealed to the British and Americans to act. In response, the Allied leaders began to formulate their policies on war crimes. In the House of Commons on September 8, 1942, British Prime Minister Winston Churchill declared that "those who are guilty of the Nazi crimes 'will have to stand up before tribunals in every land where their atrocities have been committed in order that an indelible warning may be given to future ages.'" U.S. President Franklin Roosevelt declared it to be U.S. policy "that the successful close of the war shall include provision for the surrender to the United Nations of war criminals."[14] Reeling from the Wehrmacht's furious campaign in the East, the Soviet government denounced "the barbaric violation by the German Government of the elementary rules of international law." Foreign Minister Vyacheslav Molotov alluded to "the courts of the special international tribunal," which he said would "punish according to the severity of the criminal code, any of the leaders of Fascist Germany who in the course of the war have fallen into the hands of states fighting against Hitlerite Germany."[15]

Despite their references to trials, special international tribunals, courts, retribution, organized justice, and the like, the Allies were in fact quite uncertain how to proceed against Axis criminality, and particularly how to proceed together. While eager to publicize Nazi atrocities and to join in the denunciation of these crimes, London and Washington were reluctant to move too quickly. They were unwilling to give too much voice to the governments in exile, opposed to diverting war making resources into retaliatory exercises, feared German vengeance in the event of a too aggressive policy against war criminals, and felt uneasy about working with the Soviets on the issue. Moscow, feeling perhaps that it had less to lose, went ahead on its own, setting up an Extraordinary State Commission to investigate Nazi crimes on Soviet territory and staging its own trials in 1943. For their part, the British and Americans cautiously announced the establishment of a United Nations War Crimes Commission (UNWCC) to begin investigations. The UNWCC proved to be woefully lacking in energy, however. It took a full year for it to come into being, and it did so ultimately without the Russians, who had insisted unsuccessfully on the separate representation of seven Soviet republics. Given these divisions and uncertainties, the UNWCC remained a weak instrument rather than an active forum for the elaboration of Allied policy on war criminals. In 1944, when a journalist asked its chairman, the jurist Sir Cecil Hurst, whether Adolf Hitler was on the organization's list of recommended war criminals, he replied evasively, implying that he could scarcely imagine such a thing.[16]

The bare outlines of a war crimes policy first appeared only in November 1943 when, at a meeting of the British, American, and Soviet foreign ministers in Moscow, there was some indication that the end of the war might be approaching. Keen to maintain some semblance of unity, Stalin, Roosevelt, and Churchill appended their signatures to a generally worded resolution. But most of the difficult questions remained unanswered. The Allied leaders' emphasis was on tribunals established by individual countries where crimes had been committed. At the same time, they held the door open to a quite different process for "major criminals whose offenses have no particular geographical localization" (Document 6). A few weeks later, at Teheran, Churchill, Roosevelt, and Stalin had a curious exchange on the subject of German war criminals that illustrates how far the Allied leaders were from any common policy. As Churchill himself described it, Stalin raised the issue after dinner at the Soviet embassy in the company only of their interpreters, Roosevelt's son Elliott, and a few others.

What happened next was a revealing example of the disagreement among the three war leaders on how their captured enemies were to be treated (Document 7). The issue was: Should the captured German leaders be summarily shot—and in their thousands? Stalin genially proposed the "liquidation of the German General Staff," and the shooting of "about fifty thousand officers and technicians." Churchill's version of this incident suggests that he adamantly opposed such executions. On other occasions, however, we know that he took precisely the opposite view, albeit on a drastically smaller scale than that envisioned by the Soviet dictator. In favoring executions, the prime minister was simply following the advice of legal advisers and the Foreign Office, which had warned against trials since the summer of 1942 and favored shooting top Nazis after simple identification. Regularly repeated, Whitehall's view was that an international court would take too long to establish, would be too cumbersome in practice, and would widely appear unfair to the accused. Reporting to the War Cabinet in September 1944, Lord Chancellor Sir John Simon bluntly declared that "the method by trial, conviction, and judicial sentence is quite inappropriate for notorious ringleaders such as Hitler, Himmler, Goring, Goebbels, and Ribbentrop."[17]

With the British in 1943 leaning toward summary execution of a small number of leaders and the Soviets preferring some sort of trial, Roosevelt characteristically avoided taking a stand so as not to sharpen divisions among the Allies and sought to avoid getting into details about postwar policies until it was absolutely necessary. In the months following the Teheran conference, however, Roosevelt had found himself under increasing pressure to define postwar policies on several important issues, including war criminals. By the summer of 1944, branches of the American government were hard at work on these questions, and while the president did not follow such issues closely, leading figures in his administration were hoping to win FDR's support for their own points of view.

Among those closest to Roosevelt, Secretary of the Treasury Henry Morgenthau Jr. coupled the idea of a harsh settlement for the Germans with an extremely tough approach to Nazi war criminals. Of an assimilated Jewish background, recently energized to do something on behalf of the Jews still alive in Europe, the treasury secretary burned with a sense of the heinousness and magnitude of Nazi atrocities. In a memo to the president outlining his ideas for postwar policy, Morgenthau defined his principal goal as a draconian scheme to dismantle German industrial capacity so as to prevent the country from ever disturbing world peace again. The German people, he believed, should be turned into "an agricultural population of small land-owners." Appending to this plan some thoughts on war criminals, the powerful treasury secretary disparaged judicial proceedings and contemplated "military commissions" for wrongdoers of the second rank only. "Arch-criminals," as he referred to them, were to be summarily shot (Document 8).

Convinced that the Morgenthau Plan would be a disaster for the peace, prosperity, and stability of Europe, the more urbane secretary of war, Henry L. Stimson, seventy-six years old and a patrician New York Republican, urged a radically different policy that sought to promote economic recovery and industrial development by utilizing German industrial capacity. War crimes policy, he argued, had to be part of such a constructive approach. Writing to the president in response to Morgenthau's memo, Stimson defined his differences with the treasury secretary, setting the course for the elaboration of an entirely different American approach to Nazi war criminals (Document 9).

In the months that followed, Stimson worked with his colleagues in the Pentagon, and also with the secretary of state and the attorney general, to develop an alternative to the Morgenthau Plan. Given Roosevelt's initial attraction to Morgenthau's scheme—and indeed his embracing of it at the Quebec conference with Churchill in mid-September—this may have seemed like an uphill struggle. But the president's commitment to the Morgenthau Plan at Quebec proved evanescent. Indeed, because of Roosevelt's disinclination to finish with the matter before the British and the Soviets seemed ready to do so, and in view of serious opposition to Morgenthau's approach within his administration, the president was prepared to let his principal lieutenants thrash it out before making his own decision.

This gave Stimson time. Beginning in mid-September, officials in the Pentagon worked to refine a scheme that emerged from the desk of the chief of the War Department's Special Projects Office, Lieutenant Colonel Murray Bernays. An attorney who worked in civilian life with the Securities and Exchange Commission (SEC), Bernays developed a plan that used the law of conspiracy (commonly referred to in SEC cases but hitherto unknown in international law) to organize a grand strategy for the prosecution of major Nazi war criminals.[18] Coming to grips with the practical difficulties, Bernays wanted to avoid separate prosecutions of huge numbers of individuals. Conspiracy law was one of the mechanisms he envisaged to address the singularity of Nazi criminality. Some of his basic ideas appeared in a draft signed by Stimson,

Secretary of State Cordell Hull, and Secretary of the Navy James Forrestal (Document 10).

Also at the War Department, William Chanler, a well-connected former Wall Street lawyer, championed the idea that German leadership should be charged with the planning and waging of aggressive war, held to be illegal internationally since the Kellogg-Briand Peace Pact of 1928. Two months later, utilizing Chanler's and Bernays's approach, Stimson reached agreement with the new secretary of state, Edward Stettinius Jr., and Francis Biddle, the attorney general who would later be the American judge at Nuremberg, on a broad strategy for the prosecution of Nazi war criminals. Conspiracy and aggressive war were now at the center of the War Department's plan. Also present was another of Bernays's ideas, that of charging specific organizations with criminal activity, such that upon their conviction subsequent trials could proceed without great trouble against individual members. The conspiracy/criminal-organizations plan, as it has become known, was prepared to guide Roosevelt at the Yalta conference with Churchill and Stalin in February 1945 and was thereafter refined to become U.S. policy in negotiations leading up to Nuremberg (Document 11).

While the proponents of the conspiracy/criminal-organizations plan seem to have overpowered the Morgenthau approach by the time of Yalta, the Big Three did not devote much attention to war criminals at that meeting, and the ailing president—exhausted and with only a few months to live—made no effort to win the support of Churchill and Stalin for the scheme. For their part, the British remained as opposed as ever. To understand this point of view fully, one should take into account the widespread belief at the time that the Reich was very near collapse and that the Führer and his principal henchmen might well be captured. As late as April 1945 the British warned that "Hitler and his advisers . . . may be expected to be very much alive to any opportunity of turning the tables."[19] Might a trial thereby become an unseemly platform, amidst the ruins of the Reich, for Nazi propaganda? Better that the Nazi leadership be silenced, many thought. Sharing this view, Churchill proposed to Stalin at Yalta that the Allies should prepare a list of the "grand criminals" who "should be shot as soon as they were caught and their identity established." According to Churchill's biographer, the British prime minister then asked whether Stalin preferred

> "that grand criminals should be tried before being shot," in other words, that it should be "a judicial rather than a political act."

Stalin replied that "that was so." Meanwhile Roosevelt, doubtless with an eye to charming the Soviet dictator, commented that "it should not be too judicial. He wanted to keep out newspapers and photographers until the criminals were dead."[20]

Neither Yalta nor the desultory discussions that followed between the British and American representatives in London succeeded in clarifying Allied intentions on the subject of war criminals. Then, on April 12, 1945, Roosevelt died, having barely begun his fourth term. His successor, Harry Truman, promptly accepted the wisdom of a trial following the conspiracy/criminal-organizations plan and quickly breathed life into the American proposal. And so with the new president, the American course was set. Before the end of the month Truman named Supreme Court Justice Robert H. Jackson "chief of counsel for the prosecution of Axis criminality" and set out to convince other countries to support the American approach. The scene now shifted to the founding conference of the United Nations in San Francisco, where detailed discussions were to take place in April 1945. "American idealistic fervor was burning at a white heat," notes Bradley Smith.[21]

Representing Truman on the subject of war criminals, Roosevelt speech writer Judge Samuel Rosenman, an old friend of Murray Bernays, accompanied the large American team to San Francisco—a team that included Secretary of State Stettinius, Ambassador to the Soviet Union Averell Harriman, and Assistant Secretary of War John J. McCloy. This time, the end of the war in Europe was really at hand. On April 30, Hitler killed himself in his bunker beneath the rubble of his destroyed German capital; on May 2, Berlin was securely in Russian hands, and the German army in Italy capitulated. The final German surrender was only hours away. At a crucial meeting the next day, Rosenman handed the participants in San Francisco a draft agreement for a trial of the major German war criminals. Following the State Department's plan, the draft had a section on due process for the defendants, which pointed toward future trials as well (Document 12). Immediately, a meeting of Secretary of State Stettinius with British and Soviet representatives made it clear that the time of indecision was over. Stettinius began the discussion, relaying the new, resolute tone of American policy (Document 13).

Truman's determination had a decisive impact. Faced with Washington's resolute policy, the British, and soon the French and Soviets as well, accepted the American plan in principle. What remained were the arduous technical tasks of preparing for the trial to which the major powers were now committed.

PREPARATIONS

Following agreement in principle on the U.S. proposal, American, British, French, and Russian jurists met for several weeks in London to draft the basic instrument of what was to become the Nuremberg War Crimes Trial—an agreement among the four powers to try major German war criminals and a charter outlining the mechanism by which Nazi leaders would be brought before an international military tribunal. Negotiations among the prosecutors continued for several more weeks over the list of accused, the charges to be brought against them, and the general prosecution strategy, leading to a formal indictment, signed on October 6, 1945. At this point, the opening of the trial was less than six weeks away. Throughout this period the American prosecution team drove the decision making, setting a brisk pace for their Allied colleagues and pouring more human and material resources into the enterprise than all of the latter put together.

The key figure in the American effort was the chief prosecutor for the United States, Robert H. Jackson, a strong-minded Democrat who had served in the Roosevelt administration since 1936, most importantly as attorney general for more than a year before being named an associate justice of the Supreme Court in 1941. "A vain and self-important man with intimate connections in Washington," recalled one somewhat sour observer, "Jackson was opinionated and self-seeking but not a great jurist."[22] With his formal education limited to one year at Albany (New York) Law School, Jackson "was probably the last nationally prominent lawyer to gain admission to the bar by serving an apprenticeship rather than by a law school degree," notes Telford Taylor, one of his junior colleagues at Nuremberg.[23] Dignified, brilliant, and capable of masterful oratory, Jackson was also an erratic performer, hot-tempered, and suffering, perhaps, from a streak of insecurity.

Assisted from the start by the energetic Major General William J. ("Wild Bill") Donovan, head of the Office of Strategic Services (the forerunner of the Central Intelligence Agency), Jackson went immediately to work to build a large, first-rate staff of highly motivated lawyers from both military and civilian life. Within a month Jackson not only had assembled his team but had also, as he reported to Truman on June 6,

> worked out a plan for preparation, briefing, and trial of the cases; allocated the work among the several agencies; instructed those engaged in collecting or processing evidence; visited the European Theater to expedite the examination of captured documents,

and the interrogation of witnesses and prisoners; coordinated our preparation of the main case with preparation by Judge Advocates of many cases not included in my responsibilities; and arranged co-operation and mutual assistance with the United Nations War Crimes Commission and with Counsel appointed to represent the United Kingdom in the joint prosecution.

He had been, in short, a busy man. Widely publicized in both the United States and Europe, Jackson's report to the president was drafted with a keen eye to American public opinion and to the historic significance of the proposed trial (Document 14).

On June 26, 1945, an international conference of American, British, French, and Soviet jurists assembled at Church House in London to plan the trial. Not surprisingly, given what had transpired at San Francisco in May and given also the role that Jackson and his team had played to that point, an American draft formed the basis for the discussions. Jackson dominated the proceedings. The chief British representative and Jackson's counterpart was Attorney General Sir David Maxwell-Fyfe, who yielded his place to Sir Hartley Shawcross partway through the conference when Churchill's Conservative government was defeated in the summer's elections and replaced by Labour, under Clement Atlee. Officially demoted, Maxwell-Fyfe nevertheless remained the leading personality on the British side for day-to-day discussions in London as well as during the trial itself. The French representatives included Judge Robert Falco of the Cour de Cassation in Paris, a less weighty personage, later to be the French alternate judge at Nuremberg, and Professor André Gros, who had represented his country on the United Nations War Crimes Commission and who happened for that reason to be in London. Speaking for the Soviet side was Major General Ion Timofeevich Nikitchenko, vice president of the Soviet Supreme Court—"grave, dignified, thin-lipped," according to the American judge Francis Biddle, and "capable . . . of using cruelty when it seemed appropriate."[24] Nikitchenko had presided over the infamous "show trials" of "Old Bolsheviks" in 1935—part of the orgy of judicial repression that convulsed the Soviet Union in the second half of the 1930s. He was later to be the senior Soviet judge on the International Military Tribunal. The Soviet judge was supported by Professor Aaron N. Trainin, a famous Russian specialist in international legal questions and the author of a short book on the subject.[25]

Over the next weeks, in a climate of international uncertainty, the representatives of the four powers thrashed out, often heatedly, major questions of strategy and procedure to be followed at Nuremberg. Particularly at the start of the discussions, Jackson was extremely suspicious of the Russians, fearing that they would adopt "Soviet methods" at the trial, as a British intelligence report put it.[26] Fueling mutual suspicions, Soviet-sponsored rumors were also circulating, according to which Hitler was still alive and being kept in the British zone for future machinations against Moscow. Yet Jackson and his British and French colleagues shared fundamental Soviet objectives about the structure of the proceedings. All agreed, as Jackson observed, that "political controversy" was to be avoided at the trial and that the Tribunal should not become a platform for Nazi propaganda. They further agreed that the crimes to be tried at Nuremberg should be Nazi crimes and only Nazi crimes—not, that is, crimes that might have been committed by the Allies.

Jackson raised this sensitive matter in the context of what proved to be a complex and disputed issue—the jurisdiction over "atrocities, persecutions, and deportations on political, racial, or religious grounds" committed by Germans against German nationals. How could national sovereignty, upon which the Americans themselves insisted, be reconciled with proceedings against the Germans on such matters? Ordinarily, Jackson noted, such crimes would be no business of the Allies. Even the United States did not claim to come to Nuremberg with its hands completely clean. But he nevertheless found justification for the Allied prosecution of such crimes (Document 15). "There might come a time," observed Professor Trainin in response to Jackson, "when there will be a permanent international tribunal of the United Nations organization to try all violations of international law." However, the Nuremberg Tribunal, he went on, "has a definite purpose in view, that is, to try criminals of the European Axis powers"—those crimes, and those alone.[27]

Jackson insisted on getting his way on several key issues: that the trial would take place in Nuremberg in the American-occupied zone, not in Soviet-dominated Berlin as Nikitchenko would have preferred (Jackson did concede that the formal opening of the trial would be in the former German capital, after which the proceedings would continue at Nuremberg); that the trial would focus on German aggression—later to be termed "crimes against peace"—at least as much as on war crimes and crimes against humanity; that the prosecution would adopt the American charge of conspiracy, a concept unfamiliar to Continental legal practice; and that the trial would link the conviction of groups and organizations to the actions of leading Nazi criminals so as to facilitate the subsequent prosecution of accused individuals who belonged to those groups. "[W]e have in the neighborhood of perhaps 200,000 prisoners," Jackson told his fellow planners. "We don't want to have 200,000 trials."[28] Not the most polished of diplomats, Jackson could become brittle and abrupt in the face of opposition. When the talks threatened to bog down over the Soviets' proposal of sitting in Berlin, for example, Jackson suggested that the Americans might go ahead on their own—or that he himself might quit (Document 15).

While not the only difficulty at the London conference during this period, dealing with the Soviets may have posed the greatest threat to the discussions and hence to the trial itself. All three Western delegations were aware of the Russians' notion of the trial as a mere formality, and their language—conveyed by their excellent translator Oleg Troyanovsky, the genial son of a former Soviet ambassador to the United States and a graduate of Dartmouth—could only have sounded extremely awkward to the others. The Western Allies took pains to insist that the wartime declarations of various governments were not sufficient to condemn specific individuals for war crimes, particularly for planning and launching aggressive war. To them, the purpose of the trial was to establish guilt in particular cases and to build a case against the accused. Their whole approach to trials made them reluctant to dwell on the outcome as preordained. To the Soviets, however, the real object of the trial was to punish the criminals, and they spoke about the Tribunal in frankly punitive terms. The Russians regularly insisted that the "Hitlerite Fascist criminals" had already been condemned by the Allies in wartime declarations. "The fact that the Nazi leaders are criminals has already been established," said Nikitchenko one day. "The task of the Tribunal is only to determine the measure of guilt of each particular person and to meet out the necessary punishment—the sentences"[29] (Document 27).

Most of those negotiating in London had apparently read Trainin's book *Hitlerite Responsibility under Criminal Law*, edited by the sinister orchestrator of the Soviet purge trials, Andrei Vyshinsky, and were prepared to live with its references, for example, to "bourgeois jurists [who] hinder the harnessing of the resources of criminal justice in the struggle for peace."[30] For their part, neither the Soviet professor nor his colleagues seem to have anticipated constructing an elaborate structure to try the Nazis, and they may have been mystified by the Allied insistence on this score. "Their crimes are so vast and so indisputable," Trainin contended, "that . . . the fate of Hitler and his clique can be settled by the political verdict of the victorious democratic States."[31]

Cited by others at the London meetings, Trainin's formulations were referenced respectfully throughout the debates. The general view seems to have been that the Soviets' bark was worse than their bite. Over the weeks of negotiation, as a result, the delegations made steady progress, compromised, and kept their disagreements at bay. In retrospect, the decisive circumstance governing these discussions was that all parties wanted an agreement. While the differences of opinion were serious, often related to deeply entrenched commitments of ideology and national interest, the allied representatives seem to have concluded that a four-power trial was worth having. At the Potsdam conference, which assembled a few weeks after the London discussions had begun, the British, Americans, and Soviets confirmed this priority. Jackson, having made his threats to leave, sent a message to Truman urging the president to facilitate agreement by not yielding too much to the Russians. Near the end of their meeting the Big Three sorted out their differences on war criminals, and Stalin, in all likelihood, instructed his representatives in London to close the deal.[32]

Sidney Alderman, Jackson's deputy at Nuremberg and a distinguished Washington corporate lawyer, recalled how complicated were the conversations among the four powers, each of which was negotiating simultaneously with the other three:

> It is as difficult to dissect out of the mass of the negotiations those representing distinctly American-Russian discussions as it is to dissect two eggs out of a four-egg omelet. Indeed, it is apter to say a six-egg omelet, since each of the four nations negotiated with each of the other three; so, eliminating duplications, six sets of international discussions comprised the negotiations. And, to add to the complication, all of the discussions were in three languages, by means of interpreters.[33]

Alderman later described the texture of the negotiations, and offered explanations for their success (Document 16).

The London negotiations finally bore fruit on August 8, 1945, when the participants signed the four-power agreement for a trial and appended to it a detailed charter, which became the governing instrument of the International Military Tribunal. With its crucial Article 6, defining the specific crimes falling within the jurisdiction of the Tribunal, this document became the essential legal point of reference for the prosecution, the defense, and the judges during the year-long Nuremberg Trial (Document 17).

Notwithstanding the determination of the Big Three to start a trial "at the earliest possible date," as the Potsdam conference protocol declared, the remaining tasks of preparing an indictment and choosing the defendants were arduous and time-consuming. Continuing in London, the negotiations proceeded "under . . . furious pressure," Sidney Alderman remembered.[34] As with negotiations over the charter, the Americans held the upper hand in debates over the list of defendants and the indictment — particularly because most of the likely accused were in the custody of the U.S. military. Here too the Americans had a clear objective, consistent with their prosecution strategy, which had been evolving for about a year. Their goal was to try not only the highest-ranking Nazis available — those responsible for the "common plan or conspiracy" referred to in Article 6 of the charter — but also representative groups or organizations to be deemed criminal, following a process outlined in Article 9.

The British originally had in mind a very short trial, lasting only a few weeks, with around a dozen defendants. The Americans envisioned a much more elaborate exercise, with fifty or sixty on trial. Others made suggestions, including the notion of including non-German decision makers, an idea that was rejected. One petitioner, Jacob Robinson of the World Jewish Congress's Institute of Jewish Affairs, urged Jackson to include a name for which he made a strong case: Adolf Eichmann, seen even in 1945 as a major organizer of the murder of European Jewry[35] (Document 18). Working from their designation of the principal Nazi groups and organizations and their investigation of the many prisoners in their custody, the Americans came up with various suggestions, gradually pared down in consultation with the British. Eventually, a list was further altered in discussions with the French and Soviets, the latter seeking to include two men in their own custody (Admiral Erich Raeder and propagandist Hans Fritzsche). Because of poor research and even worse communication among the trial's planners, the Allies agreed to include the industrialist Gustav Krupp von Bohlen und Halbach, who turned out to be senile and incapable of standing trial. Embarrassingly for the English and Americans, the Tribunal forcefully declared its independence of the prosecution and their political/military masters by deciding not to proceed against him, overruling Jackson's arguments on the matter.

The American staff produced a voluminous draft indictment to which the Russians essentially agreed, being concerned mainly about the need for generous discussion of crimes and aggression committed against the Soviet Union. However, detailed and difficult negotiations were required to define four counts against the various defendants, to settle last-minute disagreements over the list of accused, and to resolve questions about organizations alleged to be criminal. Toward the end, a new disagreement blew up when outlining count three — war crimes. The Soviets defined the violated U.S.S.R. as including "the Bielorussian, Ukrainian, Estonian, Latvian, Lithuanian, Karelo-Finnish, and Moldavian Soviet Socialist Republics." Unwilling to concede to the Soviets their acquisition of the Baltic states, the Americans balked, agreeing in the end to accept a Soviet assurance that their signature would not be construed as indicating diplomatic recognition of those states. The Western Allies also tried to persuade the Russians not to include reference to the Katyn Forest massacre of "925 Polish officers" (increased by the Russians, twelve days after the indictment was signed, to eleven thousand). The Russians insisted that the officers were murdered by the Germans, but the widespread view was that the Soviets had done the killing themselves. (Subsequent research has amply confirmed that the Russians had shot the Polish officers.) "We were embarrassed about including that allegation in the indictment," Sidney Alderman recalled, "but finally concluded that it was up to the Soviet Union and that if it thought it could sustain the allegation by proof, it had the right to make the charge in the indictment."[36]

Signed on October 6, only twelve days before the Tribunal held its opening session in Berlin, the indictment, with detailed appendices on the accused individuals and organizations and on the international agreements violated, was a massive document containing much more detail than was customary in Anglo-American legal practice (Document 19). One point of historical interest was the insertion of the term "genocide" into the indictment, the result of persistent and often obsessive lobbying of Dr. Raphael Lemkin, a Jewish jurist and refugee from Lithuania who had coined the term in his 1944 book, *Axis Rule in Occupied Europe*. Thanks to Lemkin's herculean efforts, the Americans accepted the inclusion of the term and persuaded their colleagues to agree. "Genocide" appeared in the description of "war crimes," however, and not, as Lemkin would have preferred, under "crimes against humanity." The term was mentioned occasionally in the deliberations of the court, but was absent from the judgment in 1946, to Lemkin's great disappointment and despite his persistent efforts. As Robert Jackson's biographer John Q. Barrett notes, Lemkin's success in 1945 was achieved as a last-minute, improvised exercise, and hardly the result of a historic decision.[37]

THE COURT

Contemporaries were struck by the gravity and solemnity of the Nuremberg Trial—especially at its beginning—a reflection of the extraordinary scope of the issues raised by the Tribunal. Many of those seated in the Nuremberg courtroom felt they were witnessing a great historic moment. Experiencing material shortages in a bombed-out city and, for the Americans in particular, far away from home and loved ones, missing good food and creature comforts, some of those present commented later about experiencing great events and being privileged to witness the beginning of a new, more hopeful world. A member of Jackson's prosecution team, Thomas J. Dodd, expressed this to his wife Grace, at home in Connecticut, in June 1946 (Document 20).

Each day, several hundred people packed into a long, wood-paneled courtroom on the second floor of Nuremberg's hastily restored Palace of Justice. Seated behind their national flags, eight jurists presided, a principal judge and an alternate from each of the four participating countries—six of them robed in black, the French with white jabots, and the Soviets in brown military-style uniforms. Twenty-one somewhat bedraggled defendants appeared in the dock in two parallel rows. Each defendant was represented by at least one counsel, and several of these lawyers spoke in addition for the six accused organizations. (The latter were the famous emblems of Nazi tyranny, noted in the indictment: the leadership corps of the Nazi Party; the Gestapo and Sicherheitsdienst, or SD; the Schutzstaffel, or SS; the Sturmabteilung, or SA; the Reich Cabinet; and the German General Staff and High Command.) Each of the four countries sent a prosecution team, of which the American team, with about fifty lawyers, was by far the largest. Filling the courtroom in addition were scores of reporters and other observers, a corps of white helmeted American guards who stood behind the defendants—looking crisp and polished for photographs, they often sagged in their places, leaning against the back wall of the room or propping themselves up against the prisoners' benches. And finally, inside a glass box, operating a novel simultaneous translating system donated by IBM, was a team of translators—"twittering unhappily," as the journalist and commentator Rebecca West noted, "like cage-birds kept awake by a bright light, feeding the microphones" with English, French, Russian, and German versions of the proceedings.[38] Except for the guards, everyone in the room wore an IBM-provided headset to hear the translation; one reporter observed, perhaps having in mind as well the wires and cables running everywhere across the floor, that the room looked like a vast (prewar) telephone exchange.[39]

The judges assembled in Nuremberg more than a month before the trial began and went quickly to work, not only settling details of form and procedure but also resolving issues raised by the prosecution and defense. From the United States came the former Roosevelt associate

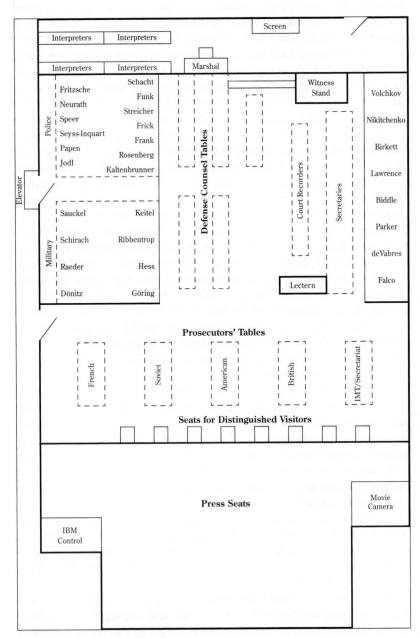

Figure 1. *The Courtroom,* 1983

Francis Biddle, a dapper Philadelphia aristocrat and former judge who had followed Robert Jackson's path from solicitor general to attorney general in 1940 and had worked closely with the chief American prosecutor in the past. Biddle's alternate was the highly experienced John Parker, a liberal U.S. circuit court judge from North Carolina who had once been considered for the Supreme Court and whose confirmation had failed by one vote in the U.S. Senate. Sir Geoffrey Lawrence, Lord Justice of Appeal since 1944, was the senior British judge, remarkably gifted, it turned out, in smoothing the ruffled feelings to which his colleagues were prone and hammering out satisfactory compromises. In early October Lawrence was elected president of the Tribunal and thereafter, according to the war hero and judges' assistant Airey Neave, turned out to be "the central figure at the Nuremberg Trial, from beginning to end." (In addition to Lawrence, only Biddle wanted the job, and as U.S. prosecutor Telford Taylor notes, after consulting senior American officials, Robert Jackson urged the American judge to back the Englishman "on the dual ground that the whole enterprise already had too much of an American cast and that if Lawrence were to preside, the British government would be committed to ensuring the success of the undertaking.")[40] A barrister for half a century before Nuremberg, Lawrence was a dignified country gentleman who was respected for his impartiality and, as a law lord, was adjudged to have the necessary social standing for the job. "He was a staunch, enduring man," wrote Neave, "who upheld the traditions respected by the world, in those far-off days, of British justice."[41] Lawrence's alternate was Sir Norman Birkett, one of the great English trial lawyers of his generation. Tall and angular, very different from the short, plump Lawrence, Birkett resented his subordinate standing relative to his British colleague; he was committed to making the trial "a very great landmark in the history of international law," however, and found his role at the end as the Tribunal's principal draftsman of the final judgment.

General Nikitchenko, who had represented the Soviet side at the London conference, reappeared as the senior Russian judge at Nuremberg. In his forties and the youngest member of the Tribunal, Nikitchenko "knew what the rest of us were like," wrote Biddle, "knew the score, [and] kept in mind a few essentials. After he got to trust us, or at least to understand us a little better, he did not bother quite so much with the meticulous passion for detail which the Russians felt called upon to exhibit during those first few slow weeks."[42] Nikitchenko was seconded by Lieutenant Colonel Alexander Federovich Volchkov, who had had once worked in the film industry, had some rudimentary

Figure 2. View of the opening of the proceedings and presentation of
evidence against the major Nazi war criminals.

United States Army Signal Corps, Harry S. Truman Library & Museum/National
Archives and Record Administration.

Figure 3. View of the translators' section in the Nuremberg courtroom.
National Archives and Record Administration.

knowledge of English but who did not always seem to understand the legal concepts put to him and his colleagues. According to historians Ann and John Tusa, "it was universally assumed that he was Nikitchenko's 'keeper'—he smacked much more of the KGB than the Bench."[43]

The senior French judge was Henri Donnedieu de Vabres, a professor from the Faculté de Droit in Paris with a scholarly style and an expertise in German law. He was "small and stocky," Rebecca West observed, "with a white mustache, and a brow kept wrinkled by the constant offenses against logic perpetrated by this chaotic universe."[44] Taking advantage of his specialty during the occupation years, Donnedieu de Vabres had not been above citing Nazi law as learned precedent—referring even to the notorious jurisprudence on *Rassenschande*, or "race defilement," laws that criminalized sexual encounters between Jews and Germans—although this does not seem to have been remembered by anyone at the time, or since.[45] His alternate was Robert Falco, a senior Paris appeals court judge. Both Falco and Nikitchenko had participated in the London conference setting up the Tribunal and had thereby had a hand in preparing the charges against the accused, an awkward point so far as their requirement of impartiality was concerned.

Francis Biddle recorded his impressions of the trial as seen from the bench and described some of the major themes of Nuremberg—the shattering evidence of atrocities, much of it new in the immediate postwar world; the periodic references to "the Germans" and their ways, notwithstanding the declared commitment of the prosecution and the judges to avoid imputations of collective guilt; and the fascination with the one significantly absent figure, Adolf Hitler, who seemed constantly present even though missing in the dock.

The accused war criminals included two of the highest-ranking and most powerful German leaders: Luftwaffe commander and for a time the second man in Nazi Germany Hermann Göring and party boss Rudolf Hess, Hitler's deputy who had spectacularly broken ranks and flown to Scotland in 1941 and who now seemed to be deranged. There were four leaders of the next rank: the semiofficial Nazi "philosopher" and head of the Ministry for the Occupied Eastern Territories, Alfred Rosenberg; Hans Frank, the party's leading jurist and wartime governor general of Poland; Reich Interior Minister Wilhelm Frick; and Reich youth leader and wartime governor of Vienna Baldur von Schirach. There were two high-level economic managers: Reich Minister of Economics Walther Funk and Hjalmar Schacht, head of the Reichsbank until 1939. There were four top military officers: Wilhelm Keitel, chief of the High Command of the Armed Forces (OKW), Hitler's own military staff; Alfred Jodl, chief of the operations staff of the OKW; Erich Raeder, grand admiral and head of the navy until 1943; and submarine chief and Hitler's designated successor, Karl Dönitz. There were three diplomats: the foreign minister from 1932 to 1938 and later Reich protector of Bohemia and Moravia, Constantin Freiherr von Neurath; Franz von Papen, Reich chancellor in 1932 and later ambassador to Turkey; and Joachim von Ribbentrop, foreign minister from 1938. There were four high functionaries and technocrats: Ernst Kaltenbrunner, SS leader and successor to Reinhard Heydrich; Arthur Seyss-Inquart, Reich governor of Austria and then Reich commissioner of the Netherlands; plenipotentiary general for labor mobilization Fritz Sauckel; and Reich minister for armaments and war production from 1942 to 1945, Albert Speer. Last were two publicists: Hans Fritzsche, propagandist and broadcaster; and Julius Streicher, Gauleiter of Franconia and editor of the pornographic anti-Semitic paper *Der Stürmer*. Three more who were mentioned in the indictment failed to appear: never captured, the administrative insider Martin Bormann,

Hitler's secretary and head of the party chancellery, was tried in absentia; industrialist Gustav Krupp von Bohlen und Halbach was declared incapable of standing trial; and Labor Front leader Robert Ley committed suicide on October 24, before the first session in Nuremberg (Document 20).

During the London negotiations, Nikitchenko had suggested a way of dividing the prosecution's case against the accused: The Americans would prepare the case against the Nazi organizations as well as the general conspiracy and the crimes against peace; the British would focus on the latter, outlining the breaches of specific treaties as well as crimes on the high seas; the French would present war crimes and crimes against humanity in the West; and the Soviets would do the same for Eastern Europe. Accepted by the Western representatives, this sensible division was broadly followed by the four prosecution teams — although, inevitably, there was plenty of overlap in presentations to the court.

On November 21, 1945, the American team began the case against the accused with a powerful address by Robert Jackson — "a very fine opening speech," wrote Norman Birkett in his diary, "on which it was a genuine pleasure to congratulate him, which I have done." "In my opinion," wrote Telford Taylor about that address, "nothing said at Nuremberg thereafter matched its force, perception, and eloquence."[46] Jackson's speech highlighted the historic importance of the trial and made a powerful legal defense of the proceedings. It also unfurled the major theme of the U.S. case — understanding each and every dimension of Nazi criminality as a reflection of a conspiratorial plan (Document 22). Like those of his colleagues from Britain, France, and the Soviet Union, Jackson's presentation came unabashedly from his own national vantage point — in this case, an optimistic, Wilsonian credo that looked to the future at least as much as to the past and that saw the trial as a blow against aggressive wars.

The elegant, handsome Sir Hartley Shawcross, attorney general in Clement Atlee's Labour government and hence an infrequent participant at Nuremberg, interrupted the American case on December 4 to make an opening address on behalf of the United Kingdom. Focusing on German aggression as a breach of international law, Shawcross claimed that during the 1930s close to a thousand treaties "embracing practically all the nations of the world" limited recourse to war, chief among the agreements being the Kellogg-Briand Pact of 1928, "that truly revolutionary enactment in modern international law" (Document 21). Shawcross then went on to underscore the individual responsibility of the defendants for the crimes of aggressive war (Document 23). The trial continued for more than a month before the French chief prosecutor, François de Menthon, rose to present what Francis Biddle thought the most moving address to that point.[47] A professor of law from Montpellier and a Christian Democrat veteran of the French Resistance, de Menthon invoked the "conscience of the peoples, who only yesterday were enslaved and tortured in both body and soul." In keeping with the Gaullist myth of the French resistance to the Germans, de Menthon portrayed a unified and martyred France from which was absent any reference to the collaborationist Vichy regime (Document 24). Concentrating on war crimes and crimes against humanity, de Menthon attributed them to ideological causes, to a flaw in what might be called "German national character." On a high rhetorical plane, in a fashion not uncommon at the time, the French prosecutor ranged across the centuries and claimed to speak, with France, in a universal idiom. Nazism, he claimed, was "the exploitation by a group of men of one of the most profound and most tragic aspects of the German soul." At the root of it all, de Menthon identified a "crime against the spirit."

Defendant Hans Frank, impressed by the Frenchman's tour de force, found the address "stimulating." "That is more like the European mentality," he told the German-born American court psychologist Gustave Gilbert.[48] Struck later by de Menthon's "jarring omission of reference to Jews and the Holocaust," Telford Taylor suggests that this may have been due, in part, to the Frenchman's having left the Eastern European crimes to the Soviets' case. But de Menthon seems also to have been reluctant, as were many in the immediate postwar period, to call attention to the Nazis' particular ideological obsession with Jews or the special victimization of European Jewry. Taylor notes the French prosecutor's sole and meager reference to the matter, toward the end of his address: "It is also known that racial discriminations provoked against citizens of the occupied countries who were catalogued as Jews, measures particularly hateful, damaging to their personal rights and to their human dignity." At the time, such circumlocution was not uncommon. Thinking about de Menthon's omission, Taylor notes that on hearing the speech he "did not mark this fact. Nor did I hear any discussion of it."[49] Within hours after completing his address, de Menthon left Nuremberg to take up a political position in Paris. His position at the Tribunal was filled by the frail and ailing Auguste Champetier de Ribes, who shared the task with future premier Edgar Faure, and with Charles Dubost, whom Jackson disliked and suspected of being a Communist.[50]

Heading the Soviet prosecution team was a forceful speaker, Roman A. Rudenko, chief prosecutor of the Ukraine: "Dumpy and plain-spoken," in Telford Taylor's description, Rudenko was "a short, pallid man wearing the brown Soviet Foreign Office uniform, with shoulder stars showing the rank of lieutenant general, a notch higher than Nikitchenko's army rank of major general." Regularly seeking instructions from Moscow—not Berlin, headquarters of the Soviet occupation authorities, as Telford Taylor, the American liaison officer to the Russians, remembered—the Soviet representatives were sometimes embarrassed by their evident lack of independence and the isolation, in social terms, in which they were obliged to live outside their professional responsibilities and official receptions.[51]

Rudenko delivered his opening statement in February, more than two months after Jackson's opening address. Seated behind him were members of the Soviet delegation, in military uniforms. Conspicuously avoiding references to Nazism, he used terminology replete with references to "Hitlerism," "Hitlerite Germany," "fascist aggressors," and the "heroic struggle against the foreign invaders and enslavers" by "freedom-loving nations." Rudenko's great challenge was to skirt any reference to the Nazi-Soviet Pact of August 1939 and the nearly two years in which his country was an ally of Nazi Germany and an occupation force in Poland—and hence, in the views of some at least, an accomplice of Nazi Germany. Rudenko's focus, instead, was on the terrible crimes committed by the Germans during their invasion of the Soviet Union. Plans for that attack, he said, "were all steps on the road to establishing Hitlerite domination in Europe and in the whole world" (Document 25).

Admired for the vigor of their addresses to the court, Rudenko and his colleagues were somewhat less appreciated for their aggressive cross-examination of witnesses—a brutal process, drawing upon Soviet practice in political trials in which the defendants, by the time they reached the witness box, were reduced to jelly and were primed to confess their crimes. "The Russian idea of cross-examination," Biddle observed, "was to read a long incriminating question, and, looking up at the witness, expect him to admit to everything." The German defendants clearly were not prepared to do so and could, occasionally, catch their interrogators off guard.

Major General G. N. Alexandrov, a Soviet prosecutor suspected of being an agent of the Soviet security forces, or NKVD, sent to keep an eye on his compatriots and to scour captured documents, blended questions with bullying denunciations in his cross-examination of the accused.[52] The process became heated during the questioning of Nazi labor boss Fritz Sauckel, and the Russian was gently rebuked by Lord Lawrence, the president of the Tribunal (Document 26).

Figure 4. General Rudenko of the Soviet delegation addressing the court.
Charles Alexander, Office of the United States Chief of Counsel, Harry S. Truman
Library & Museum/National Archives and Records Administration.

Rudenko ran into trouble on the question of the massacre of thousands
of Polish officers in the Katyn Forest, not far from Smolensk, in 1941.
The Soviets insisted on mentioning these killings in the indictment,
notwithstanding the widespread suspicions that they had themselves
committed this crime. When the question came before the Tribunal a
few days after Rudenko's opening speech, three prosecution witnesses
testified to the Nazis' guilt in the matter. Conflict arose when Dr. Otto
Stahmer, Göring's lawyer, asked the Tribunal to hear three defense
witnesses to show that the Soviets, not the Germans, had killed the

Poles. Rudenko strenuously objected and the matter went to the judges' chambers. Although Nikitchenko backed his compatriot, the Tribunal announced its determination to hear the Germans' witnesses. Francis Biddle describes what happened next (Document 27).

"Göring is the man who has really dominated the proceedings," Birkett commented in his diary. "[N]obody appears to have been prepared for his immense ability and knowledge, and his thorough mastery and understanding of the detail of the captured documents."[53] Weaned from the drugs on which he had been heavily dependent, and wrenched from his sybaritic lifestyle, a leaner, invigorated Hermann Göring stood out among the prisoners because of his swaggering show of bonhomie and his proud fidelity to the ideals of Nazism. Unrepentant and shrewd, Göring exercised an undoubted influence over his fellow prisoners with his cynical mockery of the proceedings—to the point that Gustave Gilbert, the prison psychologist who regularly visited the accused in their cells and reported on their views, was asked to draw up special lunchtime seating arrangements to segregate the troublemaker and defeat his "attempt to obstruct justice."[54]

Figure 5. Hermann Göring entering the defendants' dock at Nuremberg.

National Archives and Records Administration.

Figure 6. Main section of the prisoners' cell block in the Nuremberg jail. Cells occupied by Göring and Hess are at extreme right. Each defendant is watched by an individual guard who is constantly posted at his door. National Archives and Records Administration.

Göring testified in his own defense for three full days beginning on March 13, usually giving lengthy, detailed answers to the short, very specific inquiries of his lawyer, Otto Stahmer. It was an impressive performance, remarkable for its lucidity and intelligence (Document 28). Five days into his testimony, at noon on March 18, all eyes in the courtroom turned to the witness box to watch Göring's encounter with Robert Jackson—a cross-examination that many hoped would humiliate and diminish the boastful Reichsmarschall. To some surprise, Jackson began deferentially and lobbed questions to Göring, enabling him to go over familiar material with masterful self-control. The Reichsmarschall responded as an experienced pedagogue, lecturing the American prosecutor (Document 29).

After a short time, Jackson appeared to lose his composure, cutting off his witness. Lawrence interrupted, allowing the Reichsmarschall to continue. Thereafter, the encounter continued much as before, with Göring occasionally correcting Jackson on matters of detail, translation, or assertions of fact. During the discussion of aggressive German plans in 1936 to move troops into the demilitarized Rhineland area, the clash was sharp, and Jackson exploded.

The following morning, Jackson appealed to the bench and suffered a gentle but firm rebuke (Document 30). Gloating after his

Figure 7. Hermann Göring testifies in his own defense in the courtroom of the Palace of Justice, Nuremberg.

National Archives and Records Administration.

session with Jackson, Göring struck a pose of self-conscious heroism. Characteristically boastful, the Reichsmarschall sought Gilbert's approval. "Well, I didn't cut a *petty* figure, did I?" he asked. "Don't forget, I had the best legal brains of England, America, Russia, and France arrayed against me with their whole legal machinery—and there I was, alone!"[55]

Norman Birkett, the veteran English barrister, felt that Jackson's failure to control his witness's speechmaking sent the trial out of control. As he anticipated, other defendants took advantage of the situation to make long statements to the Tribunal in the form of answers. The trial dragged on as a result, with the attorneys on both sides generating "mountains of useless documents" for translation and consideration. Jackson's confidence seemed to have been shaken as well, a blow from which he took a long time to recover—and which rendered him more irritable than ever during the proceedings. Writing in his diary on April 10, Birkett was in a gloomy mood:

> The trial is regarded as a spectacle, a kind of gladiatorial show, with the prominent Nazis like Göring taking the place of the wild beasts

Figure 8. Justice Robert Jackson making an argument at the Nuremberg Trial.
Charles Alexander, Office of the United States Chief of Counsel. Harry S. Truman
Library & Museum.

and prosecuting counsel as the gladiators and baiters. The enormous staffs think of the trial as a means of enjoying a good time, and as most of them are young this can be forgiven: but the fact remains that much more serious work ought to be going on in almost every field, and notably in connection with the final judgment.

A month later his depression had not lifted: "When I consider the utter uselessness of acres of paper and thousands of words and that life is slipping away, I moan for this shocking waste of time."[56]

As Bradley Smith has observed, the defendants gained little or no advantage from this failure on the prosecution side—largely because the twenty-two prisoners in the dock were so deeply divided on political, ideological, social, and even personal terms. "Some of the defendants hated each other, as did Schacht and Göring," Smith notes, "while the old aristocrats treated the commoners with thinly veiled condescension. The military looked down on the civilians, and the rest of the defendants considered Streicher and Kaltenbrunner too unsavory for their company."[57] Neurath, Papen, and Schacht claimed that their responsibilities were limited to the early years of the regime, and the latter made much of having been sent to a concentration camp after the failure of the July 1944 plot against Hitler. Others hung on until the bitter end, and Dönitz had even agreed to be the Führer's successor. Rudolf Hess behaved erratically in the dock and in any case had been in British custody since May 1941. Hans Frank went through the motions of religious conversion and from time to time seemed to be genuinely contrite. But he could as well be found in Göring's camp, according to Gilbert. Quite the opposite, Albert Speer claimed to have sought to assassinate Hitler and confessed that he now appreciated the error of his ways. Kaltenbrunner, by contrast, fought tooth and nail and flatly rejected the value of much of the evidence against him.

Figure 9. In Allied custody since May 1941 after he flew to England for reasons that are still debated, former Nazi party leader Rudolf Hess is interrogated by Colonel John Owen and Colonel Smith Brookhart.

Charles Alexander, Office of the United States Chief of Counsel. Harry S. Truman Library & Museum.

Defending the accused major war criminals and the Nazi organizations was a formidable professional challenge, and one to which the entirely German team of thirty-two defense attorneys responded with quite different abilities and objectives. Anti-Nazi or unsympathetic to the regime for the most part (although not exclusively), they adopted different strategies, ranging from Otto Stahmer's providing a platform for Göring to the tenacious legal challenge to Allied war policy made by the uniformed navy judge Otto Kranzbühler on behalf of Admiral Dönitz. Unfamiliar with the Anglo-American process of cross-examining witnesses, unable to draw upon wide-ranging expertise and document-gathering personnel, and with their access to Allied archives blocked, the defense lawyers were at some disadvantage in the preparation of their cases. The prosecution had substantial control over the great mass of captured documentary evidence, and while they placed thousands of documents they intended to use in a defendants' information center, they required an elaborate procedure for having such material admitted in evidence.[58] Inevitably, some attorneys responded more effectively to these constraints than others.

Figure 10. Defendants Hermann Göring, Walther Funk, Karl Dönitz, Baldur von Schirach, and an unidentified man at lunch during the Nuremberg Trial.
Charles Alexander, Office of the United States Chief of Counsel. Harry S. Truman Library & Museum.

The German lawyers agreed to use a collective argument on only one issue, a general motion by all defense counsel on November 19, just before the trial began. In a presentation by Otto Stahmer, the lawyers made their case against the Nuremberg proceedings being based on ex post facto law (Document 31). Two days later the Tribunal rejected the defense motion, ruling that it was in conflict with Article 3 of the charter, which defined the jurisdiction of the Tribunal. Thereupon, the defense attorneys went their separate ways, adopting a variety of strategies to defend their clients against the charges in the indictment.

CRIMES AGAINST PEACE

Central to the American conception of the Nuremberg Trial was the first count in the indictment, with which all the accused were charged — the "common plan or conspiracy" to commit the crimes mentioned in the charter. Linking that count and the second, "crimes against peace" — "the planning, preparation, initiation, and waging of wars of aggression, or a war in violation of existing treaties, agreements, and assurances" — the American approach focused on aggression as the criminal core of Nazism, from which everything else flowed. "[O]ur view," Jackson said during the London conference, "is that this isn't merely a case of showing that these Nazi Hitlerite people failed to be gentlemen in war; it is a matter of their having designed an illegal attack on the international peace . . . and the other atrocities were all preparatory to it or done in execution of it."[59]

This understanding of Nazism and the Second World War animated the U.S. strategy throughout the trial: All instances of Nazi wrongdoing were understood as arising from a "common plan or conspiracy." Indeed, because of the degree to which the Americans shaped the prosecution strategy, it also, as Telford Taylor notes, threatened "to swallow the greater part of the entire case."[60] In particular, it proved impossible for the prosecution to separate the first two counts, because the evidence for one applied equally to the other and because war planning seemed similarly essential to both.

The focus on conspiracy and aggressive war derived in part from a broad legal strategy on Nazi war criminals — the decision to bring to trial and punish those who were not "major" wrongdoers yet who had contributed in important ways to the Nazi enterprise. But there was more to it than that. Remembering President Woodrow Wilson's failure to maintain the support of the American public for peacemaking in the years after the First World War, the U.S. leadership in 1945 worked hard to enlist American opinion in the settlement with Nazi Germany. At London in the summer of 1945, Jackson lectured his colleagues on how American "public psychology" differed profoundly from that of Europeans: "Our American population is at least 3,000 miles from the scene. Germany did not attack or invade the United States in violation of any treaty with us. The thing that led us to take sides in this war was that we regarded Germany's resort to war as illegal from its outset, as an illegal attack on the international peace and order." As a result, Jackson claimed, Americans wanted to show "that this war was an illegal plan of aggression." Americans persisted in "regarding this as an illegal war from the beginning and in believing that the great crime of crimes of our century was the launching of a needless war in Europe."[61] Nuremberg, Jackson felt, was to judge this "crime of crimes."

At the very beginning of the proceedings, the day after Jackson's opening address, his assistant Sidney Alderman told the Tribunal that the "planning, preparation, initiation, and waging of illegal and aggressive war" was "the heart of the case" (Document 32). Referring to the charter, Alderman explained why the United States put so much stake in count one of the indictment, "the formulation or execution of a Common Plan or Conspiracy." Clearly, the defendants differed in the degree of their criminal involvement. In the case of some, there was direct evidence of their commission of the crime of aggressive war. With others, the involvement was less direct. The conspiracy charge, however, caught them all.

In court, Alderman presented the substance of the U.S. case—an approach that had earlier divided the United States's prosecution team quite bitterly and to which not all of his own planning staff had been committed. In essence, Jackson had decided to build the U.S. arguments on a foundation of documents, a decision that included all the accused and that opposed those who would have preferred a greater reliance upon witnesses. Among the latter was Jackson's unofficial deputy, Major General William Donovan, a strong-minded war hero and head of the Office of Strategic Services (OSS), predecessor of today's Central Intelligence Agency (CIA). Jackson broke with Donovan near the beginning of the trial, opposing in particular the latter's determination to put some of the accused on the stand to help explicate sources of Nazi criminality.

Relying heavily on documentary evidence, the American prosecutors traced the central conceptions of the Nazi movement, its drive to power, its crushing of democracy, and its preparations for launching wars of aggression. In an unprecedented presentation of a film in a juridical setting, U.S. attorneys also presented a devastating documentary,

Nazi Concentration Camps, taken by Allied military cameramen to illus-
trate their contentions about war crimes and crimes against humanity.[62]
Taking much less time, the British bore down specifically on German
violation of treaties and the planning of attacks on specific countries.
Throughout, the prosecutors referred to specific defendants and their
part in the unfolding story. Breaking new ground in formally defining
aggressive war as an international crime, the prosecution made a forceful case that this view was nevertheless well grounded in international
law and the history of the interwar years. Thereby, said Sir Hartley
Shawcross, the London charter had quite properly understood the evolution of the law of nations (Document 33).

During the negotiations over the charter, the historical adviser to the
British Foreign Office, E. L. Woodward, had argued strenuously that
the American approach of a "common plan or conspiracy" to launch
aggressive war was deeply flawed. "There was indeed no plot," he
insisted. And at any event, Woodward added, "it is notoriously difficult
to prove 'intentions' from diplomatic documents."[63] Like many others,
including leaders of the French and Soviet teams, Woodward felt it was
far better to concentrate on war crimes and other atrocities. Having
rejected these arguments, the Nuremberg prosecution committed itself
to a very particular interpretation of the Nazi enterprise. The very purpose of Nazism, the prosecution claimed, had been the preparation and
waging of aggressive war. All the defendants had been co-conspirators
working toward this goal. Virtually everything the Nazis had done had
been directed to that end.

The whole notion of a "common plan or conspiracy," as historian
Michael Biddis points out, "tempted the defense to play down, and the
prosecution conversely to exaggerate, the coherence of character and
policy that existed among these men in the days of their pomp."[64] Distortion and exaggeration were indeed the results—creating an unreal
picture for subsequent historians, just as Woodward had predicted. The
first few years of Nazi rule, Sidney Alderman argued somewhat improb-
ably, were "characterized by an orderly, planned sequence of preparations for war." The remilitarization of the Rhineland in 1936, together
with the Anschluss with Austria, the crisis over Czechoslovakia in 1938,
and the occupation of that country the following year—all these were
"experiments in aggression," as Jackson put it, designed "to test the
spirit of resistance of those who lay across their path." War broke out in
1939 as a result of "conspiratorial premeditation."[65]

At what point was there a clearly articulated Nazi plan for aggression?
The prosecution's answer relied heavily on a document the Americans

discovered in the summer of 1945—the notes of Hitler's adjutant Colonel Friedrich Hossbach of a conference held at the Reich chancellery in Berlin on November 5, 1937, at which several of the defendants were present and at which Hitler revealed plans that were to be viewed as his "last will and testament." During the conference Hitler outlined his objectives of *Lebensraum*, or "living space," for the German Reich; made clear his warlike intentions; and considered several contingencies for the outbreak of war, looking to the conquest of Austria and Czechoslovakia. The Americans first put the Hossbach Memorandum, as it was subsequently called, into evidence, and Shawcross referred to it in his address to the Tribunal on December 4. The memorandum, the prosecution contended, "destroys any possible doubt concerning the Nazis' premeditation of their crimes against Peace."[66]

For their part, the defendants emphasized improvisation—and consequently far greater susceptibility to Allied counteraction had the Great Powers only chosen to act. On the Rhineland, for example, Hermann Göring stoutly denied that the German military occupation was the result of "a long-prepared affair." "It was never the case," Göring said plausibly, if incompletely, "that from the beginning, as has often been represented here, we got together and, conspiring, laid down every point of our plans for decades to come. Rather, everything arose out of the play of political forces and interests, as has always been everywhere the case, the whole world over, in matters of state policy"[67] (Document 34).

The defendants sniped away at the prosecution's contentions with respect to the Hossbach Memorandum throughout the trial—as have historians subsequently, drawing on a far richer body of evidence than was available in 1945. Göring, who was one of the participants at the conference summarized in the memorandum, criticized the prosecution's interpretation of the document—without, however, undermining the two essential points, the evidence of Hitler's aggressive intentions and his subordinates' knowledge of them (Document 35).

Kept in the limelight by the American prosecutors, the charge of crimes against peace prompted uneasiness for the Soviets at various points and sometimes also for the British. The former were vulnerable to charges on the part of the defense that they too were guilty of aggression in Finland, the Baltic states, and particularly Poland, which the Russians had attacked on September 17, 1939, and partitioned between themselves and their victorious German allies. For their part, the British knew that their plans for a surprise attack on Norway in 1940, in formal violation of international law, would be cited by defense attorneys as legitimizing the Germans' invasion of that country in April of that year.

Such charges not only threatened to embarrass the Soviets and the British regarding their conduct of the war but also raised the possibility of a defense of *tu quoque* ("you did it too") — the contention that the defendants' guilt was mitigated by the fact that the Allies had committed comparable crimes. While never explicitly forbidden by the Tribunal, the defense of *tu quoque* was arguably precluded by the charter and was a difficult argument for defense lawyers to make.

More than any other defendant, Rudolf Hess triggered anxieties on the part of the Russians. Hess's attorney from February 1946, Alfred Seidl, a former Nazi Party member from Munich, kept trying to raise the issue of Soviet culpability in order to challenge the Tribunal's authority in judging his client. Throughout the trial, Hess was a perfect focal point for Soviet suspicions. Deeply committed to an anti-Bolshevik worldview and a pioneer of Nazism, Hitler's deputy had made his daring flight to Britain on the eve of the Nazis' attack on the Soviet Union, purportedly to promote an Anglo-German accord that would crusade against the Soviets. Ever after, Stalin and his entourage seem to have feared that, one day, the British might take advantage of Hess's captivity to launch some sort of anti-Soviet maneuver.

In the glare of world attention, Hess's bizarre behavior seemed only to confirm the deep suspicions in which he was held in Moscow. Feigning, or perhaps truly suffering from, a loss of memory, he seemed sometimes mad, sometimes shrewdly scheming — it was difficult to tell which. "Hess was a clown," say historians Ann and John Tusa,

> but a Shakespearean clown. He was a grotesque figure, gaunt and with angular projections from a baggy, grey tweed suit. Everyone watched with fascination his . . . grimaces and gesticulations, his sudden paroxysms of laughter. His rabbity grin expressed no comprehensible delight. When people laughed at him — and sometimes they did — they immediately became uneasy. For hours on end Hess would show no interest in what was happening in court; he seemed to have no contact with reality. Suddenly he would shoot a piercing glance at the visitors in the gallery and smile sardonically, and spectators would feel a chill. At such moments, those who felt pity for this scarecrow, thin, miserable and old, those who believed the experts must be wrong and that Hess was too mad to be on trial, were shaken. There was a knowingness, a cunning, a shielded strength in the man. So perhaps this pathetic, ill-co-ordinated figure concealed someone capable of the influence and the crimes of which he was accused. Like the

Shakespearean clown, his presence was always disturbing, and challenged certainties.[68]

Uneasy about Hess and apprehensive about whether arguments on his and others' behalf might impugn Stalinist wartime conduct, the Soviet prosecutors reported to Deputy Foreign Minister and delegate to the United Nations Andrei Vyshinsky in Moscow on November 19, the day before the trial opened, that they were "determined to avoid delicate questions" being raised in court. The Soviet delegation prepared a list of topics that they wanted banned from the trial and discussed these with Vyshinsky when he visited Nuremberg later that month. Afterward, the Russian prosecutors raised these matters with their American, British, and French colleagues and seem to have had no trouble reaching agreement. In March, when the defense attorneys were just beginning their presentations, Rudenko and Jackson exchanged letters agreeing to invoke Article 18 of the Nuremberg charter "to firmly preclude all attempts by the defendants or counsel to take advantage of the current trial for the consideration of questions having no direct relevance to the case."[69]

It was easier said than done. On March 25, arguing on behalf of Hess, Seidl raised the Nazi-Soviet Pact of August 1939, "the skeleton in the closet of the trial," as a French commentator, Léon Poliakov, referred to it.[70] The pact was embarrassing enough in itself, suggesting that the Russians were effectively accomplices in the Nazis' conspiracy against the Poles in September. But Seidl went further, alluding to a secret protocol to the pact proposing a partition of Poland and disposing of the Baltic states—revealing an imperial motive rather than the objective of self-protection that the Soviets claimed for themselves. Attesting to this secret protocol, Seidl announced that he had a signed affidavit by Dr. Friedrich Gaus, a Foreign Office official who had drafted the Nazi-Soviet Pact. Over Rudenko's strong objections, Gaus's testimony was incorporated into the trial record a few days later. Hess's lawyer was unable, however, to produce a copy of the secret protocol itself. Seidl made the most of this evidence a week later, on April 1, when he questioned Joachim von Ribbentrop, the former Nazi foreign minister who was as eager as anyone to recall the Soviets' involvement in the attack on Poland. The exchange revealed the aggressive ambitions of the Soviets on the eve of the war (Document 36).

About the time of Ribbentrop's testimony, someone on the Allied side leaked a copy of the secret protocol to Seidl. (The source, in all likelihood, was someone on the large American prosecution team, and the motive may well have been anticommunism, according to one authority at least.)[71] On May 21, during his questioning of Ernst von Weizsäcker, the leading civil servant in the German Foreign Office under the Nazis, Hess's lawyer suddenly claimed to have the incriminating text in hand (Document 37).

By this point, Lord Lawrence's unwillingness to "put the document to the witness" was no great blow to the defense. Thanks to repeated testimony by witnesses such as Ribbentrop and Weizsäcker, the contents of the secret protocol had become public knowledge in the West. To the British, the prospects for embarrassment over Norway were considerable. The problem arose because the British and the French had been planning an invasion of the country at roughly the same time as the Germans and because the British, through the mining of the Norwegian coast and the seizure of the German ship *Altmark* in Norwegian waters in February 1940, had violated Norwegian neutrality on several occasions before the German attack. Unwilling to be put on the defensive, the British government decided to refuse both the defense and the prosecution access to its secret files, arguing that material in these documents was irrelevant to the charges in the indictment. The issue was joined during the testimony of Admiral Erich Raeder, commander in chief of the German navy in 1940. Compared with the cases against other defendants, that against Raeder on counts one and two was quite strong: He had headed the German navy since 1928, had enthusiastically pursued rearmament, and had been present at the Hossbach conference of 1937 and another on May 23, 1939, in which the Führer had been particularly explicit in declaring his war aims. On Norway, the prosecution claimed that the admiral had been especially important, that he in fact persuaded Hitler to launch the attack in April 1940.

Stiff and irritable, and on record in a statement he made in Moscow while in Soviet captivity that his junior colleague Admiral Dönitz was a "political" officer known as "Hitler-Boy Dönitz," Raeder made a poor impression, both among his fellow prisoners and on the witness stand. When questioned by his attorney, Walter Siemers, he argued credibly that he had been concerned about the possibility of a British attack on Norway almost from the beginning of the war (Document 38). According to Raeder, Hitler drew upon information supplied by the Norwegian pro-Nazi politician Vidkun Quisling. The idea—not far from the truth, it turned out—was that the British and French were seeking in 1940 to extend the war into Scandinavia by using the pretext of aid to Finland, then heavily engaged in fighting off an attack by the Soviets. Responding to attorney Siemers, Raeder challenged the notion that aggressive war was the result of a criminal conspiracy. The admiral assumed the posture of a military professional, proud of his role in Operation Weserübung, the German attack on Norway. On July 16, Siemers summed up before the Tribunal Raeder's contention that the attack on Norway was a pre-emptive strike in "forcible anticipation," justified by the "right of self-preservation." Challenged by Maxwell-Fyfe, who stoutly denied that the Germans had concrete information about Allied invasion plans, Raeder's attorney nevertheless had a plausible argument to make.[72]

The prosecution was on much more solid ground with Operation Barbarossa, the Germans' ferocious assault on the Soviet Union on June 22, 1941. Shawcross summed up the case on December 4 (Document 39). Almost all of the defendants traced the origins of the campaign to the Führer and many, thereby, denied their role in any long-established plot or conspiracy to attack the Soviet Union. Responding to the questions of his lawyer, Otto Nelte, Field Marshal Wilhelm Keitel, chief of the High Command of the Wehrmacht and almost a caricature, in Western eyes, of the obedient, uncommunicative Prussian officer, claimed that he had been opposed to the attack (Document 40).

Quite different were the arguments of General Alfred Jodl, called to the witness stand a few months later. Chief of the Wehrmacht operations staff, Jodl also emphasized Hitler's decisive role. For the stiff and soldierly war planner, however, the attack on the Soviets was really a preventive campaign. Responding to his lawyer, Franz Exner, he focused sharply on the military side of things (Document 41). Summing up, Exner reminded his client of the prosecution's claim of a "whole series of campaigns" that were the result of a "long premeditated and concerted plan of conquest which you, as a conspirator, both instigated and carried out. What have you to say to this?" Exner asked. As if regretful that planning and preparation had not been more thorough, more far-ranging, Jodl claimed that this picture was "completely distorted. . . . Everything had to be improvised for this war," he observed. "There was nothing ready except the plan of attack against Poland. There were neither enough bombs or ammunition. At that time not a single soldier thought about Norway, Belgium, Holland, Yugoslavia, Greece, or even Russia. No military agreements had been reached with Italy or with Japan."[73] If only, Jodl almost seemed to say, things had been better planned.

WAR CRIMES

War crimes were the most straightforward of the four counts against the accused at Nuremberg, in the sense that international law provided a well-worn path of custom, precedent, and legislation for their adjudication. To this day, the common view is that war criminals and hence "war crimes" were what Nuremberg was all about. "Crimes against peace" and conspiracy were central to the American prosecution, as we have just seen. "Crimes against humanity," which will be examined in the next section, were viewed as one of the original contributions of the trial to international law. But in 1945 and 1946 "war crimes" extended far into terrain commonly thought of as "crimes against humanity." Contrary to a widespread sense that the latter encompassed grave atrocities against civilians, for example, "war crimes" were understood at Nuremberg as illegal acts committed against civilian populations as well as military personnel. In the words of the charter, war crimes were "violations of the laws and customs of war," including "murder, ill-treatment or deportation to slave labor or for any other purpose of civilian population of or in occupied territory, murder or ill-treatment of prisoners of war or persons on the seas, killing of hostages, plunder of public or private property, wanton destruction of cities, towns or villages, or devastation not justified by military necessity." In keeping with its strategy, the prosecution presented Nazi war crimes as involving much more than occasional breaches of military regulations. As the French prosecutor François de Menthon put it in introducing these crimes, they were "the manifestation of a concerted and methodically executed plan" (Document 42).

The prosecutors referred to a broad array of war crimes in their opening and closing addresses: the plundering of art from every corner of Europe, notably to fill the private collection of Hermann Göring and the collections of Alfred Rosenberg's pseudo-scientific institutions; the rounding up of civilians and empressing of prisoners of war for forced labor, referred to by Robert Jackson as "the most horrible and extensive slaving operation in history"; the terrifying *Nacht und Nebel* decree, by which people were arrested and bundled off to concentration camps in Germany without leaving friends or relatives any trace of their whereabouts; the orders given for the shooting of commandos in uniform, caught in the course of military operations; the branding and massacre of Soviet prisoners of war; the deliberate policies of looting that condemned entire regions to starvation; and so on. Charles Dubost, the French deputy prosecutor, chilled the court with examples of the most ghastly wartime atrocities—"not without precedent in the Germanic practice of war," he noted pointedly. One he chose, and for which there was an abundance of cases in every occupied country, was the seizing and execution of hostages. Dubost drew heavily in his presentation on the French case, referring to nearly thirty thousand murdered civilians, many of whom were tortured before being killed (Document 43).

Much of Dubost's evidence came from German concentration camps, understood at the time as the quintessential instrument of the Nazi domination of Europe. Breaking with the American strategy, the French determined to make their case at this point through witnesses. Dubost called seven victims of concentration camps. Three of them described Mauthausen, in Austria, where many Allied prisoners of war were taken to be murdered. Two told of Buchenwald, including accounts of so-called medical experiments. Perhaps the most powerful testimony began on January 28, when Dubost called to the stand an articulate woman in a dark blue suit. Aged thirty-three, Marie Claude Vaillant-Couturier was a veteran of the French Resistance who survived more than three years of Nazi tortures and abuse, mainly in Auschwitz. A witness of great stature — she was a deputy in the French Constituent Assembly in 1946 and a decorated Resistance heroine — Vaillant-Couturier described a cascade of horrors unfamiliar to the immediate postwar audience. She told of the torture and murder of Resistance members, the unspeakable convoy to Auschwitz, the terrible regimen of the camp, the gassing of Jews, the sickness, and the medical experiments (Document 44). The courtroom hushed at Vaillant-Couturier's testimony. For some, it was simply too much to bear. The *New York Herald Tribune* reported that on hearing about the atrocities, some of the defendants removed their headphones.[74] Foolishly, when Vaillant-Couturier was finished, Julius Streicher's attorney, Dr. Hanns Marx, assisting the counsel for the SS, tried to cross-examine the witness. What followed was evidence of the integrity of her first-hand testimony (Document 45).

The prosecutors introduced many statistics about those who were murdered, not all of them correct, to be sure. In his summation, Sir Hartley Shawcross tried nobly to strike the right balance. "The mere number of victims is not the real criterion of the criminality of an act," he said.

> The majesty of death, the compassion for the innocent, the horror and detestation of the ignominy inflicted upon man — man created in the image of God — these are not the subjects of mathematical calculation. Nonetheless, somehow, numbers are relevant. For we are not dealing here with the occasional atrocities which are perhaps an incident in any war. . . . We are dealing here with something entirely different; with systematic, wholesale, consistent action, taken as a matter of deliberate calculation — calculation at the highest level.[75]

But it was only with the Soviet prosecution that the court received a full sense of the scale of Nazi war crimes—extending to literally millions of victims of German occupation and other policies. Reflecting the Soviet view of the course of the war, Roman Rudenko insisted that Nazi Germany's "main blow" was in the east, beginning with the attack on the Soviet Union in June 1941. In numbing detail, as if articulating the numbers were a kind of catharsis, the Soviet prosecutor presented an inventory of the German destruction of his country (Document 46). Among these crimes was one of stunning proportions that simply overwhelmed in magnitude the atrocities committed against captured Western servicemen—the murder of more than three million Soviet prisoners of war (Document 47).

To the documents and firsthand testimony, the prosecution added films, with scenes from German concentration camps, the Warsaw ghetto, and other horrors. The accused were also visited by leading American psychologists. Among them, Gustave Gilbert and his colleague Douglas Kelley stationed themselves at one showing to assess the reaction of the defendants. They reported a range of reactions, from contrition (Walther Funk: "covers his eyes, looks as if he is in agony, shakes his head"), to boredom (Alfred Rosenberg: "fidgets, peeks at screen, bows head, looks to see how others are reacting"), to indeterminate (Julius Streicher: "keeps watching, immobile except for an occasional squint"). In the evening, the psychologists did the rounds of the prisoners' cells to collect more impressions. Wilhelm Keitel, Gilbert reported,

> was eating, having just returned from a conference with his defense attorney. He appeared to have forgotten the film until we mentioned it. He stopped eating and said with his mouth half full, "It is terrible. When I see such things, I'm ashamed of being a German!—It was those dirty SS swine!—If I had known I would have told my son, 'I'd rather shoot you than let you join the SS.' But I didn't know.—I'll never be able to look people in the face again."[76]

Judge Norman Birkett similarly had enough, and often he saw no value in the accumulation of detail. "This evidence is building up a most terrible and convincing case of complete horror and inhumanity in the concentration camps," he wrote in his diary in the evening following Vaillant-Couturier's testimony. "But from the point of view of this trial it is a complete waste of valuable time. The case has been proved over and over again. Neither does the world need it any more, for all over the world the evidence has been published. . . . But it seems impossible to stop it, or to check the volume of it."[77]

Who was ultimately responsible for Nazi war crimes? A constant theme at Nuremberg was the defendants' efforts to pass the burden of guilt along to someone else. Alfred Rosenberg, minister for the occupied eastern territories, claimed that he had in fact been friendly toward the Soviet people but that in such matters he had been overridden by Hitler, Himmler, Göring, Sauckel, and others. A seemingly contrite Hans Frank, governor general of much of occupied Poland, claimed that he had tried in vain to restrain his superiors. Economic specialists, of whom the former Reichsbank head and minister Walther Funk was a singularly unimpressive representative, blamed the political leaders. Former Nazi Foreign Minister Joachim von Ribbentrop referred to the Führer's charismatic power: "Do you know," Gilbert recorded him saying, "even with all I know, if Hitler should come to me in this cell now, and say 'Do this!'—I would still do it.—Isn't it amazing? Can't you really feel the terrific magnetism of his personality?"[78]

Military men like Wilhelm Keitel consistently blamed the SS. To address the latter claim, American prosecutors called a high-ranking Waffen-SS officer, Erich von dem Bach-Zelewski, chief of antipartisan combat units on the eastern front at the end of 1942. Telford Taylor questioned the slight, bespectacled former officer, infamous for the murderous onslaught of his *Einsatzgruppe* (a motorized SS killing unit operating behind the front line) and his bloody repression of the uprising in the city of Warsaw in 1944 (Document 48).

Questioning the witness, Soviet Colonel Yuri Pokrovsky linked the antipartisan campaign to the wider Nazi objective. The real goal of such warfare, Bach-Zelewski admitted, was to slaughter the civilian population. Suggesting that this massacre was decided upon as part of the preparations for the attack on the Soviet Union, the witness mentioned a speech at Weselberg made "at the beginning of 1941" by Reichsführer SS Heinrich Himmler, head of the vast SS apparatus of the Third Reich: "He spoke of the purpose of the Russian campaign, which was, he said, to decimate the Slav population by 30 million." Through his questioning, Pokrovsky then sought to demonstrate that the killings were part of a predetermined plan (Document 49).

Armaments minister Albert Speer insisted on the breadth of his responsibility "for the disaster before the German people" and appeared contrite and forthcoming when he gave his testimony late in June 1946. He freely admitted using concentration camp and POW labor, and when faced with details of atrocious conditions for these workers he showed signs of impatience and offered a range of excuses (Document 50). Submarine chief Admiral Karl Dönitz presented the most vigorous legal defense against charges of war crimes, thanks in part to his brilliant attorney, Otto Kranzbühler, a thirty-eight-year old naval lawyer who was allowed to appear in court in his captain's uniform and carried the title Flottenrichter, referring to his wartime post as a naval judge advocate. Among the ablest of the defense counsel, as Biddle noted, Kranzbühler was "cool, polite but never obsequious, extraordinarily skillful, handsome."[79] Answering various charges of having breached the laws of war, Dönitz and his lawyer replied with chapter and verse: The ships his submarines attacked without warning were not "merchant vessels" at all within the meaning of the London agreement of 1936 because they were armed and they attacked submarines; U-boats did not fire on defenseless enemy crew in the water although they did, after a much discussed incident in 1942, eschew rescue as "counter to the elementary demands of warfare." In an extraordinary legal coup given the Tribunal's general disinclination to hear *tu quoque* arguments, Kranzbühler was permitted to bring to bear on his case American Admiral Chester A. Nimitz's replies to questions about the U.S. conduct of submarine warfare in the Pacific. Seen in that wider context, Kranzbühler was able to argue convincingly, German naval warfare was neither illegal nor in violation of established practices. There remained Dönitz's broader involvement in aggressive war as an adviser to Hitler, particularly his willing assumption of the position of commander in chief of the navy in 1943 and head of state in 1945, as directed by the Führer's last will and testament. Did these implicate the defendant, he was asked? Questioned by his lawyer on his relationship with Hitler, the proud and dignified admiral insisted that he was never ordered to commit war crimes. He did admit—just as did most of the accused at Nuremberg—the extraordinary impact that the Führer had on him. Dönitz claimed that he never considered that by accepting these jobs he was assuming political responsibility for the larger Nazi enterprise. Hitler gave the orders, Dönitz said, and it never occurred to the admiral to do anything but obey (Document 51).

As with the admiral, so with the field marshal. OKW head Wilhelm Keitel's lawyer told the Tribunal of his client's "highly developed soldierly conception of duty." Although the charter excluded the "defense of superior orders," as it is known, it allowed its consideration in mitigation of punishment; so while Keitel and others at times accepted some element of responsibility for what they had signed or ordered or passed along, they also dwelt earnestly on their relationship to their commander in chief. As with all the military defendants, Keitel's defense stressed his oath of loyalty to the Führer, his duty of allegiance, and his disengagement from political issues. Far from being a "yes man" according to his counsel, Otto Nelte, he "was fighting a constant battle, day after day, in every possible field, with Hitler and the forces which were influencing him on all sides."[80] Keitel himself explained how Hitler's military judgments appeared to him irrefutable, the conceptions of a genius. (Keitel was called *Lakaitel* by some of his colleagues, using a pun on the German word for *lackey*.) Questioned about war crimes by General Rudenko, Keitel offered various excuses and denials. In the end, however, as he freely admitted, he was "a loyal and obedient soldier" of his Führer and did what he was told (Document 52).

And so with the Reichsmarschall. At the very summit of the Nazi hierarchy, Hermann Göring explained his adherence to the Führer in chivalric terms. Göring had thrown in his lot with Hitler during the period before the Nazis took power, he wanted the court to know. "I gave him my hand and said: 'I unite my fate with yours for better or for worse: I dedicate myself to you in good times and in bad, even unto death.' I really meant it—and still do."[81] During the course of the trial, Göring made the only frontal challenge to the prosecution's case against Nazi war crimes. Unlike the other defendants, who strove to prove their innocence of the charges or to mitigate their guilt, the Reichsmarschall, under questioning by his attorney, Otto Stahmer, claimed that the legal foundation for the prosecution of war crimes—the Hague convention of 1907, for the most part—was simply obsolete. These agreements no longer made sense in conditions of modern warfare (Document 53).

Explaining the workings of the Führerstaat, the state ordered by the will of the Führer, Göring declared that any other course but complete obedience was unthinkable:

> [I]f a general had been able to say, "My Führer, I consider your statements wrong and not in keeping with the agreements we have made," or "This is not a policy of which we can approve," it would have defied understanding. Not because that particular general would have been shot; but I would have doubted the sanity of that man, because how does one imagine that a state can be led if, during a war, or before a war, which the political leaders have decided upon, whether wrongly or rightly, the individual general could vote whether he was going to fight or not, whether his army corps was going to stay at home or not, or could say, "I must first ask my division."[82]

In one of their final arguments, several defense attorneys seized upon the massacre of thousands of Polish officers in the Katyn Forest—quite different from *tu quoque* contentions because in this case the defense claimed that the crime was not theirs, but the Soviets'. Toward the end of the trial the Tribunal heard three defense witnesses testify that the Soviets had been the ones to murder the Poles, and three prosecution witnesses say the contrary. By general agreement, the defense made the more convincing case, to the discredit of the Russian view. In the end, however, Lawrence determined that the Tribunal should go no further with the matter and simply let it drop. When the judgment was issued months later, it was silent on this accusation that had originally been made against the accused.

Apart from occasional references to Allied air bombardment of Germany, about which the Tribunal permitted no discussion, Katyn was the only instance of its kind, and in general the defense was overwhelmed as much by the volume of evidence of war crimes as by the details. Sensing as much, the accused referred often to the Führer as having inspired Nazi war crimes. Summing up for the prosecution, Robert Jackson returned to Hitler, "the man at whom nearly every defendant has pointed an accusing finger." Together with a very few others, all of them dead or presumed dead—he mentioned Himmler, Heydrich, Goebbels, and Bormann—Hitler was supposed to have been responsible for it all. Nevertheless, the guilt of the defendants was real enough, said Jackson toward the end of his long speech (Document 54).

CRIMES AGAINST HUMANITY

The charge of "crimes against humanity" was a distinct innovation of the Nuremberg trial, and in the popular imagination it remains one of the noted achievements of the entire proceeding. Examined closely, however, it is less of a breakthrough than many believed at the time, or subsequently. As a separate count against the "major war criminals" at Nuremberg, "crimes against humanity" emerged in the summer of 1945 during the London conference that drafted the charter of the International Military Tribunal. To be sure, the term had a much longer pedigree, relating to broad humanitarian principles that had not yet been codified in positive law. The "laws of humanity" were woven into the celebrated Martens clause of the Hague convention of 1907 on land warfare, which sought to extend to entire populations the protection of "the principles of the law of nations, as established by and prevailing among civilized nations, by the laws of humanity, and the demands of public conscience." Denouncing the massacre of Armenians in 1915, the governments of France, Britain, and Russia held the Turkish government responsible for "crimes against humanity and civilization." And after World War I, the Commission of Responsibilities of the Authors of the War looked to the prosecution of those charged with "violations of the laws and customs of war and the laws of humanity" (see p. 119).[83]

During the latter part of Second World War, as jurists scrutinized alleged war crimes with a view to postwar prosecutions, "crimes against humanity" stood for grave maltreatment or atrocities committed against persons who were unprotected by law because of their nationality. Pressing this point, German anti-Nazi and other antifascist refugees from the expanded Reich understood that "war crimes" as conventionally defined might well exclude the persecutions they had suffered on Axis territory at the hands of their *own* government. German, Austrian, and Czechoslovak Jews, Social Democrats, Communists, and liberals shared this concern, and their representatives pleaded with Allied authorities to have their sufferings acknowledged in the quest for justice. Taking up their case in 1944, the American delegate to the United Nations War Crimes Commission, Herbert Pell, sought retribution for wartime atrocities committed against people on religious or racial grounds. According to the commission's official history, Pell "said that such crimes demanded the application of the 'laws of humanity,' and moved that 'crimes committed against stateless persons or against any persons because of their race or religion' represented 'crimes against humanity.'" Not long after, the commission defined such crimes explicitly as "crimes committed against any person without regard to nationality, stateless persons included, because of race, nationality, religious or political belief, irrespective of where they have been committed" — a definition not far in substance from that adopted in London and incorporated into Article 6(c) of the Nuremberg charter, entitled "Crimes against Humanity."[84]

As part of their preparation for the 1945 London conference, the American prosecution team produced several drafts of the offenses with which the Nuremberg defendants were to be charged. The challenge here was to engage the wide range of Nazi criminality, including not only wars of aggression and breaches of the "laws and customs of war," but also "atrocities and persecutions," as they were frequently termed — horrors understood to be integral to Nazism itself and that might have been sanctioned by German law at the time. Repeatedly, the American drafts referred to "persecutions on racial or religious grounds"—language, once again, that found its way into Article 6(c). As Robert Jackson explained, he had been specifically urged by émigré groups to prosecute crimes "committed inside Germany, under German law, or even in violation of German law, by authorities of the German state." As the London meetings continued, appeals from Jewish quarters argued for explicit focus on the massacre of European Jews. Sir David Maxwell-Fyfe reported pressure from Jewish groups to include some reference to persecutions on such grounds as understood by the term "crimes against humanity."[85] And the French and Russians, particularly given the suffering of their populations during the war, posed no objection to incorporating such language into the charter. The suggestion for the specific term "crimes against humanity" came to Jackson from Hersh Lauterpacht, a distinguished professor of international law at Cambridge University who had strongly pressed for a war crimes trial in 1943 and who had been keen to have the court consider atrocities committed against European Jewry.[86] The dominant force in London, Jackson introduced the heading "crimes against humanity" into one of the final drafts of the London agreement; it thus found a place in Article 6 of the Nuremberg charter and the indictment.

Would these crimes include persecutions reaching back to the Nazis' seizure of power in 1933? Jewish and other groups had argued strenuously for such inclusion, and up to the beginning of the London conference the American drafts suggested that crimes against humanity would extend to the beginning of the Nazi era. However, in keeping with his primary focus on Nazi aggression in the drafting of the charter, and uneasy about claiming jurisdiction over the internal affairs of another country, Jackson demanded that crimes against humanity be understood as part of the "common plan or enterprise of making an unjust or illegal war in which we became involved." In other words, the Americans considered such crimes to be subsidiary, deriving from the other charges against the accused. Fashioned into the language of the charter, and with the punctuation corrected by a special protocol on October 6 to underscore the point, Article 6(c) read as follows:

Crimes against Humanity: namely, murder, extermination, enslavement, deportation, and other inhumane acts committed against any civilian population, before or during the war, or persecutions on political, racial, or religious grounds in execution of or in connection with any crime within the jurisdiction of the Tribunal, whether or not in violation of the domestic law of the country where perpetrated.[87]

Addressing the Tribunal and referring to war crimes and crimes against humanity, British prosecutor Sir Hartley Shawcross said, "It is convenient to deal with these matters together for insofar as they were committed during the war, to some extent they overlap and in any case they are interconnected." In short, the boundaries between war crimes and crimes against humanity were not entirely clear.

In practice as in theory, crimes against humanity were constantly tangled with war crimes, and both in the indictment and throughout the trial there was little effort to distinguish between them. Closely circumscribed by the charter, the inclusion of crimes against humanity in the Nuremberg proceedings was therefore hardly a ringing announcement to the international community of a new category of offenses against humankind. Nevertheless, perhaps because of the contrast between the technical limitations, which few understood, and the universalistic designation of these crimes, instantly recognizable to everyone, crimes against humanity came to stand in the popular imagination—and eventually in international law—for something a good deal more. That may well be why, at the conclusion of the trial, American president Harry Truman claimed that "an undisputed gain coming out of Nürnberg is the formal recognition that there are crimes against humanity."[88]

During the trial itself few parties at Nuremberg bothered to be precise about what they meant by the term. Heedless of some of the legal complications, attorneys often alluded to crimes against humanity as a way of underscoring the particularly heinous character of Nazi wartime criminality. In his opening address to the Tribunal, the French prosecutor François de Menthon even coined an additional term (having already referred in his address to a "crime against the spirit"; see p. 28), allowing his rhetoric to sail far above Article 6. De Menthon's point was that some Nazi crimes—inspired by a kind of religious fanaticism—were an assault on the very essence of humanity. He called them "crimes against the human status" (*la condition humaine*) (Document 55).

Remarkably, in his introductory speech, which lasted for several hours and treated Nazi criminality in the most wide-ranging fashion and which was meant to deal with both war crimes and crimes against humanity, de Menthon devoted only a single sentence to Jews, a somewhat off-target reference to Nazi persecutions: "It is also known that racial discriminations were provoked against citizens of the occupied countries who were catalogued as Jews, measures particularly hateful, damaging to their personal rights and human dignity."[89] The lapse is curious, though not untypical, likely relating to the unease in postwar France and elsewhere about Jewish issues and to distortions of the popular memory having to do with wartime collaboration and popular anti-semitism. By contrast, others at Nuremberg spoke freely about Jews. Indeed, as historian Léon Poliakov observed years ago, crimes against humanity at Nuremberg more often than not meant anti-Jewish persecutions and massacres, about which there was much discussion and debate.[90] Scattered references to Gypsies appeared, but these were very few and reflected little understanding at the time of Nazi policies toward the Sinti and Roma people.

How was the wartime fate of the Jews presented at Nuremberg? Jewish organizations briefed Robert Jackson fully before the trial, and in August 1945 the American prosecutor proposed to call Chaim Weizmann, the revered president of the World Zionist Organization, to present the issue as a witness for the prosecution. The British apparently vetoed the idea, fearing that the Zionist leader's testimony, by attracting special sympathy for Jews, would have negative repercussions for the British standing as the ruling authority in Palestine. In the end it was often non-Jews who recounted the Jewish catastrophe at the trial, integrating it into their presentations—an approach that some Jewish strategists had felt in the first place was the wiser course.[91]

Neither the British nor the Americans had given much thought before the trial to the question of the circumstances of the destruction of European Jewry. Telford Taylor, a U.S. army colonel in 1945, a prosecutor at Nuremberg, and a leader of the prosecution team that took over subsequent proceedings—someone of unquestioned sympathy toward Jews—recalled many years later that as the trial was being prepared he knew little about what we call "the Holocaust": "like so many others, I remained ignorant of the mass extermination camps in Poland, and the full scope of the Holocaust did not dawn on me until several months later, at Nuremberg."[92] One measure of this incomprehension was the prosecution's miscasting of defendant Julius Streicher, a repellent but clearly second-rate Jew-baiter—"the filthy Streicher," as Jackson put it in his summation—as a mastermind of count four of the indictment, inciting and "directing" others in the persecution of the Jews. Repellant Streicher certainly was; but he was no mastermind.

Both the Americans and the British set the murder of European Jews in what is to us a familiar historical perspective—including references to six million killed, establishing that figure for the first time with the authority of a non-Jewish international agency. Some basic elements were missed, however: Notably, the prosecutors failed to distinguish between concentration camps, where there had been great cruelty and loss of life but not systematic mass murder, and the death camps of

Poland, where close to four million had been killed as if on an assembly line. There was certainly an acknowledgment of the magnitude of the catastrophe. Jackson, in his summary, had this to say: "The Nazi movement will be of evil memory in history because of its persecution of the Jews, the most far-flung and terrible racial persecution of all time."[93] Shawcross, in the same vein, declared a day later: "There is one group to which the method of annihilation was applied on a scale so immense that it is my duty to refer separately to the evidence. I mean the extermination of the Jews. If there were no other crime against these men, this one alone, in which all of them were implicated, would suffice. History holds no parallel to these horrors."[94]

Both the Americans and the British, and to a much lesser extent the French, gave evidence to the Tribunal of essential details of what we now understand as the Holocaust. Introducing the American case, for example, Jackson referred to a bizarre and ghoulish document that has since become famous—the richly illustrated report on the suppression of the Warsaw ghetto uprising of 1943 by SS commander Jürgen Stroop. Presented by American prosecutor Major William F. Walsh and followed by photographs projected on a screen in a darkened courtroom, the account was almost certainly the most extensive publicity the world had yet received of the 1943 Jewish revolt (Document 56).

Soviet prosecutors spared nothing so far as the Nazi assault on the Jews was concerned. They detailed the slaughters of the *Einsatzgruppen* and others who followed in the wake of the Wehrmacht into Soviet territory, shooting Jews by the hundreds of thousands; the gas vans that were later used to such deadly effect; the terrorizing of entire ghettos and the massacre of their inhabitants; and the death camps in the east—particularly Auschwitz, about which they now disseminated previously little-known information. Among the relatively few witnesses they called were ordinary Jews who told what they had seen with their own eyes. Chief counselor L. N. Smirnov, for example, called to the stand the Jewish writer and former partisan fighter, Abram Suzkever (Document 57).

Soviet prosecutor Roman Rudenko, who assessed this and other testimony for the Tribunal, had no doubt whatever about scope or premeditation: "The fascist conspirators planned the extermination to the last man of the Jewish population of the world and carried out this extermination throughout the whole of their conspiratorial activity from 1933 onward."[95] But what the Soviets did not explain was why Jews had been singled out by the Nazis. Indeed, Rudenko claimed that *all* inhabitants of Eastern Europe "were subjected to merciless persecution and mass extermination": entire populations of occupied Europe "and of the Slavic countries above all others—especially Russians, Ukrainians, Bielorussians, Poles, Czechs, Serbians, Slovenes, Jews." Particularly with reference to the Soviet Union, the Soviet prosecutor was eager to underscore that the Nazis' murderous goals—"the merciless annihilation of the Soviet people for political and racial reasons"—involved more than a quarrel with the Jews.[96] While prominent in the list of victims, therefore, the Jews were not held to be the object of a distinctive, obsessive, high-priority Nazi war aim.

Other approaches to the murder of European Jews at Nuremberg may seem odd from the vantage point of more than a half century's discussion of the matter. Smirnov's words may have revealed more than a translation problem when he denounced "the excessive anti-Semitism of the Hitlerite criminals." Maxwell-Fyfe still had much to learn in the summer of 1945 when he announced that the Majdanek concentration camp "could only have been run with the approval of the German government."[97] American colonel John Amen's interrogation of *Einsatzgruppe* D commander Otto Ohlendorff did not make it clear that the unit's ninety thousand victims between June 1941 and June 1942 were almost entirely Jews.[98] Although he was in Allied custody, no one on the prosecution side moved to call as a witness Rudolf Höss, the former commandant of Auschwitz. Höss appeared, giving some of the most chilling and historically important testimony of the entire trial, but as a *defense* witness—called by Kaltenbrunner's lawyer, Kurt Kauffmann, to demonstrate his client's distance from the killing process (Document 58). Notwithstanding the unconvincing character of Höss's testimony for mitigating Kaltenbrunner's personal guilt, his appearance was almost certainly a disaster for the defense, blackening the defendant (and by implication others, and the SS) with some of the most heinous crimes of the Second World War.

Reference to crimes against humanity, specifically the persecution of the Jews, came up regularly in the examination of the defendants, but with varying degrees of emphasis. It dominated the testimony of Julius Streicher, alone among those charged only with this count and the conspiracy charge. Streicher's testimony and cross-examination were noteworthy mainly for what they revealed about the accused—a coarse, garrulous, repulsive fanatic whom even Nazi loyalists found embarrassing. The other defendants made at least an effort at respectability. Most freely admitted their own prewar and even wartime anti-semitism, but all, even Göring, denied wanting to see all Jews killed. Here as elsewhere, the Reichsmarschall stood out; his outline of Nazi Jewish policy was characteristically unrepentant (Document 59).

Should there have been a more explicit focus at Nuremberg on the murder of European Jews—perhaps even a separate count in the indictment? Allied representatives in London in the planning phases of the Nuremberg Trial considered this issue in general terms, but understood Jewish appeals as similar to those of émigrés such as the Poles and others. The general view was that it would be unwise to single out any particular group. As late as 1947, when he was in charge of the American-organized Subsequent Proceedings, Telford Taylor faced a demand "to have an entire case which would concern itself only with the charge that the Nazis exterminated approximately 6,000,000 European Jews." Taylor sounded out his staff on the question, but was clearly skeptical. In the end, the matter seems to have been passed over without much deliberation (Document 60).

At the trial itself, most defendants simply denied knowledge or responsibility. Göring disclaimed involvement; like many other defendants, he said he favored Jewish emigration somewhere (he did not give details) and indicated that this was his understanding in an ominous communication to Reinhard Heydrich on July 31, 1941, calling for "a total solution to the Jewish question within the area of Jewish influence in Europe." Göring's approach matched what Alfred Rosenberg called a "chivalrous solution" of the Jewish question. Alfred Thoma, Rosenberg's attorney, summed up this well-worn line of argument when speaking for his client at the end of the trial. Thoma's speech provoked an interruption and stout protest by the Soviet prosecutor Roman Rudenko, which was smoothly ignored by Lord Lawrence (Document 61).

How much did the defendants know about the crimes against humanity, about the murders in the east, about the "final solution," the concentration camps, or Auschwitz? Göring remained a loyalist to the end: He did not know, he claimed; and probably neither did Hitler. He would not even allow that atrocities had occurred systematically; the most that he would concede was that there might have been "isolated cases" of liquidations.[99] Kaltenbrunner, Heydrich's successor as head of the vast Main Office for Reich Security (*Reichssicherheitshauptamt*)—the vast SS police apparatus—said he did not know of the final solution before 1943. "Immediately after receiving knowledge of this fact," he told the Tribunal,

> I fought, just as I had done previously, not only against the final solution, but also against this type of treatment of the Jewish problem. . . . [I] protested to Hitler and the next day to Himmler. I did not only draw their attention to my personal attitude and my

completely different conception which I had brought over from Austria and to my humanitarian qualms, but immediately from the first day, I concluded practically every one of my situation reports right to the very end by saying that there was no hostile power that would negotiate with a Reich which had burdened itself with this guilt.

Chiefly thanks to his intervention, Kaltenbrunner ventured, the persecution of Jews ended in October 1944.[100] At various points in the trial, other defendants protested that they had helped Jews at specific moments—among them Schacht, Ribbentrop, Papen, Schirach, Seyss-Inquart, and Speer.

There was some contrition at Nuremberg, although few noteworthy instances. Hans Frank, once determined to rid the Generalgouvernement[101] of Jews, handed over to the Americans his voluminous diary of the days when he ruled in Kraków and claimed in prison to have committed himself anew to Catholicism. "A thousand years will pass and still Germany's guilt will not have been erased," he told the court.[102] Walther Funk, president of the Reichsbank, accused of having received deposits of gold taken from the teeth of gassed Jewish victims, was singularly unimpressive—"a broken heap of flesh," wrote Norman Birkett in his diary, "half-asleep during most of the days, apathetic and listless, and raising blinking eyes to the bright lights installed in the Court for the benefit of the cinematograph operators."[103] Testifying about his pretrial interrogation, in which he had broken into tears, Funk told his attorney that he had just been released from the hospital at the time (Document 62).

Most of the accused gave more articulate reasons why they should not be convicted on the count of crimes against humanity or why history should look kindly upon them. Göring made a persuasive case that such crimes should in no manner be understood as part of a pre-1939 plot to launch an aggressive war. Some placed the blame on Hitler, others on the SS. Still others claimed that they did not know or that they were powerless. Why had they not spoken out? The military men referred to their soldierly obligations: As soldiers, they had sworn an oath to Adolf Hitler. Civilians often protested their inability to have any impact on affairs of state. Toward the end of his cross-examination of the crafty, arrogant Franz von Papen, Sir David Maxwell-Fyfe put a key moral question to him. Papen was—or at least ought to have been, Maxwell-Fyfe thought — moved by the Nazi murders of his close friends and associates. One after another they had been cut down as Hitler consolidated his power and as Papen himself remained a pillar of the regime and moved along—from vice chancellor to minister in Vienna and then Ankara. One of only two defendants *not* charged with crimes against humanity, Papen may have felt freer to answer the British prosecutor's direct questioning. His reasons for not standing up to Hitler were not cowardly, he claimed, but patriotic (Document 63).

LAST WORDS

"We had become friends over the long months of the trial," wrote Francis Biddle about his fellow judges at Nuremberg, "and were consequently less reluctant to criticize each other than in those early days in Berlin when, eyeing our opposite numbers politely, yet with a certain distrust, we had solemnly discussed what we should wear in court."[104] Toward the end of June, while the presentations on behalf of the defendants droned on, Biddle and his colleagues began to sort out what Airey Neave has called "the biggest judicial headache of all time."[105] In June 1946, still hearing testimony and arguments by day, the judges met in the evenings to debate drafts of a final judgment, many of them prepared by the British alternate Sir Norman Birkett. The latter, who was becoming particularly short-tempered over translation difficulties, windy rhetoric, and sloppy courtroom performance, had a particular talent for legal draftsmanship, and the president of the court, Lord Lawrence, seems to have done well to pass the task along to his British colleague.

The court remained in session until August 31, the last day of the trial, its two hundred and sixteenth day. As provided by the charter, Lawrence now accorded the accused an opportunity to speak—for "a few minutes each"—from their places in the dock, aided by a microphone at the end of a pole, held by a guard. In keeping with his preeminence, always acknowledged by the Tribunal, Göring was the first to rise. His speech was forthright, unremarkable, and oddly anticlimactic (Document 64). Next to address the Tribunal was Rudolf Hess, whose speech turned into "a ghoulish and sad fiasco," Telford Taylor felt. Beginning intelligibly, with oblique references to the Soviet show trials, he soon degenerated into gibberish and ended under pressure from the president (Document 65). Joachim von Ribbentrop followed, with a dreary, self-righteous statement, enlivened only by a sarcastic reference to his talks with Stalin in 1939—a theme to which the Tribunal was by now habituated:

When I went to see Marshal Stalin in Moscow in 1939, he did not discuss with me the possibility of a peaceful settlement of the German-Polish conflict within the framework of the Kellogg-Briand Pact; but rather he hinted that if in addition to half of Poland and the Baltic countries he did not receive Lithuania and the harbor of Libau, I might as well return home.[106]

One after another the accused addressed the Tribunal. Most disclaimed responsibility — some more, some less. Some acknowledged distress at the crimes of Nazism, and a few showed signs of remorse. There were moments of arrogant self-righteousness, but also quiet dignity and restraint. Some defendants seemed torn between the two, making signs of contrition but showing flashes of anger for finding themselves where they were. Among the most widely anticipated speeches was that of Albert Speer, who spoke near the end. His theme was the peril of modem technology — a threat, he claimed pointedly, to "every country in the world" (Document 66).

As these statements were being made, work on the final judgment was already well advanced. It was finally ready on September 30, when the court reassembled and the judges began to read their decision aloud — starting with Lord Lawrence and then passing to one of the others every three-quarters of an hour. Some fifty thousand words in its final form, the judgment took two days to read. The climax came on October 1, when the four voting judges reached the sections dealing with specific defendants, announcing nineteen convictions, three acquittals (Schacht, Papen, and Fritzsche), and the sentences of the court.

The judgment opened with a rather dry, factual historical section outlining the origins and aims of the Nazi Party, the Nazi seizure of power in 1933, and the consolidation of power and the process of German rearmament, seen as part of the preparation for war. On history, there was little controversy. The judgment set the Nazi regime in context by emphasizing the role of the Nazi Party and a small number of zealots, led by Hitler and including many of the defendants — Streicher, Frick, Hess, and Göring for the period before 1933 and most of the others thereafter. This emphasis continued in the description of the consolidation phase, the period of rearmament, and planning for war. Notably, there was not the slightest imputation of blame for the German people or German traditions in the account of what happened.

The survey of the evidence then proceeded to several sections on the "common plan or conspiracy and aggressive war" — the basis for counts one and two of the indictment. Adhering to the line that the

American prosecution followed from the beginning, the judges emphasized the central importance of the first two counts. "To initiate a war of aggression . . . is not only an international crime," they said, "it is the supreme international crime differing only from other war crimes in that it contains within itself the accumulated evil of the whole."[107] War, they underscored, was premeditated. Referring to three conferences called by Hitler, beginning with the Hossbach meeting of November 5, 1937, and to two "acts of aggression"—the seizures of Austria and Czechoslovakia — the judges concluded that Germany had indeed been bent on war. The judgment then outlined the steps to an ever wider conflict: first the aggression against Poland in 1939 (sketched historically, but omitting reference to the Nazi-Soviet Pact or the Soviet attack on that country); the attack on Denmark and Norway; the invasion of Belgium, the Netherlands, and Luxembourg; the war against Yugoslavia and Greece; the onslaught on the Soviet Union; and the declaration of war against the United States. "The Charter defines as a crime the planning or waging of war that is a war of aggression or a war in violation of international treaties," the judges said. "The Tribunal has decided that certain of the defendants planned and waged aggressive wars against 10 nations, and were therefore guilty of this series of crimes."[108]

How did the judges respond to the legal challenges made by the defendants to the charges of waging aggressive war and responsibility for crimes against international law? Here, as elsewhere, they took shelter in the Tribunal's charter. In the final paragraph of this section of their judgment, the judges referred to the "doctrine of 'superior orders'" — the claim, made particularly by the military defendants, that in committing some crimes they should not bear responsibility because they had acted under the orders of their military commander, Adolf Hitler. Referring to Article 8 of the charter, the judges disallowed this defense, but in so doing they also provided a test for the establishment of guilt that, notes one legal authority, "resounded throughout the whole international legal world and [has been] profusely quoted in the subsequent cases as well as in the juristic literature"[109] (Document 67).

The judges then turned to the "common plan or conspiracy" (count one of the indictment), which proved to be the most controversial issue the Tribunal had to resolve. Would the judges accept the contention of the American prosecution that the accused had conspired to commit the crimes outlined in the charter? In the judges' debates, the British firmly embraced the notion of conspiracy, precisely along the lines that the American Robert Jackson had argued in court. Ion Nikitchenko and his Soviet colleague were similarly inclined. But the French Donnedieu de

Vabres, supported by Robert Falco, made the opposite case. As Biddle recalled, Donnedieu de Vabres reminded everyone that conspiracy was a crime unknown in international and Continental law: "To the French it was a shocking idea that under the wide range of the English law of conspiracy an individual could be punished. The substantive crime, they insisted, absorbs the conspiracy, which becomes useless once the substantive crime is committed, and we have no need to resort to a theory which involves psychological as well as moral difficulties." By focusing on conspiracy, the French felt, the Tribunal would reduce the responsibility of the Germans "by shifting the blame to the secret plots of a small group." Biddle noted Donnedieu de Vabres as saying that "Hitlerian crimes have their roots deep in the German people." The French judges wanted count one simply thrown out. Interestingly, Biddle sympathized strongly with the French, having acquired a strong dislike of conspiracy indictments in the United States. Unlike the French, however, he feared that a conviction on the conspiracy charge and a finding that organizations were part of this conspiracy would draw into the net far too many ordinary Germans.[110] Here, as so often at Nuremberg, disagreement was resolved through compromise — in this case a finding that there had indeed been a conspiracy, or rather several conspiratorial plans, going back at least to the time of the Hossbach conference of November 1937, but that the purpose of this conspiracy was not so wide as the prosecution had contended. Specifically, the judges limited the role of the conspiracy to the acts of aggressive war — excluding a conspiracy to commit war crimes or crimes against humanity. Toward the end of this section, the judges raised the issue of the degree of responsibility of the defendants in the context of a Hitlerian dictatorship (Document 68). The judgment next proceeded to summarize the evidence on war crimes and crimes against humanity — the murder and ill-treatment of prisoners of war and civilians, the pillage of private and public property, and slave labor.

In their discussion of crimes against humanity, the judges clarified what became known as the "war nexus" — an important finding, taken from the wording (and punctuation) of the Nuremberg charter, that these crimes, when committed before the formal declaration of war in 1939, had to be linked with the other crimes specified in the charter. "To constitute Crimes against Humanity," the judges found, these crimes

> must have been in the execution of, or in connection with, any crime within the jurisdiction of the Tribunal. The Tribunal is of the opinion that revolting and horrible as many of these crimes

were, it has not been satisfactorily proved that they were done in execution of, or in connection with, any such crime. The Tribunal therefore cannot make a general declaration that the acts before 1939 were Crimes against Humanity within the meaning of the Charter, but from the beginning of the war in 1939, War Crimes were committed on a vast scale, which were also Crimes against Humanity; and insofar as the inhumane acts charged in the Indictment, and committed after the beginning of the war, did not constitute War Crimes, they were all committed in execution of, or in connection with, the aggressive war, and therefore constituted Crimes against Humanity.[111]

Notably, the judges had a separate section on the persecution of the Jews (Document 69). Important here was the judges' isolation of "the 'final solution of the Jewish question' in Europe," using the German terminology which, the judges made crystal clear, "meant the extermination of the Jews."

Next in the judgment came the organizations. Considering the various organizations claimed by the prosecution to have been criminal, the judges proceeded cautiously, out of fear that individuals might simply be convicted wholesale of the crime of membership in such an organization and be sentenced to death. At stake was the fate of as many as four million Germans, who had belonged to the six organizations accused of criminality. Collecting evidence on these had proven to be a major logistical challenge. The court held extensive hearings, a huge task managed by a British war hero, Colonel Airey Neave, in the spring of 1946. In the end, these hearings collected affidavits signed by 313,000 people, and almost 100,000 declarations from members of the SS claiming that they knew nothing of atrocities. Hundreds came to Nuremberg as potential witnesses, and in the end twenty-two testified before the Tribunal. Sorting out the legal implications proved to be a major challenge.[112] Inevitably, compromises were necessary, with Nikitchenko favoring sweeping declarations of criminality and Biddle at one point opposing altogether declaring entire organizations criminal. A declaration of criminality, the judges said finally, "should be exercised in accordance with well-settled legal principles, one of the most important of which is that criminal guilt is personal, and that mass punishment should be avoided." They set clear limits, then, for criminal designation in the future (Document 70).

The judges discussed each of the five indicted organizations, rendering their judgments: the leadership corps of the Nazi Party (criminal, if above a specified rank and under specified conditions of membership or participation); the Gestapo and SD, taken together (most units criminal, above low-level service personnel); the SS (most elements criminal, except conscripts who had committed no crimes); the SA (not criminal); the Reich Cabinet (not criminal); the General Staff and High Command (not a criminal organization, although some members were "a disgrace to the honorable profession of arms").

Finally, the court concluded with a detailed consideration of each defendant and the pronouncements of the Tribunal on the counts on which they had been indicted. Reassembled after an hour's break, those convicted heard Lawrence read the sentences of the court:

Göring: indicted on all four counts; convicted on all four; sentenced to death by hanging

Ribbentrop: indicted on all four counts; convicted on all four; sentenced to death by hanging

Keitel: indicted on all four counts; convicted on all four; sentenced to death by hanging

Jodl: indicted on all four counts; convicted on all four; sentenced to death by hanging

Rosenberg: indicted on all four counts; convicted on all four; sentenced to death by hanging

Frick: indicted on all four counts; convicted on counts two, three, and four; sentenced to death by hanging

Seyss-Inquart: indicted on all four counts; convicted on counts two, three, and four; sentenced to death by hanging

Sauckel: indicted on all four counts; convicted on counts three and four; sentenced to death by hanging

Bormann: indicted on counts one, three, and four; convicted on counts three and four; sentenced in absentia to death by hanging

Kaltenbrunner: indicted on counts one, three, and four; convicted on counts three and four; sentenced to death by hanging

Frank: indicted on counts one, three, and four; convicted on counts three and four; sentenced to death by hanging

Streicher: indicted on counts one and four; convicted on count four; sentenced to death by hanging

Raeder: indicted on counts one, two, and three; convicted on counts one, two, and three; sentenced to imprisonment for life

Funk: indicted on all four counts; convicted on counts two, three, and four; sentenced to imprisonment for life

Hess: indicted on all four counts; convicted on counts one and two; sentenced to imprisonment for life

Figure 11. The defendants look on as the verdicts are read.
AP Photo.

Speer: indicted on all four counts; convicted on counts three and four; sentenced to twenty years' imprisonment

Schirach: indicted on counts one and four; convicted on count four; sentenced to twenty years' imprisonment

Neurath: indicted on all four counts; convicted on all four counts; sentenced to fifteen years' imprisonment

Dönitz: indicted on counts one, two, and three; convicted on counts two and three; sentenced to ten years' imprisonment

Fritzsche: indicted on counts one, three, and four; acquitted

Papen: indicted on counts one and two; acquitted

Schacht: indicted on counts one and four; acquitted

As Biddle recalled the deliberations among the judges, the Russians had become increasingly impatient as the debates wore on and agreements were struck over several defendants whose cases seemed to some particularly difficult. Airey Neave thought that pressures on Nikitchenko increased as the discussions often went against the Russians and it became suspected, "in the closed circle of the Nuremberg delegations," that the senior Russian judge was under "Western influence." "He appeared drunk at dances with his evil-looking alternative Volchkov," Neave wrote in 1978.

> I have a clear vision of Nikitchenko with his maroon and gold epaulettes, staggering around the room. The Western Allies looked away. . . . He was continually defeated by a majority. When a Western judge failed to win his point, this was a rejection of his personal interpretation of the law. When Nikitchenko failed to persuade his colleagues, it meant that he had not obtained the verdict ordered by Stalin.[113]

In a public show of disagreement at the end, Nikitchenko announced his dissent—disputing the acquittal of three defendants and challenging the failure to declare the Reich Cabinet and the General Staff criminal organizations. The Tribunal took appropriate notice of the Soviet judge's opinion, but after a year of argument and speeches everyone's patience had worn thin. At Nuremberg, most Western participants and observers were desperate to go home. Younger American prosecutors and a contingent of new judges were ready to try new defendants. The trial of the major war criminals was finally over, and Nikitchenko's dissent had little echo beyond the courtroom itself.

ASSESSMENT

Nuremberg stands for much more than the International Military Tribunal and its work, or even than the wider process of judging Nazi war criminals in the wake of the Second World War. Administratively, it sometimes signifies, in popular discourse, not only the trial before the International Military Tribunal, the subject of this book, but also the twelve "subsequent proceedings" held under American auspices and formally known as the trials before the Nuremberg Military Tribunals. As the person in charge of the latter, Telford Taylor observed, Nuremberg is "a name which conjures up the moral and legal issues raised by applying judicial methods and decisions to challenged wartime acts."[114] As such, there is a special import associated with the assessments made of it over the years, and observers have tended to be more prone to criticize Nuremberg than they might be with other events of more than a half century ago. The proceedings examined in this book were not without opposition at the time, and critical voices may have grown stronger as the years passed because assessments speak to important present-day concerns. Controversy over major issues remains vigorous, and the manifest failure of the world community to live up to the hopes in particular of the International Military Tribunal's architects has been seen as confirming the critics' judgment at the time. Since aggressive war, war crimes, and crimes against humanity have continued unchecked by the application of law, it is said, Nuremberg appears more and more as an exception, a calling of one group of defendants to account while wrongdoing of the sort for which they were tried remains a familiar and even accepted part of the international landscape—including wrongdoing by those who purport to be the judges. In addition, ever since wartime illusions about one of the participating countries, the Soviet Union, were shed, the International Military Tribunal's claims of impartiality seem particularly difficult to sustain.

This book considers a different way of looking at that trial than through the prism of moral and legal concerns. The task here is less to judge than to understand in historical terms—and to do so with an eye to the values, characters, and circumstances of the time. Thus it is particularly concerned with three categories of historical assessment: political, legal, and cultural.

In the political sphere, academic or legal assessments of Nuremberg counted for relatively little at the time. Popular opinion, however, counted for much. Worldwide interest in the proceedings was considerable, reflected by the fact that, as the American commentator Janet Flanner claimed when the International Military Tribunal first met, the courtroom held the largest assembly of journalists ever gathered to cover a single event—more than 160 reporters.[115] (Coverage was intense in the United States, but less so in Europe, where much of the evidence presented in court remained unreported in daily newspapers — in part owing to the shortage of newsprint.)

With its message beamed to nonspecialists, the Nuremberg court was not appreciated by its millions of onlookers as a chapter in legal theory or political philosophy. Rather, the trial was first and foremost understood as a way of dealing with the leaders of the Third Reich. Everywhere in the Allied world, the question of what to do with the Nazi leadership posed itself insistently in the last months of the war. And everywhere, it must be appreciated, responses to the question were extremely harsh. Opinion surveys in Britain and the United States showed large pluralities or majorities supporting the swift execution, without trial, of Nazi leaders. When the French were asked in October 1944 about what to do with Hitler, 40 percent favored the option "shoot, kill, hang him," while 30 percent wanted "torture before killing him" (39 percent of women chose torture, reported the pollster, and only 23 percent of men). Opinion everywhere, particularly in the occupied countries, favored a very severe treatment of Germany. The recourse to judicial proceedings was always the preference of a minority, sometimes a tiny minority.[116]

So in practical terms, the real alternative to Nuremberg was not a wider inquiry into war crimes committed by victors as well as vanquished or a new venture into international adjudication by incorporating judges from countries that had not participated in the war, including judges from the defeated Axis powers. The real alternative, and what most people from Allied countries seemed to prefer, were summary proceedings followed by speedy punishment—in all likelihood death. Without American pressure, this would probably have taken place. This powerful popular mood explains why the often vocal denunciations of Nuremberg as "victor's justice," which were occasionally heard in the United States, for example, had such faint echo anywhere at the time. In October 1946, for example, in the immediate wake of the verdict of the Nuremberg court, a Republican senator from Ohio, Robert A. Taft, lambasted the proceedings, calling them an act of vengeance and retrospective judgment that would discredit the idea of justice in

Europe for years to come. While certainly some Americans agreed with Taft, they were unquestionably in the minority, a minuscule proportion of the American public. "All newspaper editors, commentators, and politicians who were sensitive to the mood of the nation, whether they personally approved or disapproved of the trials, assumed that the man on the street favored the Tribunal," notes historian William Bosch. "Seventy-five percent of Americans polled approved the postwar trials of the German leaders," he reports. "This judgment was echoed by 69 per cent of the columnists, 73 per cent of the newspapers, and 75 per cent of the periodicals."[117]

Writing in January 1947, former secretary of war Henry L. Stimson offered a practical defense of Nuremberg tinged with an idealism thought by some to be typically American (Document 71). While referring formally to "the victorious Powers," Stimson seems to have understood "we" to mean the American people, to whom he appealed in his final sentence. In this, the American statesman seems to have reflected a wider consensus about the trial. For all the talk about an international effort at Nuremberg, William Bosch observes, "Americans and Europeans, supporters and opponents, all considered the Tribunal essentially an American show."[118] Reflecting the hope and optimism in the United States, foreseeing an era of peace through prosperity and cooperation with the Soviet Union, American defenders of Nuremberg assimilated the process and results of the trial into a wider mission in the world.

Nuremberg was also understood as a last act of the Allied coalition against Nazi Germany. When Sidney Alderman, who had worked with Robert Jackson at the London conference, contributed an article in 1951 to a volume entitled *Negotiating with the Russians*, he drew a lesson from the Nuremberg trial that was born of personal experience:

> You can successfully negotiate with the Soviet Union if your ultimate ends and theirs are the same. There will always be difficulties as to language and as to concepts. There will always be differences as to procedures. But on a mission like ours, where the ultimate aims are not in conflict, all difficulties are readily overcome. They are skillful negotiators and can be extremely cooperative.[119]

Nuremberg, in this line of thought, seemed to justify those strategists of international affairs who foresaw international peace and concord by working together on concrete, limited problems.

Since "negotiating with the Russians" was such a high Allied priority at Nuremberg, reflecting a global priority as the war drew to a close, both judges and prosecutors studiously avoided confrontation with the Soviets over such issues as the Nazi-Soviet Pact and its secret protocol, the Soviet attack on Poland in 1939, and the massacre of Polish officers and others in the Katyn Forest. In retrospect, Nuremberg can be seen as occurring just as Cold War storm clouds were gathering—as tensions were rising and disputes were evident, but when the Allies, certainly the Americans, were eagerly hoping that these difficulties would be resolved. Again and again westerners responsible for the trial were prepared to look the other way when it came to the Russians, preferring not to scrutinize their Soviet interlocutors too closely. A fine illustration of the mood of those times is drawn by Francis Biddle, describing what happened when the orchestrator of the Soviet purge trials, Andrei Vyshinsky, came to Nuremberg in November 1945 (Document 72).

On the legal side, criticisms rained down on Nuremberg as lawyers followed the proceedings closely and pronounced judgment on it. Those on the bench "were not jurists of long experience or towering stature," historian Bradley Smith observes. Several of the leading judicial personalities in the United States and Britain had declined to serve on the Tribunal. "None of the members of the Court had experience in international relations, and only one, Francis Biddle, had held a cabinet-level post in government."[120] "The standard of the court does not compare favorably with the highest Courts in England," Norman Birkett wrote during the trial,

> and there has been much weakness and vacillation, and, above all, a failure to appreciate that the trial is only in form a judicial process and its main importance is political. For that, of course, what was required was not only a knowledge of law but a knowledge of history, particularly German history, a knowledge of men and world affairs, and an instinct to apply these things at every stage of this most remarkable case.[121]

German critics of Nuremberg pointed to the severe imbalance between the prosecution and the defense and challenged both the wider conception of the trial as well as the procedures adopted. Admiral Dönitz's attorney, Otto Kranzbühler, made a strong case that the procedures decided on in London and at Nuremberg put the accused at a significant disadvantage (Document 73). For his part, defending what was to a large degree his handiwork, Henry Stimson contended that the judgment of the Tribunal was essentially fair, even if too lenient in some cases (Document 74). So far as the law of the Nuremberg trial is concerned, learned disputation was part of the trial itself, flourished in its wake, and is likely to continue indefinitely on the most fundamental questions. Examined historically, however, much of this debate may seem beside the point. Given the circumstances of 1945–1946 it is impossible to imagine that opinion in the Allied countries would have countenanced, for example, turning a trial over to judges from neutral countries. Neutrality had no aura of rectitude in 1945, and particularly in formerly occupied Europe there was a widespread view that neutral countries had failed to take a courageous stand, had been intimidated by the Nazis, or had profited from the agony of other countries, first leaning to the side of Hitler and then, when their victory was in sight, to that of the Allies. German opinion, one should add—or at least that opinion allowed expression by the Allied occupation—hardly suggested a more independent-minded environment for a trial, assuming that the Allies would ever have permitted Germans to take over the proceedings or participate in the judiciary. The vindictive reaction of anti-Nazi Germans to the acquittal of Fritzsche, Papen, and Schacht, insisting that they face trial once again, is a case in point.

Similarly, it is highly implausible that any court judging high-ranking Nazis would have allowed a searching exploration of the injustices of the Treaty of Versailles in 1919. Defense attorneys repeatedly sought to present evidence on this great evil that they contended was at the root of Nazism; they should not have been surprised that they were forbidden to make this case. By the same token, there was not the slightest chance that the court would hear arguments on the devastating Allied aerial bombardment of Germany—on the question, raised by the defense, of whether this strategy had violated the laws and customs of war. Leaving aside the issue of whether clean hands are or are not necessary to render a just decision, there was simply no way that Allied governments or societies in 1945 were going to put the conduct of their military operations before the same tribunal that was judging accused Nazi war criminals—or any other tribunal, for that matter. In his summation, Sir Hartley Shawcross dealt with this complex legal question in terms that no layperson could fail to understand: "Do two wrongs make a right? Not in that international law which this Tribunal will administer."[122]

Examining Nuremberg historically—considering the impact on the proceedings of circumstances and opinions peculiar to the time—may also be a way of understanding some of the verdicts rendered by the court. It seems certain, for example, that Albert Speer's energetic anticommunism and polished efforts to curry sympathy with the West told, in the end, in his favor; he received a sentence of twenty years, despite his having been deeply implicated in the use of slave labor and responsible for the deaths of hundreds of thousands. "Murder in occupied Europe and in the gas chambers had been exposed and condemned, but murder in the factories and mines had gone unpunished," writes one critic.[123] Moreover, the contrast of Speer's fate with that of the rough-hewn minister of labor Fritz Sauckel, who was sentenced to hang, struck many at the time as anomalous. Concerns to punish "German militarism," seemingly embodied in Wilhelm Keitel and Alfred Jodl, may well have moved the judges to sentence both of them to death—a verdict which rankled, one should add, many Allied soldiers at the time. Likewise, foul-mouthed and loathsome as he was, Julius Streicher, in the views of many, ought not to have been sentenced to hang. The judges came hastily to their decision about him, and it seems likely that they did so at least as much out of revulsion against his personality and the wartime crimes against the Jews (in which he played no active part) as out of reaction to his own wrongdoing. In these examples, as in others that various authors raise, an understanding of Nuremberg can only gain from the historical perspective.

More generally, Nuremberg must be understood within the framework of Allied worries about the continuing threat of Nazism to Germany and to Europe. Hundreds of thousands of Nazi-sympathizing officers, judges, police, bureaucrats, and industrialists remained part of the German scene in 1945, and in the West, at least, it was assumed that they were an inescapable part of the future Germany. Nuremberg prosecutors and judges were highly conscious of their responsibilities for the future of Germany and Europe to pronounce a stern verdict against Nazism. Invited by Articles 10, 11, and 22 of the charter to look to subsequent trials, the court could not ignore its impact on this task, so much discussed at the time.

As suggested at the beginning of this section with reference to the wider resonance of the term *Nuremberg*, the trial of the major war criminals has entered into our culture, and this too prompts some historical reflection. Inevitably, with the passage of time, our views of Nazism, the Holocaust, and the Second World War are becoming more historical — freed progressively from the grip of partisanship and a perspective overwhelmed by grief or anger. Accepted by some as inevitable, this process is worth supporting as an educational and cultural goal. Coming to terms with these great scars in the last century is one of the challenges of our time, and if we really believe we are capable of preventing such catastrophes in the future we had better ensure that we have as objective an evaluation as possible of what went so wrong in the past.

In this process of understanding, Nuremberg has had an important place. It brought forward an extraordinarily vast body of documentation — "evidence far exceeding that previously presented to any tribunal in history," Shawcross pointed out.[124] More than many of the organizers ever hoped, Nuremberg has been a voice for history, in the form of thousands of documents on the Third Reich assembled by the court and released for the scrutiny of historians and writers coming from every possible vantage point. The prosecution and, to a lesser degree, the defense used the trial to introduce evidence that has been pored over by a whole generation. It is perhaps worth stressing to an audience accustomed to demanding "full disclosure" and still in the process of absorbing a new hoard of documentation from the former Soviet Union and its allies just how unprecedented this process was—despite the obvious limitation of disclosure not extending to the Allied side. "There is no parallel in history," wrote one participant, "to this baring of contemporary official papers to the public eye and to expert scrutiny."[125] But this "orgy of revelation" is not to be taken for granted; the process was driven by the Nuremberg prosecution, in particular Jackson's much-criticized prosecution strategy to rely on documentary evidence rather than the testimony of witnesses.

At its best moments, Nuremberg set an example for a kind of historical judgment—impartial, but not necessarily dispassionate; fair-minded, but not without moral compass; searching in its quest for truth, while recognizing the formal limitations that attend to the endeavor in an adversary proceeding. Nuremberg was not perfect, by any means, and it is possible to believe that its warts and blemishes—or even its structural faults—may be the most important things to discuss today. But most would agree that there are other dimensions too and that some of these speak to our efforts to understand and contend with the history of our time. One thinks, for example, of Lord Lawrence's calm insistence on fair play at heated moments in the trial; of the efforts, practically for the first time outside Jewish circles, to grasp the awful significance of the murder of European Jews; of the painful recognition, when hearing the case of Karl Dönitz, that Allied methods of submarine warfare had to be considered along with those of the Reich; of the rejection of the claim of those in high places that they were always bound to obey "superior orders"; and finally of the sincere appeals, from many quarters, to establish some rule of law in a perilous world of nation-states.

NOTES

[1]The Nuremberg War Crimes Trial of 1945–1946 is distinguished from the subsequent Nuremberg proceedings, commonly referred to in the plural as the Nuremberg War Crimes Trials, held under the auspices of the American occupation authorities between December 1946 and April 1949. Partial records of the latter trials, twelve in all, are contained in *Trials of War Criminals before the Nuremberg Military Tribunals under Control Council Law No. 10*, 15 vols. (Washington, D.C.: Government Printing Office, 1951–1952). As the Nuremberg Trial of 1945–1946 proceeded, many thought that it should be followed by a second international trial of the major war criminals. In the end this did not happen. For a discussion and explanation see Donald Bloxham, "'The Trial That Never Was': Why There Was No Second International Trial of Major War Criminals at Nuremberg," *History*, 87 (2002), 41–60.

[2]Robert K. Woetzel, *The Nuremberg Trials in International Law, with a Postlude on the Eichmann Case* (London: Stevens and Sons, 1962), 24.

[3]James F. Willis, *Prologue to Nuremberg: The Politics and Diplomacy of Punishing War Criminals of the First World War* (Westport, CT.: Greenwood Press, 1981), 45, 63–64.

[4]Willis, *Prologue*, 69.

[5]Willis, *Prologue*, 139; Peter Calvocoressi, *Nuremberg: The Facts, the Law, and the Consequences* (London: Chatto and Windus, 1947), 20; Woetzel, *Nuremberg Trials*, 31–34. For a different and somewhat defensive view, see Claud Mullins, *The Leipzig Trials: An Account of the War Criminals' Trials and a Study of the German Mentality* (London: H. F. and G. Witherby, 1921).

[6]*Report of Robert H. Jackson, United States Representative to the International Conference on Military Trials, London, 1945* (Washington, DC: Department of State, 1949), 368; Willis, *Prologue*, 174.

[7]International Military Tribunal, *Trial of the Major War Criminals before the International Military Tribunal, Nuremberg, 14 November 1945–1 October 1946*, 42 vols. 2: 98–155.

[8]Adam Roberts, "Land Warfare: From Hague to Nuremberg," in Michael Howard, George J. Andreopoulos, and Mark R. Shulman, eds., *The Laws of War: Constraints on Warfare in the Western World* (New Haven: Yale University Press, 1994), 125, 128.

[9]The Covenant of the League of Nations, The Avalon Project, Yale University, http://avalon.law.yale.edu/20th_century/leagcov.asp. Last cited, April 17, 2017.

[10]Alfred Zimmern, *The League of Nations and the Rule of Law, 1918–1935* (London: Macmillan, 1936), 384. Emphasis in original.

[11]International Military Tribunal, *Trial of the Major War Criminals*, 3: 100, 5: 386.

[12]Bradley F. Smith, *The Road to Nuremberg* (New York: Basic Books, 1981), 114–15; Bradley F. Smith, *Reaching Judgment at Nuremberg* (New York: Basic Books, 1977), 34.

[13]Inter-Allied Information Committee, *Punishment for War Crimes: The Inter-Allied Declaration Signed at St. James's Palace, London, on 13th January 1942 and Relative Documents*, 2 vols. ([London]: His Majesty's Stationery Office, [1942]), 1: 3–4.

[14]Roger Daniels, *Franklin D. Roosevelt: The War Years* (Urbana-Champaign: University of Illinois Press, 2016), 293; Arieh Kochavi, *Prelude to Nuremberg: Allied War Crimes Policiy and the Question of Punishment* (Chapel Hill, North Carolina: University of North Carolina Press, 1998), 33; Richard Breitman and Allan J. Lichtman, *FDR and the Jews* (Cambridge, Mass.: Belknap, 2013), 198. Although the founding conference of the United Nations organization, held in San Francisco, did not occur until the spring of 1945, the term "United Nations" was widely used by the Allies after the Declaration of United Nations of January 1, 1942—a call for a united war effort against Germany and Japan, originally signed by twenty-six nations, including the Soviet Union.

[15]Inter-Allied Information Committee, *Punishment for War Crimes*, 2: 6–10.

[16]Arieh J. Kochavi, *Prelude to Nuremberg: Allied War Crimes Policy and the Question of Punishment* (Chapel Hill: University of North Carolina Press, 1998), Ch. 2; Jonathan Bush, "'The Supreme . . . Crime' and Its Origins: The Lost Legislative History of the Crime of Aggressive War," *Columbia Law Review*, 102 (2002), 2345–7; Eric Stover, Victor Paskin, and Alexa Koenig, *The Pursuit of War Criminals* (Berkeley: University of California Press, 2016), 27.

[17]John Simon Memorandum, September 4, 1944, Prime Minister's Papers, 4/100/10 (London: Public Record Office).

[18]John F. Murphy, "Norms of Criminal Procedure at the International Military Tribunal," in George Ginsburgs and V. N. Kudriavtsev, *The Nuremberg Trial and International Law* (Dordrecht: Martinus Nijhoff Publishers, 1990), 63.

[19]*Report of Robert H. Jackson*, 19.

[20]Martin Gilbert, *Winston S. Churchill, 1941–1945: Road to Victory* (London: William Heinemann, 1986), 1201–2. The American president played very little part in the articulation of his subordinates' trial plan although he followed and embraced their reasoning. In failing health, he endorsed the evolving scheme being worked out by Stimson's subordinates, approving their views on the importance of conspiracy/criminal organizations and the place of aggressive war as the essence of German criminality. See Telford Taylor, *The Anatomy of the Nuremberg Trials: A Personal Memoir* (Boston: Little, Brown, 1992), 38–39; Smith, *The Road to Nuremberg*, 120; and Bush, "'The Supreme . . . Crime', 2363. See also Joseph Lelyveld, *His Final Battle: The Last Months of Franklin Roosevelt* (New York: Knopf, 2016).

[21]Bradley F. Smith, *The American Road to Nuremberg: The Documentary Record, 1944–1945* (Stanford, CA: Hoover Institution Press, 1982), 139.

[22]Walter Goldstein, "War Crimes and the Lessons of Nuremberg," *Dimensions*, 8, no. 1 (1994): 33.

[23]Taylor, *Anatomy of the Nuremberg Trials*, 43.

[24]Francis Biddle, *In Brief Authority* (Garden City, NY: Doubleday, 1962), 381.

[25]On Nikitchenko's role in the 1935 trial, see Robert Conquest, *The Great Terror: Stalin's Purge of the Thirties* (New York: Macmillan, 1973), 153–54, 361.

[26]Brief for P.M. [Prime Minister], August 1, 1945. Prime Minister's Papers, 4/100/12 (London: Public Record Office).

[27]*Report of Robert H. Jackson*, 333–34.

[28]*Report of Robert H. Jackson*, 130.

[29]*Report of Robert H. Jackson*, 303.

[30]A. N. Trainin, *Hitlerite Responsibility under Criminal Law*, ed. A. Y. Vyshinsky, trans. A. Rothstein (London: Hutchinson, [1945]), 12.

[31]*Hitlerite Responsibility*, 93.

[32]John Wheeler-Bennett and Anthony Nicholls, *The Semblance of Peace: The Political Settlement after the Second World War* (New York: Norton, 1974), 401–2; Francine Hirsch, "The Soviets at Nuremberg: International Law, Propaganda, and the Making of the Postwar Order," *American Historical Review*, 113 (2008), 701–30.

[33]Sidney S. Alderman, "Negotiating on War Crimes Prosecutions, 1945," in Raymond Dennett and Joseph E. Johnson, eds., *Negotiating with the Russians* (Boston: World Peace Foundation, 1951), 49.

[34]Alderman, "Negotiating on War Crimes Prosecutions," 51.

[35]Michael R. Marrus, "A Jewish Lobby at Nuremberg: Jacob Robinson and the Institute of Jewish Affairs, 1945–46," *Cardozo Law Review*, Vol. 27 (February 2006), 1651–65.

[36]"Negotiating on War Crimes Prosecutions," 96–97. Seventy years after the killings, in 2010, the Russian parliament finally admitted that it was Stalin who had ordered the murder of the Polish officers and thousands of prominent persons in 1940. It is now believed that as many as 22,000 Poles were murdered at Katyn, with the massacres carried out by the NKVD. See "Russia Posts Katyn Massacre Documents Online," *The Guardian*, April 28, 2010.

[37]John Q. Barrett, "Raphael Lemkin and Genocide at Nuremberg," in Christoph Safferling and Eckhardt Conze, eds., *The Genocide Convention Sixty Years After Its Adoption* (The Hague: Asser Press, 2010), 45; Joel Cooper, *Raphael Lemkin and the Struggle for the Genocide Convention* (New York: Palgrave Macmillan, 2008), Ch. 4.

[38]Rebecca West, *A Train of Powder* (New York: Viking Press, 1965), 7.

[39]Ann Tusa and John Tusa, *The Nuremberg Trial* (London: Macmillan, 1983), 147.

[40]Taylor, *Anatomy of the Nuremberg Trials*, 123.

[41]Airey Neave, *Nuremberg: A Personal Record of the Major Nazi War Criminals* (London: Hodder and Stoughton, 1978), 252.

[42]Neave, *Nuremberg*, 381.

[43]Tusa and Tusa, *Nuremberg Trial*, 111.

[44]West, *Train of Powder*, 18.

[45]Henri Donnedieu de Vabres, *Recueil critique*, 1943, 89–90; 94–97. I am grateful to Jean-Marc Beraud of the Faculty of Law at the University of Lyon for referring me to these articles.

[46]H. Montgomery Hyde, *Norman Birkett: The Life of Lord Birkett of Ulverston* (London: Hamish Hamilton, 1964), 500; Taylor, *Anatomy of the Nuremberg Trials*, 167.

[47]Biddle, *In Brief Authority*, 407.

[48]G. M. Gilbert, *Nuremberg Diary* (New York: Signet, 1947), 119. Gilbert's position was curious, involving conflicts normally considered unacceptable in criminal proceedings. As a German-speaking intelligence officer in the United States army, Gilbert had interrogated German prisoners and civilians prior to the Nazi collapse. He was designated prison psychologist for the Nuremberg trial and kept a diary of his activities. "My principal duty was to maintain close daily contact with the prisoners in order to keep the prison commandant, Colonel B. C. Andrus, aware of the state of their morale," he wrote, "and to help in any way possible to assure their standing trial with orderly discipline." Dispensing cigarettes and chocolate bars, Gilbert visited the prisoners regularly and at times had lengthy conversations with them about the proceedings. He visited each of them to obtain their first reactions to the indictment, for example, and recorded their reactions. Some of the prisoners responded volubly, reporting extensively on their lives before and during the trial. Gilbert also worked with other psychiatrists in administering various psychological tests on the accused. Hardly a neutral observer, Gilbert passed along information about the accused to the American chief prosecutor Jackson from time to time, as Telford Taylor notes. See Gilbert, *Nuremberg Diary*, 9; Taylor, *Anatomy of Nuremberg Trials*, 187.

[49]Taylor, *Anatomy of Nuremberg Trials*, 296.

[50]Taylor, *Anatomy of Nuremberg Trials*, 103.

[51]Taylor, *Anatomy of Nuremberg Trials*, 100, 209, 307.

[52]On Alexandrov see Joseph E. Persico, *Nuremberg: Infamy on Trial* (New York: Viking, 1994), 244, and Robert E. Conot, *Justice at Nuremberg* (New York: Harper and Row, 1983), 88.

[53]Hyde, *Norman Birkett*, 510.

[54]Gilbert, *Nuremberg Diary*, 149.

[55]Gilbert, *Nuremberg Diary*, 192.

[56]Hyde, *Norman Birkett*, 514, 518.

[57]Smith, *Reaching Judgment at Nuremberg*, 110.

[58]John Mendelsohn, "Trial by Document: The Problem of Due Process for War Criminals at Nuremberg," *Prologue*, 7 (Winter 1975): 230.

[59]*Report of Robert H. Jackson*, 299.

[60]Taylor, *Anatomy of the Nuremberg Trials*, 80.

[61]*Report of Robert H. Jackson*, 383–84.

[62]Lawrence Douglas, "Film as Witness: Screening *Nazi Concentration Camps* before the Nuremberg Tribunal," *Yale Law Journal* 105 (1995): 449–81.

[63]Smith, *Reaching Judgment at Nuremberg*, 72.

[64]Michael Biddis, "The Nuremberg Trial: Two Exercises in Judgment," *Journal of Contemporary History* 16 (1981): 602.

[65]International Military Tribunal, *Trial of the Major War Criminals*, 2: 131, 256, 257.

[66]International Military Tribunal, *Trial of the Major War Criminals*, 2: 262.

[67]International Military Tribunal, *Trial of the Major War Criminals*, 9: 309.

[68]Tusa and Tusa, *The Nuremberg Trial*, 294.

[69]Yuri Zorya and Natalia Lebedeva, "The Year 1939 in the Nuremberg Files," *International Affairs*, 10 (October 1989): 119–22.

[70]Léon Poliakov, *Le Procès de Nuremberg* (Paris: Julliard, 1971), 112.

[71]Smith, *Reaching Judgment at Nuremberg*, 105.

[72]See the excellent discussion of this matter in Patrick Salmon, "Crimes against Peace: The Case of the Invasion of Norway at the Nuremberg Trials," in Richard Langhorne, ed., *Diplomacy and Intelligence during the Second World War: Essays in Honour of F. H. Hinsley* (Cambridge: Cambridge University Press, 1985), 245–69.

[73]International Military Tribunal, *Trial of the Major War Criminals*, 15: 398.

[74]Tusa and Tusa, *The Nuremberg Trial*, 193–94.

[75]International Military Tribunal, *Trial of the Major War Criminals*, 19: 467.

[76]Gilbert, *Nuremberg Diary*, 48–49.

[77]Hyde, *Norman Birkett*, 505.

[78]Gilbert, *Nuremberg Diary*, 67.

[79]Biddle, *In Brief Authority*, 450.

[80]International Military Tribunal, *Trial of the Major War Criminals*, 18: 1–2.

[81]International Military Tribunal, *Trial of the Major War Criminals*, 9: 440.

[82]International Military Tribunal, *Trial of the Major War Criminals*, 9: 311.

[83]Carnegie Endowment for International Peace, Division of International Law, *Violation of the Laws and Customs of War: Reports of Majority and Dissenting Reports of American and Japanese Members of the Commission of Responsibilities, Conference of Paris 1919*, pamphlet no. 32 (Oxford: Clarendon Press, 1919), 26; also see Roger S. Clark, "Crimes against Humanity," in George Ginsburgs and V. N. Kudriavtsev, *The Nuremberg Trial and International Law* (Dordrecht: Martinus Nijhoff Publishers, 1990), 177–212.

[84]United Nations War Crimes Commission, *History of the United Nations War Crimes Commission and the Development of the Laws of War* (London: United Nations War Crimes Commission, 1948), 175–76.

[85]*Report of Robert H. Jackson,* 329, 333. On Jewish appeals see Michael R. Marrus, "Three Jewish Emigrés at Nuremberg: Hersh Lauterpacht, Jacob Robinson, and Raphael Lemkin," in Ezra Mendelsohn, Steffani Hoffman, and Richard Cohen, eds., *Against the Grain: Jewish Intellectuals in Hard Times* (New York: Berghahn Books, 2014), 240–54.

[86]Jacob Robinson, "The International Military Tribunal and the Holocaust: Some Legal Reflections," *Israel Law Review* 7 (1972): 3; H. Lauterpacht, "The Law of Nations

and the Punishment of War Crimes," *British Year Book of International Law* 21 (1944): 58–95; Elihu Lauterpacht, *The Life of Sir Hersch Lauterpacht, QC, FBA, LLD* (Cambridge: Cambridge University Press, 2010), 268–83 and passim. See especially Philippe Sands, *East West Street: On the Origins of 'Genocide' and 'Crimes Against Humanity'* (New York: Knopf, 2016).

[87]See pages 1–2. Not long after the appearance of the text of the completed London Charter, someone noticed a discrepancy in the text of article 6(c), defining Crimes against Humanity. The French and English versions had a semicolon after "before or during the war"; and the Russian version had a comma. A meeting in Berlin in October 1945 resolved the issue with an agreement among the four powers who made up the tribunal in favor of the Russian text. The effects were hardly trivial. By introducing a comma instead of a semicolon after *war*, the Berlin protocol ensured the limited scope of *all* crimes against humanity—limited, that is, to acts committed "in connection with any crime within the jurisdiction of the Tribunal." This now required link of Crimes Against Humanity with Crimes Against Peace and War Crimes became known as the "war nexus." Was the original discrepancy inadvertent, undertaken without a full awareness of its implications, or was there a deliberate effort, on the part of the court and prosecutors who noticed the discrepancy to limit the purview of crimes against humanity? Whatever the case, the implications were important, and soon apparent.

[88]Egon Schwelb, "Crimes against Humanity," *British Year Book of International Law* 23 (1946): 225. See Sydney L. Goldenberg, "Crimes against Humanity—1945–1970," *Western Ontario Law Review* 10 (1971): 1–55.

[89]International Military Tribunal, *Trial of the Major War Criminals*, 5: 412.

[90]Poliakov, *Le Procès de Nuremberg*, 209. For an overview of crimes against Jews at Nuremberg see Michael R. Marrus, "The Holocaust at Nuremberg," *Yad Vashem Studies*, 26 (1998), 4–45.

[91]Leonard Stein to Chaim Weizmann, August 28, 1945 (Rehovot, Israel: Weizmann Archives, Weizmann Papers, File 2600).

[92]Taylor, *Anatomy of the Nuremberg Trials*, xi. See also Jonathan Bush, "Nuremberg: The Modern Law of War and its Limitations," *Columbia Law Review*, 93 (1993), 2022–86.

[93]International Military Tribunal, *Trial of the Major War Criminals*, 19: 404. Lauterpacht, who was in the courtroom, described his reactions in a letter to his wife: "It was a great satisfaction to watch the faces of the accused when Jackson was unfolding the story of the Jewish atrocities. It was a historic speech which lasted a day and a great personal triumph for Jackson. I shook [him] by the hand for a long minute. My table was at a distance of about 15 yards from the accused." Lauterpacht, *Life of Lauterpacht*, 277.

[94]International Military Tribunal, *Trial of the Major War Criminals*, 19: 501.

[95]International Military Tribunal, *Trial of the Major War Criminals*, 7: 192.

[96]International Military Tribunal, *Trial of the Major War Criminals*, 7: 153, 192.

[97]International Military Tribunal, *Trial of the Major War Criminals*, 7: 294; Smith, *Reaching Judgment at Nuremberg*, 48.

[98]International Military Tribunal, *Trial of the Major War Criminals*, 3: 311–30.

[99]International Military Tribunal, *Trial of the Major War Criminals*, 9: 618–19.

[100]International Military Tribunal, *Trial of the Major War Criminals*, 11: 275–76.

[101]Those parts of German-occupied Poland captured in 1939 and not incorporated into the Reich. As governor general, Hans Frank was administrative head of the Generalgouvernement, with his capital in Kraków.

[102]International Military Tribunal, *Trial of the Major War Criminals*, 12: 2. For the reaction of his fellow defendants to this remark see Sands, *East West Street*, 299.

[103]Hyde, *Norman Birkett*, 505.

[104]Biddle, *In Brief Authority*, 466.

[105]Neave, *Nuremberg*, 336.

[106]International Military Tribunal, *Trial of the Major War Criminals*, 22: 374.

[107]International Military Tribunal, *Trial of the Major War Criminals*, 1: 186.

[108]International Military Tribunal, *Trial of the Major War Criminals*, 1: 216.

[109]Yoram Dinstein, *The Defence of 'Obedience to Superior Orders' in International Law* (Leyden: A. W. Sijthoff, 1965), 147–48.

[110]Biddle, *In Brief Authority*, 466–67; Francis Biddle Papers, Folder 3, Box 14.

[111]For a focused discussion of this entire matter, together with the requisite texts, see Beth Van Schaack, "The Definition of Crimes Against Humanity: Resolving the Incoherence," *Columbia Journal of International Law*, 37 (1998–1999), 804, and passim. See also M. Cherif Bassiouni, *Crimes Against Humanity: Historical Evolution and Contemporary Application* (New York: Cambridge University Press, 2011), Ch. 3.

[112]Conot, *Justice at Nuremberg*, 456. See also Jonathan A. Bush, "The Prehistory of Corporations and Conspiracy in International Criminal Law: What Nuremberg Really Said," *Columbia Law Review*, 109 (2009), 1094–1262.

[113]Neave, *Nuremberg*, 339.

[114]Taylor, *Anatomy of the Nuremberg Trials*, 626. See Kevin Jon Heller, *The Nuremberg Military Tribunals and the Origins of International Criminal Law* (Oxford: Oxford University Press, 2011).

[115]Genêt [Janet Flanner], "Letter from Nuremberg," *New Yorker*, March 16, 1946, 84.

[116]William J. Bosch, *Judgment on Nuremberg: American Attitudes toward the Major German War-Crime Trials* (Chapel Hill: University of North Carolina Press, 1970), 90–94; "The Quarter's Polls," *Public Opinion Quarterly* 8 (1944): 586–95.

[117]Bosch, *Judgment on Nuremberg*, 91, 109.

[118]Bosch, *Judgment on Nuremberg*, 115.

[119]Alderman, "Negotiating on War Crimes Prosecutions," 97–98.

[120]Smith, *Reaching Judgment at Nuremberg*, 114.

[121]Hyde, *Norman Birkett*, 515.

[122]International Military Tribunal, *Trial of the Major War Criminals*, 19: 449.

[123]Tom Bower, *The Pledge Betrayed: America and Britain and the Denazification of Postwar Germany* (Garden City, NY: Doubleday, 1982), 325.

[124]International Military Tribunal, *Trial of the Major War Criminals*, 19: 435.

[125]Calvocoressi, *Nuremberg*, 125.

PART TWO

The Documents

1

Historical Precedents

1

COMMISSION OF RESPONSIBILITIES

Majority Report

March 29, 1919

The Commission desire to state expressly that . . . there is no reason why rank, however exalted, should in any circumstances protect the holder of it from responsibility when that responsibility has been established before a properly constituted tribunal. This extends even to the case of Heads of States. An argument has been raised to the contrary based upon the alleged immunity, and in particular the alleged inviolability, of a Sovereign of a State. But this privilege, where it is recognised, is one of practical expedience in municipal law, and is not fundamental. However, even if, in some countries, a Sovereign is exempt from being prosecuted in a national court of his own country the position from an international point of view is quite different.

We have later on in our Report proposed the establishment of a High Tribunal composed of judges drawn from many nations, and included the possibility of the trial before that Tribunal of a former Head of a State with the consent of that State itself secured by

Carnegie Endowment for International Peace, Division of International Law, *Violation of the Laws and Customs of War: Reports of Majority and Dissenting Reports of American and Japanese Members of the Commission of Responsibilities, Conference of Paris 1919*, pamphlet no. 32. Oxford: Clarendon Press, 1919, 19–25.

articles in the Treaty of Peace.[1] If the immunity of a Sovereign is claimed to extend beyond the limits above stated, it would involve laying down the principle that the greatest outrages against the laws and customs of war and the laws of humanity, if proved against him, could in no circumstances be punished. Such a conclusion would shock the conscience of civilized mankind.

In view of the grave charges which may be preferred against—to take one case—the ex-Kaiser—the vindication of the principles of the laws and customs of war and the laws of humanity which have been violated would be incomplete if he were not brought to trial and if other offenders less highly placed were punished. Moreover, the trial of the offenders might be seriously prejudiced if they attempted and were able to plead the superior orders of a Sovereign against whom no steps had been or were being taken.

There is little doubt that the ex-Kaiser and others in high authority were cognisant of and could at least have mitigated the barbarities committed during the course of the war. A word from them would have brought about a different method in the action of their subordinates on land, at sea and in the air. . . .

. . . the Commission is of opinion that, having regard to the multiplicity of crimes committed by those Powers which a short time before had on two occasions at the Hague protested their reverence for right and their respect for the principles of humanity, the public conscience insists upon a sanction which will put clearly in the light that it is not permitted cynically to profess a disdain for the most sacred laws and the most formal undertakings.

Two classes of culpable acts present themselves: —

(a.) Acts which provoked the world war and accompanied its inception.
(b.) Violations of the laws and customs of war and the laws of humanity.

(a.) Acts Which Provoked the War and Accompanied Its Inception

In this class the Commission has considered acts not strictly war crimes, but acts which provoked the war or accompanied its inception, such, to take outstanding examples, as the invasion of Luxemburg and Belgium.

---

[1]The Treaty of Versailles, which would be signed in May 1919.

The premeditation of a war of aggression, dissimulated under a peaceful pretense, then suddenly declared under false pretexts, is conduct which the public conscience reproves and which history will condemn, but by reason of the purely optional character of the Institutions at The Hague for the maintenance of peace (International Commission of Enquiry, Mediation and Arbitration) a war of aggression may not be considered as an act directly contrary to positive law, or one which can be successfully brought before a tribunal such as the Commission is authorised to consider under its Terms of Reference.

Further, any enquiry into the authorship of the war must, to be exhaustive, extend over events that have happened during many years in different European countries, and must raise many difficult and complex problems which might be more fitly investigated by historians and statesmen than by a tribunal appropriate to the trial of offenders against the laws and customs of war. The need of prompt action is from this point of view important. Any tribunal appropriate to deal with the other offences to which reference is made might hardly be a good court to discuss and deal decisively with such a subject as the authorship of the war. The proceedings and discussions, charges and counter-charges, if adequately and dispassionately examined, might consume much time, and the result might conceivably confuse the simpler issues into which the tribunal will be charged to enquire. While this prolonged investigation was proceeding some witnesses might disappear, the recollection of others would become fainter and less trustworthy, offenders might escape, and the moral effect of tardily imposed punishment would be much less salutary than if punishment were inflicted while the memory of the wrongs done was still fresh and the demand for punishment was insistent.

We therefore do not advise that the acts which provoked the war should be charged against their authors and made the subject of proceedings before a tribunal. . . .

(b.) Violations of the Laws and Customs of War and of the Laws of Humanity

Every belligerent has, according to international law, the power and authority to try the individuals alleged to be guilty of the crimes of which an enumeration has been given [earlier][2] on Violations of the Laws and Customs of War, if such persons have been taken prisoners or have otherwise fallen into its power. Each belligerent has, or has power to set up, pursuant to its own legislation, an appropriate tribunal, military or civil, for the trial of such cases. These courts would be able to try the incriminated persons according to their own procedure, and much complication and consequent delay would be avoided which would arise if all such cases were to be brought before a single tribunal.

There remain, however, a number of charges: —

(a.) Against persons belonging to enemy countries who have committed outrages against a number of civilians and soldiers of several Allied nations, such as outrages committed in prison camps where prisoners of war of several nations were congregated or the crime of forced labour in mines where prisoners of more than one nationality were forced to work;

(b.) Against persons of authority, belonging to enemy countries, whose orders were executed not only in one area or on one battle front, but whose orders affected the conduct of operations against several of the Allied armies;

(c.) Against all authorities, civil or military, belonging to enemy countries, however high their position may have been, without distinction of rank, including the heads of States, who ordered, or, with knowledge thereof and with power to intervene, abstained from preventing or taking measures to prevent, putting an end to or repressing, violations of the laws or customs of war (it being understood that no such abstention should constitute a defence for the actual perpetrators);

(d.) Against such other persons belonging to enemy countries as, having regard to the character of the offence or the law of any belligerent country, it may be considered advisable not to proceed before a court other than the High Tribunal hereafter referred to.

For the trial of outrages falling under these four categories the Commission is of opinion that a High Tribunal is essential. . . .

---

[2]The list included murders, massacres, and "systematic terrorism"; killing of hostages, torturing or deliberately starving civilians, rape; and "abduction of girls and women for enforced prostitution."

UNITED STATES REPRESENTATIVES ON THE COMMISSION OF RESPONSIBILITIES

Memorandum of Reservations to the Majority Report

April 4, 1919

Nevertheless, the report of the Commission does not, as in the opinion of the American Representatives it should, confine itself to the ascertainment of the facts and to their violation of the laws and customs of war, but, going beyond the terms of the mandate, declares that the facts found and acts committed were in violation of the laws and of the elementary principles of humanity. The laws and customs of war are a standard certain, to be found in books of authority and in the practice of nations. The laws and principles of humanity vary with the individual, which, if for no other reason, should exclude them from consideration in a court of justice, especially one charged with the administration of criminal law. The American Representatives, therefore, objected to the references to the laws and principles of humanity, to be found in the report, in what they believed was meant to be a judicial proceeding, as, in their opinion, the facts found were to be violations or breaches of the laws and customs of war, and the persons singled out for trial and punishment for acts committed during the war were only to be those persons guilty of acts which should have been committed in violation of the laws and customs of war. . . .

The conclusion which the Commission reached, and which is stated in the report, is to the effect that "all persons belonging to enemy countries, however high their position may have been, without distinction of rank, including Chiefs òf States, who have been guilty of offences against the laws and customs of war or the laws of humanity, are liable to criminal prosecution." The American Representatives are unable to agree with this conclusion, in so

Carnegie Endowment for International Peace, Division of International Law, *Violation of the Laws and Customs of War: Reports of Majority and Dissenting Reports of American and Japanese Members of the Commission of Responsibilities, Conference of Paris 1919,* pamphlet no. 32. Oxford: Clarendon Press, 1919, 64–65, 69–70, 71–73.

far as it subjects to criminal, and, therefore, to legal prosecution, persons accused of offences against "the laws of humanity," and in so far as it subjects Chiefs of States to a degree of responsibility hitherto unknown to municipal or international law, for which no precedents are to be found in the modern practice of nations. . . .

With the portion of the report devoted to the "constitution and procedure of a tribunal appropriate for the trial of these offences," the American Representatives are unable to agree, and their views differ so fundamentally and so radically from those of the Commission that they found themselves obliged to oppose the views of their colleagues in the Commission and to dissent from the statement of those views as recorded in the report.

In a matter of such importance affecting not one but many countries and calculated to influence their future conduct, the American Representatives believed that the nations should use the machinery at hand, which had been tried and found competent, with a law and a procedure framed and therefore known in advance, rather than to create an international tribunal with a criminal jurisdiction for which there is no precedent, precept, practice, or procedure. They further believed that, if an act violating the laws and customs of war committed by the enemy affected more than one country, a tribunal could be formed of the countries affected by uniting the national commissions or courts thereof, in which event the tribunal would be formed by the mere assemblage of the members, bringing with them the law to be applied, namely, the laws and customs of war, and the procedure, namely, the procedure of the national commissions or courts. . . .

In an earlier stage of the general report, indeed, until its final revision, [enemy authorities] were declared liable because they "abstained from preventing, putting an end to, or repressing, violations of the laws or customs of war." To this criterion of liability the American Representatives were unalterably opposed. It is one thing to punish a person who committed, or, possessing the authority, ordered others to commit an act constituting a crime; it is quite another thing to punish a person who failed to prevent, to put an end to, or to repress violations of the laws or customs of war. . . .

. . . The American Representatives believe that the Commission has exceeded its mandate in extending liability to violations of the laws of humanity, inasmuch as the facts to be examined are solely violations of the laws and customs of war. They also believe that the Commission erred in seeking to subject Heads of States to trial and punishment by a tribunal to whose jurisdiction they were not subject when the alleged offences were committed.

As pointed out by the American Representatives on more than one occasion, war was and is by its very nature inhuman, but acts consistent with the laws and customs of war, although these acts are inhuman, are nevertheless not the object of punishment by a court of justice. A judicial tribunal only deals with existing law and only administers existing law, leaving to another forum infractions of the moral law and actions contrary to the laws and principles of humanity. A further objection lies in the fact that the laws and principles of humanity are not certain, varying with time, place, and circumstance, and according, it may be, to the conscience of the individual judge. There is no fixed and universal standard of humanity. . . .

3

The Treaty of Versailles
1919

ARTICLE 227

The Allied and Associated Powers publicly arraign William II of Hohenzollern, formerly German Emperor, for a supreme offence against international morality and the sanctity of treaties.

A special tribunal will be constituted to try the accused, thereby assuring him the guarantees essential to the right of defence. It will be composed of five judges, one appointed by each of the following Powers: namely, the United States of America, Great Britain, France, Italy, and Japan.

In its decision the tribunal will be guided by the highest motives of international policy, with a view to vindicating the

Carnegie Endowment for International Peace, Division of International Law, *Violation of the Laws and Customs of War: Reports of Majority and Dissenting Reports of American and Japanese Members of the Commission of Responsibilities, Conference of Paris 1919*, pamphlet no. 32. Oxford: Clarendon Press, 1919, vii–viii.

solemn obligations of international undertakings and the validity of international morality. It will be its duty to fix the punishment which it considers should be imposed.

The Allied and Associated Powers will address a request to the Government of the Netherlands for the surrender to them of the ex-Emperor in order that he may be put on trial.

ARTICLE 228

The German Government recognizes the right of the Allied and Associated Powers to bring before military tribunals persons accused of having committed acts in violation of the laws and customs of war. Such persons shall, if found guilty, be sentenced to punishments laid down by law. This provision will apply notwithstanding any proceedings or prosecution before a tribunal in Germany or in the territory of her allies.

The German Government shall hand over to the Allied and Associated Powers, or to such one of them as shall so request, all persons accused of having committed an act in violation of the laws and customs of war, who are specified either by name or by the rank, office, or employment which they held under the German authorities.

ARTICLE 229

Persons guilty of criminal acts against the nationals of one of the Allied and Associated Powers will be brought before the military tribunals of that Power.

Persons guilty of criminal acts against the nationals of more than one of the Allied and Associated Powers will be brought before military tribunals composed of members of the military tribunals of the Powers concerned.

In every case the accused will be entitled to name his own counsel.

ARTICLE 230

The German Government undertakes to furnish all documents and information of every kind, the production of which may be considered necessary to ensure the full knowledge of the incriminating acts, the discovery of offenders, and the just appreciation of responsibility. . . .

4

Kellogg-Briand Pact
1928

ARTICLE I

The High Contracting Parties solemnly declare in the names of their respective peoples that they condemn recourse to war for the solution of international controversies, and renounce it as an instrument of national policy in their relations with one another.

ARTICLE II

The High Contracting Parties agree that the settlement or solution of all disputes or conflicts of whatever nature or of whatever origin they may be, which may arise among them, shall never be sought except by pacific means.

ARTICLE III

The present Treaty shall be ratified by the High Contracting Parties named in the Preamble in accordance with their respective constitutional requirements, and shall take effect as between them as soon as all their several instruments of ratification shall have been deposited at Washington.

This Treaty shall, when it has come into effect as prescribed in the preceding paragraph, remain open as long as may be necessary for adherence by all the other Powers of the world. Every instrument evidencing the adherence of a Power shall be deposited at Washington and the Treaty shall immediately upon such deposit become effective as between the Power thus adhering and the other Powers parties hereto. . . .

In faith whereof the respective Plenipotentiaries have signed this Treaty in the French and English languages both texts having equal force, and hereunto affix their seals.

Done at Paris, the twenty-seventh day of August in the year one thousand nine hundred and twenty-eight.

Treaties, Conventions, International Acts, Protocols, and Agreements between the United States of America and Other Powers, 1923–37. Washington, DC: Government Printing Office, 1937, 5132–33.

5

HENRY L. STIMSON

Speech before the Council on
Foreign Relations, New York

August 8, 1932

War between nations was renounced by the signatories of the Briand-Kellogg Pact. This means that it has become illegal throughout practically the entire world. It is no longer to be the source and subject of rights. It is no longer to be the principle around which the duties, the conduct, and the rights of nations revolve. It is an illegal thing. Hereafter when two nations engage in armed conflict either one or both of them must be wrongdoers — violators of the general treaty. We no longer draw a circle about them and treat them with the punctilios of the duelist's code. Instead we denounce them as lawbreakers.

By that very act we have made obsolete many legal precedents and have given the legal profession the task of re-examining many of its codes and treatises.

The language of the Briand-Kellogg Treaty and the contemporaneous statements of its founders make its purpose clear. Some of its critics have asserted that the Pact was really not a treaty at all; that it was not intended to confer rights and impose liabilities; that it was a mere group of unilateral statements made by the signatories, declaring a pious purpose on the part of each, of which purpose that signatory was to be the sole judge and executor, and for a violation of which no other signatory could call him to account.

If such an interpretation were correct, it would reduce the Pact to a mere gesture. If its promises conferred no rights as between the members of the community of signatories, it would be a sham. It would be worse than a nullity, for its failure would carry down the faith of the world in other efforts for peace.

But such critics are wrong. There is nothing in the language of the Pact nor in its contemporaneous history to justify any such an interpretation. . . .

Henry L. Stimson, "The Pact of Paris: Three Years of Development." *Foreign Affairs* II, Special Supplement (1932): iv.

2

Background

6

WINSTON S. CHURCHILL, FRANKLIN D. ROOSEVELT, AND JOSEPH STALIN

Moscow Declaration

November 1, 1943

The United Kingdom, the United States and the Soviet Union have received from many quarters evidence of the atrocities, massacres and cold-blooded mass executions which are being perpetrated by the Hitlerite forces in many of the countries they have overrun and from which they are now being steadily expelled.

The brutalities of Hitlerite domination are no new thing and all peoples or territories in their grip have suffered from the worst form of government by terror.

What is new is that many of these territories are now being redeemed by the advancing armies of the liberating powers and that, in their desperation, the recoiling Hitlerite Huns are redoubling their ruthless cruelties. This is now evidenced with particular clearness by the monstrous crimes of the Hitlerites on the territory of the Soviet Union which is being liberated from the Hitlerites and on French and Italian territory.

United Nations War Crimes Commission, *History of the United Nations War Crimes Commission and the Development of the Laws of War.* London: United Nations War Crimes Commission, 1948, 107–8.

Accordingly, the aforesaid three Allied Powers, speaking in the interest of the 32 United Nations, hereby solemnly declare and give full warning of their declaration as follows:

At the time of the granting of any armistice to any Government which may be set up in Germany, those German officers and men and members of the Nazi Party who have been responsible for or have taken a consenting part in the above atrocities, massacres and executions will be sent back to the countries in which their abominable deeds were done in order that they may be judged and punished according to the laws of these liberated countries and of the Free Governments which will be erected therein. Lists will be compiled in all possible detail from all these countries, having regard especially to the invaded parts of the Soviet Union, to Poland and Czechoslovakia, to Yugoslavia and Greece, including Crete and other islands, to Norway, Denmark, the Netherlands, Belgium, Luxembourg, France and Italy.

Those, Germans who take part in wholesale shootings of Italian officers or in the execution of French, Dutch, Belgian or Norwegian hostages or of Cretan peasants, or who have shared in the slaughters inflicted on the people of Poland, or in the territories of the Soviet Union which are now being swept clear of the enemy, will know that they will be brought back to the scene of their crimes and judged on the spot by the peoples they have outraged.

Let those who have hitherto not imbrued their hands with innocent blood beware lest they join the ranks of the guilty, for most assuredly the three Allied Powers will pursue them to the uttermost ends of the earth and will deliver them to the accusers in order that justice may be done.

The above declaration is without prejudice to the case of the major criminals whose offences have no particular geographical location and who will be punished by a joint decision of the Governments of the Allies.

7

WINSTON S. CHURCHILL

An Exchange with Roosevelt and Stalin at Teheran
November 29, 1943

Stalin . . . indulged in a great deal of "teasing" of me, which I did not at all resent until the Marshal entered in a genial manner upon a serious and even deadly aspect of the punishment to be inflicted upon the Germans. The German General Staff, he said, must be liquidated. The whole force of Hitler's mighty armies depended upon about fifty thousand officers and technicians. If these were rounded up and shot at the end of the war, German military strength would be extirpated. On this I thought it right to say: "The British Parliament and public will never tolerate mass executions. Even if in war passion they allowed them to begin, they would turn violently against those responsible after the first butchery had taken place. The Soviets must be under no delusion on this point."

Stalin however, perhaps only in mischief, pursued the subject. "Fifty thousand," he said, "must be shot." I was deeply angered. "I would rather," I said, "be taken out into the garden here and now and be shot myself than sully my own and my country's honour by such infamy."

At this point the President intervened. He had a compromise to propose. Not fifty thousand should be shot, but only forty-nine thousand. By this he hoped, no doubt, to reduce the whole matter to ridicule. Eden[1] also made signs and gestures intended to reassure me that it was all a joke. But now Elliott Roosevelt rose in his place at the end of the table and made a speech, saying how cordially he agreed with Marshal Stalin's plan and how sure he was that the United States Army would support it. At this intrusion I got up and left the table, walking off into the next room, which was in semi-darkness. I had not been there a minute before

---

[1] Anthony Eden, British secretary of state for foreign affairs (1935–1938, 1940–1945).

Winston S. Churchill, *The Second World War.* Vol. 5, *Closing the Ring.* New York: Bantam Books, 1962, 319–20.

hands were clapped upon my shoulders from behind, and there was Stalin, with Molotov at his side, both grinning broadly, and eagerly declaring that they were only playing, and that nothing of a serious character had entered their heads. Stalin has a very captivating manner when he chooses to use it, and I never saw him do so to such an extent as at this moment. Although I was not then, and am not now, fully convinced that all was chaff and there was no serious intent lurking behind, I consented to return, and the rest of the evening passed pleasantly. . . .

8

HENRY MORGENTHAU JR.

Memorandum for President Roosevelt (The Morgenthau Plan)
September 5, 1944

A list of the arch-criminals of this war whose obvious guilt has generally been recognized by the United Nations shall be drawn up as soon as possible and transmitted to the appropriate military authorities. The military authorities shall be instructed with respect to all persons who are on such list as follows:

(a) They shall be apprehended as soon as possible and identified as soon as possible after apprehension, the identification to be approved by an officer of the General rank.

(b) When such identification has been made the person identified shall be put to death forthwith by firing squads made up of soldiers of the United Nations.

(2) *Certain Other War Criminals*

(a) Military commissions shall be established by the Allied Military Government for the trial of certain crimes which have been committed against civilization during this war. As soon as practicable, representatives of the liberated countries of Europe shall be

Bradley F. Smith, *The American Road to Nuremberg: The Documentary Record, 1944–1945*. Stanford, CA: Hoover Institution Press, 1982, 28–29.

included on such commissions. These crimes shall include those crimes covered by the following section and such other crimes as such military commissions may be ordered to try from time to time.

(b) Any person who is suspected of being responsible for (through the issuance of orders or otherwise), or having participated in causing the death of any human being in the following situations shall be arrested and tried promptly by such military commissions, unless prior to trial one of the United Nations has requested that such person be placed in its custody for trial on similar charges for acts committed within its territory:

(i) The death was caused by action in violation of the rules of war.

(ii) The victim was killed as a hostage in reprisal for the deeds of other persons.

(iii) The victim met death because of his nationality, race, color, creed, or political conviction.

(c) Any person who is convicted by the military commissions of the crimes specified in paragraph (b) shall be sentenced to death, unless the military commissions, in exceptional cases, determine that there are extenuating circumstances, in which case other punishment may be meted out, including deportation to a penal colony outside of Germany. Upon conviction, the sentence shall be carried out immediately.

B. Detention of Certain Groups

All members of the following groups should be detained until the extent of the guilt of each individual is determined:

(a) The SS.
(b) The Gestapo.
(c) All high officials of the police, SA and other security organizations.
(d) All high Government and Nazi Party officials.
(e) All leading public figures closely identified with Nazism.

C. Registration of Males

An appropriate program will be formulated for the re-registration as soon as possible of all males of the age of 14 or over. The registration shall be on a form and in a manner to be prescribed by the

military authorities and shall show, among other things, whether
or not the person registering is a member of the Nazi Party or
affiliated organizations, the Gestapo, SS, SA or Kraft Korps . . .

9

HENRY L. STIMSON

Memorandum Opposing the Morgenthau Plan
September 9, 1944

SECRET

It is not a question of a soft treatment of Germany or a harsh treatment of Germany. We are all trying to devise protection against
recurrence by Germany of her attempts to dominate the world.
We differ as to method. The fundamental remedy of Mr. Morgenthau
is to provide that the industry of Germany shall be substantially
obliterated. . . .

I am unalterably opposed to such a program for the reasons
given in my memorandum dated September 5 which is already
before the President. I do not think that the reasons there stated
need again be elaborated. In substance, my point is that these
resources constitute a natural and necessary asset for the pro-
ductivity of Europe. In a period when the world is suffering from
destruction and from want of production, the concept of the total
obliteration of these values is to my mind wholly wrong. My insistence is that these assets be conserved and made available for
the benefit of the whole of Europe, including particularly Great
Britain. . . .

The other fundamental point upon which I feel we differ is
the matter of the trial and punishment of those Germans who
are responsible for crimes and depredations. Under the plan proposed by Mr. Morgenthau, the so-called arch-criminals shall be
put to death by the military without provision for any trial and

Foreign Relations of the United States: The Conference at Quebec, 1944. Washington, DC:
Government Printing Office, 1972, 123–25.

upon mere identification after apprehension. The method of dealing with these and other criminals requires careful thought and a well-defined procedure. Such procedure must embody, in my judgment, at least the rudimentary aspects of the Bill of Rights, namely, notification to the accused of the charge, the right to be heard and, within reasonable limits, to call witnesses in his defense. I do not mean to favor the institution of state trials or to introduce any cumbersome machinery but the very punishment of these men in a dignified manner consistent with the advance of civilization, will have all the greater effect upon posterity. Furthermore, it will afford the most effective way of making a record of the Nazi system of terrorism and of the effort of the Allies to terminate the system and prevent its recurrence.

I am disposed to believe that at least as to the chief Nazi officials, we should participate in an international tribunal constituted to try them. They should be charged with offences against the laws of the Rules of War in that they have committed wanton and unnecessary cruelties in connection with the prosecution of the war. This law of the Rules of War has been upheld by our own Supreme Court and will be the basis of judicial action against the Nazis.

Even though these offences have not been committed against our troops, I feel that our moral position is better if we take our share in their conviction. Other war criminals who have committed crimes in subjugated territory should be returned in accordance with the Moscow Declaration [see pp. 131–133] to those territories for trial by national military commissions having jurisdiction of the offence under the same Rules of War. I have great difficulty in finding any means whereby military commissions may try and convict those responsible for excesses committed within Germany both before and during the war which have no relation to the conduct of the war. I would be prepared to construe broadly what constituted a violation of the Rules of War but there is a certain field in which I fear that external courts cannot move. Such courts would be without jurisdiction in precisely the same way that any foreign court would be without jurisdiction to try those who were guilty of, or condoned, lynching in our own country. . . .

10

CORDELL HULL, HENRY L. STIMSON, AND JAMES FORRESTAL

Draft Memorandum for the President

November 11, 1944

The criminality with which the Nazi leaders and groups are charged does not consist of scattered individual outrages such as may occur in any war, but represents the results of a purposeful and systematic pattern created by them to the end of achieving world domination. The objective in the prosecution of Nazi war crimes should be not only to punish the individual criminals, but also to expose and condemn the criminal purpose behind each individual outrage.

The writings and statements of the Nazi leaders themselves indicate that beginning even prior to the assumption of power by the Nazis in Germany, there has been a continuing conspiracy necessarily involving the commission of the atrocities which the United Nations have pledged themselves to punish. We believe that further research will develop the full scope of this conspiracy and enable its demonstration according to accepted judicial standards before a fair tribunal.

To such a state of facts the well recognized principles of the law of criminal conspiracy are plainly applicable, and may be employed. An indictment upon a charge of conspiracy will properly include the leaders of State, the governmental and party agencies such as the SS and Gestapo, and other individuals and groups who during the time in question have been in control of formulating and executing Nazi policy. . . .

The proceeding will be judicial rather than political. It will rest securely upon traditionally established legal concepts. Not only will the guilty of this generation be brought to justice according to due process of law, but in addition, the conduct of the Axis will have been solemnly condemned by an international adjudication of guilt that cannot fail to impress the generations to come. The

Bradley F. Smith, *The American Road to Nuremberg: The Documentary Record, 1944–1945.* Stanford, CA: Hoover Institution Press, 1982, 42–44.

Germans will not again be able to claim, as they have been claiming with regard to the Versailles Treaty, that an admission of war guilt was exacted from them under duress. It may be noted, in addition, that those of the criminals who have been or may hereafter be taken prisoners of war will lose their protected status under the Geneva Prisoners of War Convention,[1] and can be dealt with freed from the restrictions of that Convention. . . .

[1]The Geneva convention on the treatment of prisoners of war was signed in 1929 by representatives of all the major countries except the Soviet Union. This international agreement built upon previous conventions that defined "the laws and customs of war." The most important of these were the wide-ranging Hague Conventions Respecting the Laws and Customs of War on Land of 1899 and 1907 (signed by more than forty nations), and the Red Cross Convention of 1906 (signed by thirty-six nations), a refinement of the original 1864 Red Cross Convention for the Amelioration of the Condition of the Wounded in Armies in the Field.

11

HENRY L. STIMSON, EDWARD R. STETTINIUS JR., AND FRANCIS BIDDLE

Memorandum for the President

January 22, 1945

After Germany's unconditional surrender the United Nations could, if they elected, put to death the most notorious Nazi criminals, such as Hitler or Himmler, without trial or hearing. We do not favor this method. While it has the advantages of a sure and swift disposition, it would be violative of the most fundamental principles of justice, common to all the United Nations. This would encourage the Germans to turn these criminals into martyrs, and, in any event, only a few individuals could be reached in this way.

We think that the just and effective solution lies in the use of the judicial method. Condemnation of these criminals after a trial, moreover, would command maximum public support in our own

Report of Robert H. Jackson, United States Representative to the International Conference on Military Trials, London 1945. Washington, DC: Department of State, 1949, 6–8.

times and receive the respect of history. The use of the judicial method will, in addition, make available for all mankind to study in future years an authentic record of Nazi crimes and criminality.

We recommend the following:

The German leaders and the organizations employed by them, such as those referred to above (SA, SS, Gestapo), should be charged both with the commission of their atrocious crimes, and also with joint participation in a broad criminal enterprise which included and intended these crimes, or was reasonably calculated to bring them about. The allegation of the criminal enterprise would be so couched as to permit full proof of the entire Nazi plan from its inception and the means used in its furtherance and execution, including the pre-war atrocities and those committed against their own nationals, neutrals, and stateless persons, as well as the waging of an illegal war of aggression with ruthless disregard for international law and the rules of war. Such a charge would be firmly founded upon the rule of liability, common to all penal systems and included in the general doctrines of the laws of war, that those who participate in the formulation and execution of a criminal plan involving multiple crimes are jointly liable for each of the offenses committed and jointly responsible for the acts of each other. Under such a charge there are admissible in evidence the acts of any of the conspirators done in furtherance of the conspiracy, whether or not these acts were in themselves criminal and subject to separate prosecution as such.

The trial of this charge and the determination of the guilty parties would be carried out in two stages:

The United Nations would, in the first instance, bring before an international tribunal created by Executive Agreement, the highest ranking German leaders to a number fairly representative of the groups and organizations charged with complicity in the basic criminal plan. Adjudication would be sought not only of the guilt of those individuals physically before the court, but also of the complicity of the members of the organizations included within the charge. The court would make findings adjudicating the facts established, including the nature and purposes of the criminal plan, the identity of the groups and organizations guilty of complicity in it, and the acts committed in its execution. The court would also sentence those individual defendants physically before it who are convicted.

The above would complete the mission of this international tribunal.

Thereafter, there would be brought before occupation courts the individuals not sent back for trial under the provisions of the

Moscow Declaration [see pp. 134–135], and members of the organizations who are charged with complicity through such membership, but against whom there is not sufficient proof of specific atrocities. In view of the nature of the charges and the representative character of the defendants who were before the court in the first trial, the findings of that court should justly be taken to constitute a general adjudication of the criminal character of the groups and organizations referred to, binding upon all the members thereof in their subsequent trials in occupation courts. In these subsequent trials, therefore, the only necessary proof of guilt of any particular defendant would be his membership in one of those organizations. Proof would also be taken of the nature and extent of the individual's participation. The punishment of each defendant would be made appropriate to the facts of his particular case. In appropriate cases, the penalty might be imprisonment at hard labor instead of the death penalty, and the offenders could be worked in restoring the devastated areas.

Individual defendants who can be connected with specific atrocities will be tried and punished in the national courts of the countries concerned, as contemplated in the Moscow Declaration. . . .

12

American Draft of Definitive Proposal, Presented to Foreign Ministers at San Francisco

April 1945

Due Process for Defendants

In order to insure fair trial for defendants charged with crime pursuant to this Agreement, it is declared that the following is required in order to constitute due process in their behalf:

a. Reasonable notice shall be given to the defendants of the charges against them and of the opportunity to defend. Such notice

Report of Robert H. Jackson, United States Representative to the International Conference on Military Trials, London 1945. Washington, DC: Department of State, 1949, 24–25.

may be actual or constructive. Any tribunal before which charges are tried pursuant to this Agreement shall have the right to determine what constitutes reasonable notice in any given instance.

b. The defendants physically present before the tribunal (a) will be furnished with copies, translated into their own language, of any indictment, statement of charges or other document of arraignment upon which they are being tried, and (b) will be given fair opportunity to be heard in their defense personally and by counsel. The tribunal shall determine to what extent proceedings against defendants maybe taken without their presence.

c. Organizations, official or unofficial, may be charged pursuant to this Agreement with criminal acts or with complicity therein by producing before the tribunal and putting on trial such of their number as the tribunal may determine to be fairly representative of the group or organization in question.

d. Upon conviction of an organization hereunder, the tribunal shall make written findings and enter written judgment finding and adjudicating the charges against such organization and the representative members on trial. . . . Upon proof of such membership the burden shall be upon the defendant to establish any circumstances relating to his membership or participation therein which are relevant either in defense or in mitigation. . . .

13

Memorandum of Conversation of Edward R. Stettinius Jr. and Samuel Rosenman with Vyacheslav Molotov and Anthony Eden, in San Francisco

May 3, 1945

2. Judge Rosenman stated that he had been sent here by the President to place the U.S. proposals for the treatment of war criminals before the Foreign Ministers of the United Kingdom,

Foreign Relations of the United States, 1945, vol. 3, *European Advisory Commission; Austria; Germany.* Washington, DC: Government Printing Office, 1968, 1162–64.

U.S.S.R., and France who with the United States were the four powers represented on the Control Council for Germany. . . . The U.S. is very much interested in settling these matters and feels that an agreement must be reached promptly.

3. Judge Rosenman summarized the American proposal as follows: We believe that there should be organized an international military tribunal rather than a civilian tribunal. This court should consist of one representative of each of the four powers represented on the Control Council for Germany. There should also be organized immediately a committee of one representative of each of the four powers to start collecting evidence and preparing for the trials to come. It was our thought that the representatives on this committee would act in the capacity of council to try the cases before the international military tribunal. The President had already appointed Justice Jackson for this purpose.

4. Judge Rosenman said there were several categories of criminals concerned:

(a) there were the top Nazis. We had formerly considered these to be Hitler, Goering, Goebbels, Mussolini, and two or three others. It now looked as though we might not have to concern ourselves with these men.

(b) there were also the criminals which were going to be returned to the country where their crimes had been committed.

(c) there were others whose crimes were not geographically located.

(d) there would be numerous others who had committed crimes but could not be proven because of the fact that the witnesses were dead or there was no evidence still in existence. He gave, for example, the case of Gestapo and SS troops who had undoubtedly committed crimes but we would not be able to prove them.

(e) It was the U.S. belief that these crimes must be sought out and punished, not only to punish the guilty for its moral value but also because these men would certainly provide the nucleus of a future Nazi party and would lead any future uprising.

5. Judge Rosenman stated that we had a plan which we felt would solve this difficulty. We proposed to place on trial the Nazi organizations themselves rather than the individuals and to convict them and all their members of engaging in a criminal conspiracy to control the world, to persecute minorities, to break treaties, to invade other nations and to commit crimes. We are convinced

we can convict these organizations of these crimes. Once having proved the organizations to be guilty, each person who had joined the organization voluntarily would *ipso facto* be guilty of a war crime. While we do not necessarily want to put all the guilty persons to death, we would definitely want to sentence them at least to hard labor to rehabilitate the countries which the Germans had despoiled. . . .

7. The Secretary stated that before we proceeded further, he wanted to settle the matter of bringing the French into these discussions. Mr. Molotov and Mr. Eden stated that they had no objection to bringing the French in. . . .

8. Mr. Eden stated that his colleagues in London had been considering this matter of war crimes for some time. Their position was that the major war criminals, the top 7 or 8 Nazis, should not be tried by judicial procedures. Their position had, however, recently changed greatly due to the fact that many of these top Nazis had already been killed and no doubt many more would be killed within the next few days. The War Cabinet still saw objections to a formal state trial of war criminals for the most notorious Nazis whose crimes had no geographic location. If, however, their two great Allies definitely wanted a judicial trial of such men, the British were willing to bow to them in the matter. They would, however, like to review the proposed procedure. The War Cabinet favored the proposed procedure as outlined by Judge Rosenman for a criminal conspiracy to convict members of the Gestapo and other similar Nazi organizations. They would like to review the proposals in detail. . . .

9. Mr. Molotov stated that he felt Judge Rosenman had made proposals on a matter of great importance and that we should pay great attention to them. He reserved the right to express the views of his Government on the documents which had been submitted, stating that it was difficult to make any comment on such short notice. He asked for time to study the documents and thought that after they had done so, it might be appropriate to have the experts discuss the questions. . . .

3

Preparations

14

ROBERT H. JACKSON

Report to the President

June 6, 1945

1. The American case is being prepared on the assumption that an inescapable responsibility rests upon this country to conduct an inquiry, preferably in association with others, but alone if necessary, into the culpability of those whom there is probable cause to accuse of atrocities and other crimes. We have many such men in our possession. What shall we do with them? We could, of course, set them at large without a hearing. But it has cost unmeasured thousands of American lives to beat and bind these men. To free them without a trial would mock the dead and make cynics of the living. On the other hand, we could execute or otherwise punish them without a hearing. But undiscriminating executions or punishments without definite findings of guilt, fairly arrived at, would violate pledges repeatedly given, and would not set easily on the American conscience or be remembered by our children with pride. The only other course is to determine the innocence or guilt of the accused after a hearing as dispassionate as the times and horrors we deal with will permit, and upon a record that will leave our reasons and motives clear.

Report of Robert H. Jackson, United States Representative to the International Conference on Military Trials, London 1945. Washington, DC: Department of State. 1949, 46–50.

2. These hearings, however, must not be regarded in the same light as a trial under our system, where defense is a matter of constitutional right. Fair hearings for the accused are, of course, required to make sure that we punish only the right men and for the right reasons. But the procedure of these hearings may properly bar obstructive and dilatory tactics resorted to by defendants in our ordinary criminal trials. . . .

3. Whom will we accuse and put to their defense? We will accuse a large number of individuals and officials who were in authority in the government, in the military establishment, including the General Staff, and in the financial, industrial, and economic life of Germany who by all civilized standards are provable to be common criminals. We also propose to establish the criminal character of several voluntary organizations which have played a cruel and controlling part in subjugating first the German people and then their neighbors. It is not, of course, suggested that a person should be judged a criminal merely because he voted for certain candidates or maintained political affiliations in the sense that we in America support political parties. The organizations which we will accuse have no resemblance to our political parties. Organizations such as the Gestapo and the S.S. were direct action units, and were recruited from volunteers accepted only because of aptitude for, and fanatical devotion to, their violent purposes.

In examining the accused organizations in the trial, it is our proposal to demonstrate their declared and covert objectives, methods of recruitment, structure, lines of responsibility, and methods of effectuating their programs. In this trial, important representative members will be allowed to defend their organizations as well as themselves. The best practicable notice will be given, that named organizations stand accused and that any member is privileged to appear and join in their defense. If in the main trial an organization is found to be criminal, the second stage will be to identify and try before regular military tribunals individual members not already personally convicted in the principal case. Findings in the main trial that an organization is criminal in nature will be conclusive in any subsequent proceedings against individual members. The individual member will thereafter be allowed to plead only personal defenses or extenuating circumstances, such as that he joined under duress, and as to these defenses he should have the burden of proof. . . .

4. Our case against the major defendants is concerned with the Nazi master plan, not with individual barbarities and perversions which occurred independently of any central plan. The groundwork of our case must be factually authentic and constitute a well-documented history of what we are convinced was a grand, concerted pattern to incite and commit the aggressions and barbarities which have shocked the world. We must not forget that when the Nazi plans were boldly proclaimed they were so extravagant that the world refused to take them seriously. Unless we write the record of this movement with clarity and precision, we cannot blame the future if in days of peace it finds incredible the accusatory generalities uttered during the war. We must establish incredible events by credible evidence.

5. What specifically are the crimes with which these individuals and organizations should be charged, and what marks their conduct as criminal?

. . . We can save ourselves from . . . pitfalls if our test of what legally is crime gives recognition to those things which fundamentally outraged the conscience of the American people and brought them finally to the conviction that their own liberty and civilization could not persist in the same world with the Nazi power.

Those acts which offended the conscience of our people were criminal by standards generally accepted in all civilized countries, and I believe that we may proceed to punish those responsible in full accord with both our own traditions of fairness and with standards of just conduct which have been internationally accepted. I think also that through these trials we should be able to establish that a process of retribution by law awaits those who in the future similarly attack civilization. . . .

Once these international brigands, the top leaders of the Nazi party, the S.S., and the Gestapo, had firmly established themselves within Germany by terrorism and crime, they immediately set out on a course of international pillage. They bribed, debased, and incited to treason the citizens and subjects of other nations for the purpose of establishing their fifth columns[1] of corruption

---

[1]A term originating in the siege of Madrid during the Spanish civil war (1936–1939), *fifth column* refers to forces of internal subversion during an external military threat. In Spain, four Nationalist military columns were advancing on Madrid, and Republican defenders feared that a "fifth column" would support the Nationalists from within the city.

and sabotage within those nations. They ignored the commonest obligations of one state respecting the internal affairs of another. They lightly made and promptly broke international engagements as a part of their settled policy to deceive, corrupt, and overwhelm. They made, and made only to violate, pledges respecting the demilitarized Rhineland, and Czechoslovakia, and Poland, and Russia. They did not hesitate to instigate the Japanese to treacherous attack on the United States. Our people saw in this succession of events the destruction of the minimum elements of trust which can hold the community of nations together in peace and progress. Then, in consummation of their plan, the Nazis swooped down upon the nations they had deceived and ruthlessly conquered them. They flagrantly violated the obligations which states, including their own, have undertaken by convention or tradition as a part of the rules of land warfare, and of the law of the sea. They want only destroyed cities like Rotterdam for no military purpose. They wiped out whole populations, as at Lidice, where no military purposes were to be served. They confiscated property of the Poles and gave it to party members. They transported in labor battalions great sectors of the civilian populations of the conquered countries. They refused the ordinary protections of law to the populations which they enslaved. The feeling of outrage grew in this country, and it became more and more felt that these were crimes committed against us and against the whole society of civilized nations by a band of brigands who had seized the instrumentality of a state.

I believe that those instincts of our people were right and that they should guide us as the fundamental tests of criminality. We propose to punish acts which have been regarded as criminal since the time of Cain and have been so written in every civilized code.

In arranging these trials we must also bear in mind the aspirations with which our people have faced the sacrifices of war. After we entered the war, and as we expended our men and our wealth to stamp out these wrongs, it was the universal feeling of our people that out of this war should come unmistakable rules and workable machinery from which any who might contemplate another era of brigandage would know that they would be held personally responsible and would be personally punished. Our people have been waiting for these trials in the spirit of Woodrow Wilson, who hoped to "give to international law the kind of vitality which it can only have if it is a real expression of our moral judgment." . . .

15

Minutes of the London Conference
for the Preparation of the Trial

July 23, 1945

MR. JUSTICE JACKSON: We have some regrettable circumstances at times in our own country in which minorities are unfairly treated. We think it is justifiable that we interfere or attempt to bring retribution to individuals or states only because the concentration camps and the deportations were in pursuance of a common plan or enterprise of making an unjust or illegal war in which we became involved. We see no other basis on which we are justified in reaching the atrocities which were committed inside Germany, under German law, or even in violation of German law, by authorities of the German state. Without substantially this definition, we would not think we had any part in the prosecution of those things. . . .

. . . I am really getting very discouraged about this, I must say. And it seems to me that there are one or two or three things to do. I am getting very discouraged about the possibility of conducting an international trial with the different viewpoints. It isn't the fault of anybody, but we have very different viewpoints. I think the United States might well withdraw from this matter and turn our prisoners over to the European powers to try, or else agree on separate trials, or something of that sort. It seems to me our difference in viewpoint is too great to work without so much difficulty and delay that it is going to be impractical to try these people within the length of time I can commit the United States to this venture. The matter has taken a different shape than when I came here authorized to sign on behalf of my Government, and it looks quite discouraging, I must say. . . .

. . . The difficulty with the proposition here is that, if the United States is going to take responsibility as host for these trials at Nürnberg, we must put a staff to work getting physical

Report of Robert H. Jackson, United States Representative to the International Conference on Military Trials, London 1945. Washington, DC: Department of State, 1949, 333.

plans ready, and the same is true any place else. The Army has told me again and again, "Don't come at us without consultation months ahead of time because it takes time." Now we could not even find out under the proposal now before us where the trial could be held until the other prosecutors are appointed. It would be the middle of September before we could know whether we could even go ahead, and I cannot wait that long. I shall have to say to my Government that they will have to put someone else to this task because I must be back to the Supreme Court. That is not your trouble, of course, but it is a very practical one for me. I think this agreement should fix the place for the first trial so that we can be at work at once getting it ready. I have tried to point out the facilities at Nürnberg. I am willing to give a list of my prisoners and lay all my cards on the table, but if you let this thing drag we will be running into different currents of public sentiment and people will be disgusted with too much delay. I don't see how we can, as lawyers responsible to our people, permit it. . . .

16

SIDNEY ALDERMAN

On Negotiating with the Russians
1951

There is one outstanding, yet quite simple, reason why these London negotiations were successful, whereas so many recent negotiations with the Soviet Union have been complete failures. It is a reason inherent in human nature rather than in any peculiar characteristics of the Russian nature or temperament. It is the very plain fact that there was no difference or conflict among the four powers as to the ultimate aim of these negotiations. There were differences in concepts as to judicial process,

Sidney S. Alderman, "Negotiating on War Crimes Prosecutions, 1945," in Raymond Dennett and Joseph E. Johnson, eds., *Negotiating with the Russians.* Boston: World Peace Foundation, 1951, 52–53.

as to procedure, as to what constitutes a fair trial, as to where the trial should be held, even as to substantive international law and definitions of war crimes. But there was no difference as to the one ultimate aim, the creation of an international military tribunal and the indictment, trial, conviction and punishment of the major European Axis war criminals. . . .

A second important reason for the success of these negotiations is that they were all conducted in secret, confidential sessions. The press was never present. No press releases were ever given as to the details of the discussions, although, as inevitably happens, there were some leaks to or speculations by the press as to supposed differences among the four negotiators. Nevertheless, the Agreement and Charter was an "open covenant" secretly, not openly, arrived at. As a result there was no temptation to make the debates and discussions a sounding-board for home consumption in the four nations or for propaganda by any one nation directed to public opinion in the others or elsewhere.

For these reasons we never had any acrimonious debates. . . . The Russians were second to none in politeness and tact. They were characteristically stubborn on any matter on which they took a definite position or on which apparently, they were under instructions from Moscow. But they were never rude. They could sit tight on a matter for days and weeks, remaining totally impervious to the arguments of others, without ever giving any offense or departing in the slightest from an attitude of perfect politeness. They would agree to a matter one day and repudiate the agreement the next, evidently having communicated with Moscow in the meantime, without any appearance of embarrassment at the inconsistency and with the blandest suavity of manner. These acts or tactics often harassed, sometimes vexed, the other conferees, but neither the words nor the manners of the Russians ever did. There was a complete absence of any such diatribes and invectives as [Soviet leaders] have accustomed us to in recent years.

Individually the Russians were charming, courteous and friendly. Our individual conversations with them were hampered by the constant necessity of an interpreter, but that necessity in no wise prevented, only slowed down, social communication. Sometimes such slowing down of conversation is a good thing. It gives each participant the chance to weigh carefully what the other has said and what his reply will be. It helps to avoid the hasty *faux pas.* They entertained elaborately and well, usually at the Savoy. At one of their parties at the Savoy, I said to Professor Trainin that only good, sound capitalists could afford to live and entertain at such an expensive hotel. He enjoyed the jibe hugely. In the course of our conversation he asked me what I did in "civil" life. I told him that I represented "special interests." He laughed again and said slyly, "Ah, you know, we have some of those in Russia too." They were not only gracious hosts but also genial guests. We formed very close personal attachments for each of them. Not one of us has heard a word, even by indirection, from any of them since they returned behind the "Iron Curtain." Several of us have tried to communicate but never a word of acknowledgment or response. We think we know why. . . .

17

Charter of the International Military Tribunal
August 8, 1945

ARTICLE 1

In pursuance of the Agreement signed on the 8th day of August 1945 by the Government of the United States of America, the Provisional Government of the French Republic, the Government of the United Kingdom of Great Britain and Northern Ireland, and the Government of the Union of Soviet Socialist Republics, there shall be established an International Military Tribunal (hereinafter called "the Tribunal") for the just and prompt trial and punishment of the major war criminals of the European Axis.

ARTICLE 2

The Tribunal shall consist of four members, each with an alternate. One member and one alternate shall be appointed by each of the Signatories. . . .

International Military Tribunal, *Trial of the Major War Criminals before the International Military Tribunal, Nuremberg, 14 November 1945–1 October 1946*, 42 vols. Nuremberg: International Military Tribunal, 1947, 1:10–16.

ARTICLE 6

The Tribunal established by the Agreement referred to in Article 1 hereof for the trial and punishment of the major war criminals of the European Axis countries shall have the power to try and punish persons who, acting in the interests of the European Axis countries, whether as individuals or as members of organizations, committed any of the following crimes.

The following acts, or any of them, are crimes coming within the jurisdiction of the Tribunal for which there shall be individual responsibility:

   (a) *Crimes against Peace:* namely, planning, preparation, initiation or waging of a war of aggression, or a war in violation of international treaties, agreements or assurances, or participation in a Common Plan or Conspiracy for the accomplishment of any of the foregoing;

   (b) *War Crimes:* namely, violations of the laws or customs of war. Such violations shall include, but not be limited to, murder, ill-treatment or deportation to slave labor or for any other purpose of civilian population of or in occupied territory, murder or ill-treatment of prisoners of war or persons on the seas, killing of hostages, plunder of public or private property, wanton destruction of cities, towns, or villages, or devastation not justified by military necessity;

   (c) *Crimes against Humanity:* namely, murder, extermination, enslavement, deportation, and other inhumane acts committed against any civilian population, before or during the war,[1] or persecutions on political, racial, or religious grounds in execution of or in connection with any crime within the jurisdiction of the Tribunal, whether or not in violation of domestic law of the country where perpetrated.

Leaders, organizers, instigators, and accomplices participating in the formulation or execution of a Common Plan or Conspiracy to commit any of the foregoing crimes are responsible for all acts performed by any persons in execution of such plan.

---

[1]Comma substituted in place of semicolon by Protocol of 6 October 1945. See pages 79–80, and also page 114, n. 87.

ARTICLE 7

The official position of defendants, whether as Heads of State or responsible officials in Government departments, shall not be considered as freeing them from responsibility or mitigating punishment.

ARTICLE 8

The fact that the defendant acted pursuant to order of his Government or of a superior shall not free him from responsibility, but may be considered in mitigation of punishment if the Tribunal determine that justice so requires.

ARTICLE 10

In cases where a group or organization is declared criminal by the Tribunal, the competent national authority of any Signatory shall have the right to bring individuals to trial for membership therein before national, military, or occupation courts. In any such case the criminal nature of the group or organization is considered proved and shall not be questioned.

ARTICLE 13

The Tribunal shall draw up rules for its procedure. These rules shall not be inconsistent with the provisions of this Charter.

ARTICLE 16

In order to ensure fair trial for the defendants, the following procedure shall be followed:

(a) The Indictment shall include full particulars specifying in detail the charges against the defendants. A copy of the Indictment and of all the documents lodged with the Indictment, translated into a language which he understands, shall be furnished to the defendant at a reasonable time before the Trial.

(b) During any preliminary examination or trial of a defendant he shall have the right to give any explanation relevant to the charges made against him.

(c) A preliminary examination of a defendant and his trial shall be conducted in, or translated into, a language which the defendant understands.

(d) A defendant shall have the right to conduct his own defense before the Tribunal or to have the assistance of counsel.

(e) A defendant shall have the right through himself or through his counsel to present evidence at the Trial in support of his defense, and to cross-examine any witness called by the Prosecution. . . .

ARTICLE 18

The Tribunal shall:

(a) confine the Trial strictly to an expeditious hearing of the issues raised by the charges,

(b) take strict measures to prevent any action which will cause unreasonable delay, and rule out irrelevant issues and statements of any kind whatsoever,

(c) deal summarily with any contumacy, imposing appropriate punishment, including exclusion of any defendant or his counsel from some or all further proceedings, but without prejudice to the determination of the charges.

ARTICLE 19

The Tribunal shall not be bound by technical rules of evidence. It shall adopt and apply to the greatest possible extent expeditious and nontechnical procedure, and shall admit any evidence which it deems to have probative value. . . .

ARTICLE 26

The judgment of the Tribunal as to the guilt or the innocence of any defendant shall give the reasons on which it is based, and shall be final and not subject to review.

ARTICLE 27

The Tribunal shall have the right to impose upon a defendant on conviction, death or such other punishment as shall be determined by it to be just.

18

JACOB ROBINSON TO ROBERT JACKSON ON ADOLF EICHMANN

July 27, 1945

The newspapers recently carried lists of a few dozen top Nazi leaders who are to appear before the Inter-Allied Tribunal. It was a great disappointment not to find in these lists the name of a man who is probably more directly responsible for the destruction of the Jews than any other single Nazi. He is SS Obersturmfuehrer Adolf Aichman [sic] . . .

His activities covered the whole of Europe, wherever Jewish problems had to be "solved". . . . There is hardly a single geographical section of Europe where the Jews were liquidated, that did not benefit from the direct guidance of Eichmann. . . . I think it would be very important to have him apprehended (if this has not already be[en] done) and, in view of his direct guilt, arraigned along with other criminals at the great trial.

Truman Presidential Museum & Library, The War Crimes Trials at Nuremberg, letter from Jacob Robinson to Robert H. Jackson, July 27, 1945, http://www.trumanlibrary .org/whistlestop/study_collections/nuremberg/index.php?action=docs#1945

19

INTERNATIONAL MILITARY TRIBUNAL

Indictment

October 6, 1945

INTERNATIONAL MILITARY TRIBUNAL

The United States of America, the French Republic, the United Kingdom of Great Britain and Northern Ireland, and the Union of Soviet Socialist Republics

— against —

International Military Tribunal, *Trial of the Major War Criminals before the International Military Tribunal, Nuremberg, 14 November 1945–1 October 1946,* 42 vols. Nuremberg: International Military Tribunal, 1947, 1:27, 29–31, 35–67.

Hermann Wilhelm Göring, Rudolf Hess, Joachim von Ribbentrop, Robert Ley, Wilhelm Keitel, Ernst Kaltenbrunner, Alfred Rosenberg, Hans Frank, Wilhelm Frick, Julius Streicher, Walter Funk, Hjalmar Schacht, Gustav Krupp von Bohlen und Halbach, Karl Dönitz, Erich Raeder, Baldur von Schirach, Fritz Sauckel, Alfred Jodl, Martin Bormann, Franz von Papen, Arthur Seyss-Inquart, Albert Speer, Constantin von Neurath, and Hans Fritzsche, individually and as members of any of the following groups or organizations to which they respectively belonged; namely: Die Reichsregierung (Reich Cabinet); Das Korps der Politischen Leiter der Nationalsozialistischen Deutschen Arbeiterpartei (Leadership Corps of the Nazi Party); Die Schutzstaffeln der Nationalsozialistischen Deutschen Arbeiterpartei (commonly known as the "SS") and including Der Sicherheitsdienst (commonly known as the "SD"); Die Geheime Staatspolizei (Secret State Police, commonly known as the "Gestapo"); Die Sturmabteilungen der NSDAP (commonly known as the "SA"); and the General Staff and High Command of the German Armed Forces, all as defined in Appendix B. . . .

COUNT ONE—THE COMMON PLAN OR CONSPIRACY

(Charter, Article 6, especially 6 (a))

III. Statement of the Offense

All the defendants, with divers other persons, during a period of years preceding 8 May 1945, participated as leaders, organizers, instigators, or accomplices in the formulation or execution of a common plan or conspiracy to commit, or which involved the commission of, Crimes against Peace, War Crimes, and Crimes against Humanity, as defined in the Charter of this Tribunal, and, in accordance with the provisions of the Charter, are individually responsible for their own acts and for all acts committed by any persons in the execution of such plan or conspiracy. The common plan or conspiracy embraced the commission of Crimes against Peace, in that the defendants planned, prepared, initiated, and waged wars of aggression, which were also wars in violation of international treaties, agreements, or assurances. In the development and course of the common plan or conspiracy it came to embrace the commission of War Crimes, in that it contemplated, and the defendants determined upon and carried out, ruthless wars against countries and populations, in violation of the rules and customs of war, including as typical and systematic means by which the wars were prosecuted, murder, ill-treatment, deportation for slave labor and for other purposes of civilian populations of occupied territories, murder and ill-treatment of prisoners of war and of persons on the high seas, the taking and killing of hostages, the plunder of public and private property, the indiscriminate destruction of cities, towns, and villages, and devastation not justified by military necessity. The common plan or conspiracy contemplated and came to embrace as typical and systematic means, and the defendants determined upon and committed, Crimes against Humanity, both within Germany and within occupied territories, including murder, extermination, enslavement, deportation, and other inhumane acts committed against civilian populations before and during the war, and persecutions on political, racial, or religious grounds, in execution of the plan for preparing and prosecuting aggressive or illegal wars, many of such acts and persecutions being violations of the domestic laws of the countries where perpetrated. . . .

COUNT TWO—CRIMES AGAINST PEACE

(Charter, Article 6 (a))

V. Statement of the Offense

All the defendants with divers other persons, during a period of years preceding 8 May 1945, participated in the planning, preparation, initiation, and waging of wars of aggression, which were also wars in violation of international treaties, agreements, and assurances. . . .

COUNT THREE—WAR CRIMES

(Charter, Article 6, especially 6 (b))

VIII. Statement of the Offense

All the defendants committed War Crimes between 1 September 1939 and 8 May 1945, in Germany and in all those countries and territories occupied by the German Armed Forces since

1 September 1939, and in Austria, Czechoslovakia, and Italy, and on the High Seas.

All the defendants, acting in concert with others, formulated and executed a Common Plan or Conspiracy to commit War Crimes as defined in Article 6 (b) of the Charter. This plan involved, among other things, the practice of "total war" including methods of combat and of military occupation in direct conflict with the laws and customs of war, and the commission of crimes perpetrated on the field of battle during encounters with enemy armies, and against prisoners of war, and in occupied territories against the civilian population of such territories. . . .

These methods and crimes constituted violations of international conventions, of internal penal laws and of the general principles of criminal law as derived from the criminal law of all civilized nations, and were involved in and part of a systematic course of conduct. . . .

COUNT FOUR—CRIMES AGAINST HUMANITY

(Charter, Article 6, especially 6 (c))

X. Statement of the Offense

All the defendants committed Crimes against Humanity during a period of years preceding 8 May 1945 in Germany and in all those countries and territories occupied by the German armed forces since 1 September 1939 and in Austria and Czechoslovakia and in Italy and on the High Seas.

All the defendants, acting in concert with others, formulated and executed a common plan or conspiracy to commit Crimes against Humanity as defined in Article 6 (c) of the Charter. This plan involved, among other things, the murder and persecution of all who were or who were suspected of being hostile to the Nazi Party and all who were or who were suspected of being opposed to the common plan alleged in Count One.

The said Crimes against Humanity were committed by the defendants and by other persons for whose acts the defendants are responsible (under Article 6 of the Charter) as such other persons, when committing the said War Crimes, performed their acts in execution of a common plan and conspiracy to commit the said War Crimes, in the formulation and execution of which plan and conspiracy all the defendants participated as leaders, organizers, instigators, and accomplices.

These methods and crimes constituted violations of international conventions, of internal penal laws, of the general principles of criminal law as derived from the criminal law of all civilized nations and were involved in and part of a systematic course of conduct. The said acts were contrary to Article 6 of the Charter.

The Prosecution will rely upon the facts pleaded under Count Three as also constituting Crimes against Humanity.

(A) MURDER, EXTERMINATION, ENSLAVEMENT, DEPORTATION, AND OTHER INHUMANE ACTS COMMITTED AGAINST CIVILIAN POPULATIONS BEFORE AND DURING THE WAR

For the purposes set out above, the defendants adopted a policy of persecution, repression, and extermination of all civilians in Germany who were, or who were believed to be, or who were believed likely to become, hostile to the Nazi Government and the common plan or conspiracy described in Count One. They imprisoned such persons without judicial process, holding them in "protective custody" and concentration camps, and subjected them to persecution, degradation, despoilment, enslavement, torture, and murder. . . . These acts and policies were continued and extended to the occupied countries after 1 September 1939, and until 8 May 1945.

(B) PERSECUTION ON POLITICAL, RACIAL, AND RELIGIOUS GROUNDS IN EXECUTION OF AND IN CONNECTION WITH THE COMMON PLAN MENTIONED IN COUNT ONE

As above stated, in execution of and in connection with the common plan mentioned in Count One, opponents of the German Government were exterminated and persecuted. These persecutions were directed against Jews. They were also directed against persons whose political belief or spiritual aspirations were deemed to be in conflict with the aims of the Nazis.

Jews were systematically persecuted since 1933; they were deprived of their liberty, thrown into concentration camps where they were murdered and ill-treated. Their property was confiscated. Hundreds of thousands of Jews were so treated before 1 September 1939.

Since 1 September 1939, the persecution of the Jews was redoubled: millions of Jews from Germany and from the occupied Western Countries were sent to the Eastern Countries for extermination.

4

The Court

20

Thomas J. Dodd to Mary Grace Murphy Dodd
June 1, 1946

Grace my dearest one . . .

I feel that we are doing something so important that it is awesome—it is almost purifying. It has a deep religious meaning, of that I feel certain. Surely it is God's wish that men not wage wars of aggression. The proof here is absolutely overwhelming. I would never have believed that men could be so evil, so determined on a course of war; of murder; of slavery; of dreadful tyranny. Never before has such a record been written and men will read it for a thousand years in amazement and wonder how it ever happened.

Christopher J. Dodd, ed. *Letters from Nuremberg: My Father's Narrative of a Quest for Justice*. New York: Crown Publishers, 2007, 313.

21

FRANCIS BIDDLE

Description of the Court

1962

. . . Hitler's ghost haunted the courtroom, we could all see its outline, standing contemptuously at Göring's elbow; frowning at Schacht as he spoke of the Führer's enormous reading, of his juggling with his knowledge, in certain respects a man of genius, a mass psychologist of really diabolical genius, who finally fell victim to the spell he cast over the masses, for whoever seduces them is finally led and seduced by them. Streicher, who had been thoroughly under his spell, described Hitler after speaking for three hours in the Munich beer cellar in 1921, as "drenched in perspiration, radiant." General Keitel was impressed with the great man's knowledge of tactics, of operations, of strategy, of organization, of the details of armament, of the equipment of all the armies, of the classic authorities on the science of war — Clausewitz, Moltke, Schlieffe[n]. But Jodl, summarizing his views in a last speech, said that the "Wehrmacht was confronted with the impossible task of conducting a war they did not want, under a commander they did not trust, to fight with troops and police forces not under their command" — by no means an inaccurate description.

We watched the defendants day after day, these drab men once great, most of them now turning on the Führer who had led them to their brief spasm of violent triumph. A few were still "loyal." Some felt that it was not "correct" to attack a dead man who had been head of the State. Others transferred their guilt to the man who, they said, was alone responsible, from whom, they pleaded, orders came to them that had to be obeyed: theirs but to do or die, they argued; how could there be a conspiracy, a meeting of the minds, when one man's mind commanded all the others? . . .

Day after day the horrors accumulated — tortures by the Gestapo in France, scientific "experiments" on prisoners who died

---

Francis Biddle, *In Brief Authority*. Garden City, NY: Doubleday, 1962, 434–46.

in agony, the gas chambers, the carefully planned liquidation of the Jews. Hour on hour the twenty-one men in the dock listened, and the shame spread, and steadily washed to the rocks of their loyalty to the man who was responsible for it all. After one day's evidence Hans Fritzsche was physically ill in his cell. And when Hans Frank, the notorious Governor General of Poland, made his cheap, dramatic confession — "a thousand years will pass and still this guilt of Germany will not have been erased" — Schacht observed to [court psychologist Gustave] Gilbert that Göring's united front of loyalty and defiance seemed to have collapsed. After Gisevius had testified, the legend was warped and tarnished. Speer tried in his testimony to destroy it forever. The Führer principle, he had at last realized, the authoritarian system, was fundamentally wrong. In 1945 when the situation had become hopeless Hitler "attributed the outcome of the war in an increasing degree to the failure of the German people, but he never blamed himself. . . . The German people remained faithful to Adolf Hitler to the end. He knowingly betrayed them."

22

ROBERT H. JACKSON

Opening Address for the United States
November 21, 1945

May it please Your Honors:

The privilege of opening the first trial in history for crimes against the peace of the world imposes a grave responsibility. The wrongs which we seek to condemn and punish have been so calculated, so malignant, and so devastating, that civilization cannot tolerate their being ignored, because it cannot survive their being repeated. That four great nations, flushed with victory and stung with injury stay the hand of vengeance and voluntarily submit

International Military Tribunal, *Trial of the Major War Criminals before the International Military Tribunal, Nuremberg, 14 November 1945–1 October 1946,* 42 vols. Nuremberg: International Military Tribunal, 1947, 2:98–103, 104–5, 153–54.

their captive enemies to the judgment of the law is one of the most significant tributes that Power has ever paid to Reason.

This Tribunal, while it is novel and experimental, is not the product of abstract speculations nor is it created to vindicate legalistic theories. This inquest represents the practical effort of four of the most mighty of nations, with the support of 17 more, to utilize international law to meet the greatest menace of our times — aggressive war. The common sense of mankind demands that law shall not stop with the punishment of petty crimes by little people. It must also reach men who possess themselves of great power and make deliberate and concerted use of it to set in motion evils which leave no home in the world untouched. It is a cause of that magnitude that the United Nations will lay before Your Honors.

In the prisoners' dock sit twenty-odd broken men. . . .

What makes this inquest significant is that these prisoners represent sinister influences that will lurk in the world long after their bodies have returned to dust. We will show them to be living symbols of racial hatreds, of terrorism and violence, and of the arrogance and cruelty of power. They are symbols of fierce nationalisms and of militarism, of intrigue and war-making which have embroiled Europe generation after generation, crushing its manhood, destroying its homes, and impoverishing its life. They have so identified themselves with the philosophies they conceived and with the forces they directed that any tenderness to them is a victory and an encouragement to all the evils which are attached to their names. Civilization can afford no compromise with the social forces which would gain renewed strength if we deal ambiguously or indecisively with the men in whom those forces now precariously survive. . . .

In justice to the nations and the men associated in this prosecution, I must remind you of certain difficulties which may leave their mark on this case. Never before in legal history has an effort been made to bring within the scope of a single litigation the developments of a decade, covering a whole continent, and involving a score of nations, countless individuals, and innumerable events. Despite the magnitude of the task, the world has demanded immediate action. This demand has had to be met, though perhaps at the cost of finished craftsmanship. In my country, established courts, following familiar procedures, applying well-thumbed precedents, and dealing with the legal consequences of local and limited events seldom commence a trial within a year of the event in litigation. Yet less than 8 months ago today the courtroom in which you sit was an enemy fortress in the hands of German SS troops. Less than 8 months ago nearly all our witnesses and documents were in enemy hands. The law had not been codified, no procedures had been established, no tribunal was in existence, no usable courthouse stood here, none of the hundreds of tons of official German documents had been examined, no prosecuting staff had been assembled, nearly all of the present defendants were at large, and the four prosecuting powers had not yet joined in common cause to try them. I should be the last to deny that the case may well suffer from incomplete researches and quite likely will not be the example of professional work which any of the prosecuting nations would normally wish to sponsor. It is, however, a completely adequate case to the judgment we shall ask you to render, and its full development we shall be obliged to leave to the historians. . . .

Unfortunately, the nature of these crimes is such that both prosecution and judgment must be by victor nations over vanquished foes. The worldwide scope of the aggressions carried out by these men has left but few real neutrals. Either the victors must judge the vanquished or we must leave the defeated to judge themselves. After the first World War, we learned the futility of the latter course. The former high station of these defendants, the notoriety of their acts, and the adaptability of their conduct to provoke retaliation make it hard to distinguish between the demand for a just and measured retribution, and the unthinking cry for vengeance which arises from the anguish of war. It is our task, so far as humanly possible, to draw the line between the two. We must never forget that the record on which we judge these defendants today is the record on which history will judge us tomorrow. To pass these defendants a poisoned chalice is to put it to our own lips as well. We must summon such detachment and intellectual integrity to our task that this Trial will commend itself to posterity as fulfilling humanity's aspirations to do justice.

At the very outset, let us dispose of the contention that to put these men to trial is to do them an injustice entitling them to some special consideration. These defendants may be hard pressed but they are not ill used. Let us see what alternative they would have to being tried. . . .

If these men are the first war leaders of a defeated nation to be prosecuted in the name of the law, they are also the first to be given a chance to plead for their lives in the name of the law. Realistically, the Charter of this Tribunal, which gives them a hearing, is also the source of their only hope. It may be that these men of troubled conscience, whose only wish is that the world forget them, do not regard a trial as a favor. But they do have a fair opportunity to defend themselves — a favor which these men, when in power, rarely extended to their fellow countrymen. Despite the fact that public opinion already condemns their acts, we agree that here they must be given a presumption of innocence, and we accept the burden of proving criminal acts and the responsibility of these defendants for their commission.

When I say that we do not ask for convictions unless we prove crime, I do not mean mere technical or incidental transgression of international conventions. We charge guilt on planned and intended conduct that involves moral as well as legal wrong. And we do not mean conduct that is a natural and human, even if illegal, cutting of corners, such as many of us might well have committed had we been in the defendants' positions. It is not because they yielded to the normal frailties of human beings that we accuse them. It is their abnormal and inhuman conduct which brings them to this bar.

We will not ask you to convict these men on the testimony of their foes. There is no count in the Indictment that cannot be proved by books and records. The Germans were always meticulous record keepers, and these defendants had their share of the Teutonic passion for thoroughness in putting things on paper. Nor were they without vanity. They arranged frequently to be photographed in action. We will show you their own films. You will see their own conduct and hear their own voices as these defendants re-enact for you, from the screen, some of the events in the course of the conspiracy.

We would also make clear that we have no purpose to incriminate the whole German people. We know that the Nazi Party was not put in power by a majority of the German vote. We know it came to power by an evil alliance between the most extreme of the Nazi revolutionists, the most unrestrained of the German reactionaries, and the most aggressive of the German militarists. If the German populace had willingly accepted the Nazi program, no Storm-troopers would have been needed in the early days of the Party and there would have been no need for concentration camps or the Gestapo, both of which institutions were inaugurated as soon as the Nazis gained control of the German State. Only after these lawless innovations proved successful at home were they taken abroad.

The German people should know by now that the people of the United States hold them in no fear, and in no hate. It is true that the Germans have taught us the horrors of modern warfare, but the ruin that lies from the Rhine to the Danube shows that we, like our Allies, have not been dull pupils. If we are not awed by German fortitude and proficiency in war, and if we are not persuaded of their political maturity, we do respect their skill in the arts of peace, their technical competence, and the sober, industrious, and self-disciplined character of the masses of the German people. . . .

In general, our case will disclose these defendants all uniting at some time with the Nazi Party in a plan which they well knew could be accomplished only by an outbreak of war in Europe. Their seizure of the German State, their subjugation of the German people, their terrorism and extermination of dissident elements, their planning and waging of war, their calculated and planned ruthlessness in the conduct of warfare, their deliberate and planned criminality toward conquered peoples — all these are ends for which they acted in concert; and all these are phases of the conspiracy, a conspiracy which reached one goal only to set out for another and more ambitious one. We shall also trace for you the intricate web of organizations which these men formed and utilized to accomplish these ends. We will show how the entire structure of offices and officials was dedicated to the criminal purposes and committed to the use of the criminal methods planned by these defendants and their co-conspirators, many of whom war and suicide have put beyond reach.

It is my purpose to open the case, particularly under Count One of the Indictment, and to deal with the Common Plan or Conspiracy to achieve ends possible only by resort to Crimes against Peace, War Crimes, and Crimes against Humanity. My emphasis will not be on individual barbarities and perversions which may have occurred independently of any central plan. One of the dangers ever present is that this Trial may be protracted by details of particular wrongs and that we will become lost in a "wilderness of single instances." Nor will I now dwell on the activity of individual defendants except as it may contribute to exposition of the common plan.

The case as presented by the United States will be concerned with the brains and authority back of all the crimes. These defendants were men of a station and rank which does not soil its own hands with blood. They were men who knew how to use lesser folk as tools. We want to reach the planners and designers, the inciters and leaders without whose evil architecture the world would not have been for so long scourged with the violence and lawlessness, and wracked with the agonies and convulsions, of this terrible war. . . .

Among the nations which unite in accusing these defendants the United States is perhaps in a position to be the most dispassionate, for having sustained the least injury, it is perhaps the least animated by vengeance. Our American cities have not been bombed by day and by night, by humans, and by robots. It is not our temples that had been laid in ruins. Our countrymen have not had their homes destroyed over their heads. The menace of Nazi aggression, except to those in actual service, has seemed less personal and immediate to us than to European peoples. But while the United States is not first in rancor, it is not second in determination that the forces of law and order be made equal to the task of dealing with such international lawlessness as I have recited here.

Twice in my lifetime, the United States has sent its young manhood across the Atlantic, drained its resources, and burdened itself with debt to help defeat Germany. But the real hope and faith that has sustained the American people in these great efforts was that victory for ourselves and our Allies would lay the basis for an ordered international relationship in Europe and would end the centuries of strife on this embattled continent.

Twice we have held back in the early stages of European conflict in the belief that it might be confined to a purely European affair. In the United States, we have tried to build an economy without armament, a system of government without militarism, and a society where men are not regimented for war. This purpose, we know now, can never be realized if the world periodically is to be embroiled in war. The United States cannot, generation after generation, throw its youth or its resources on to the battlefields of Europe to redress the lack of balance between Germany's strength and that of her enemies, and to keep the battles from our shores.

The American dream of a peace-and-plenty economy, as well as the hopes of other nations, can never be fulfilled if those nations are involved in a war every generation so vast and devastating as to crush the generation that fights and burden the generation that follows. But experience has shown that wars are no longer local. All modern wars become world wars eventually. And none of the big nations at least can stay out. If we cannot stay out of wars, our only hope is to prevent wars.

I am too well aware of the weaknesses of juridical action alone to contend that in itself your decision under this Charter can prevent future wars. Judicial action always comes after the event. Wars are started only on the theory and in the confidence that they can be won. Personal punishment, to be suffered only in the event the war is lost, will probably not be a sufficient deterrent to prevent a war where the warmakers feel the chances of defeat to be negligible.

But the ultimate step in avoiding periodic wars, which are inevitable in a system of international lawlessness, is to make statesmen responsible to law. And let me make clear that while this law is first applied against German aggressors, the law includes, and if it is to serve a useful purpose it must condemn aggression by any other nations, including those which sit here now in judgment. We are able to do away with domestic tyranny and violence and aggression by those in power against the rights of their own people only when we make all men answerable to the law. This trial represents mankind's desperate effort to apply the discipline of the law to statesmen who have used their powers of state to attack the foundations of the world's peace and to commit aggressions against the rights of their neighbors. . . .

23

HARTLEY SHAWCROSS

Opening Address for the United Kingdom

December 4, 1945

In [the] General Treaty for the Renunciation of War [the Kellogg-Briand Pact], practically the whole civilized world abolished war as a legally permissible means of enforcing the law or of changing it. The right of war was no longer of the essence of sovereignty. Whatever the position may have been at the time of the Hague Convention, whatever the position may have been in 1914, whatever it may have been in 1918 — and it is not necessary to discuss it — no international lawyer of repute, no responsible statesman, no soldier concerned with the legal use of armed forces, no economist or industrialist concerned in his country's war economy could doubt that with the Pact of Paris on the statute book a war of aggression was contrary to international law. Nor have the repeated violations of the Pact by the Axis Powers in any way affected its validity. Let this be firmly and clearly stated. Those very breaches, except perhaps to the cynic and the malevolent, have added to the strength of the treaty; they provoked the sustained wrath of peoples angered by the contemptuous disregard of this great statute and determined to vindicate its provisions. The Pact of Paris is the law of nations. This Tribunal will declare it. . . .

The General Treaty for the Renunciation of War, this great constitutional instrument of an international society awakened to the deadly dangers of another Armageddon, did not remain an isolated effort soon to be forgotten in the turmoil of recurrent international crises. It became, in conjunction with the Covenant of the League of Nations or independently of it, the starting point for a new orientation of governments in matters of peace, war, and neutrality. . . .

International Military Tribunal, *Trial of the Major War Criminals before the International Military Tribunal, Nuremberg, 14 November 1945–1 October 1946,* 42 vols. Nuremberg: International Military Tribunal, 1947, 3:99–100, 103, 105–6, 143–44.

What statesman or politician in charge of the affairs of nations could doubt, from 1928 onwards, that aggressive war, or that all war, except in self-defense or for the collective enforcement of the law, or against a state which had itself violated the Pact of Paris, was unlawful and outlawed? What statesman or politician embarking upon such a war could reasonably and justifiably count upon an immunity other than that of a successful outcome of the criminal venture? What more decisive evidence of a prohibition laid down by positive international law could any lawyer desire than that which has been adduced before this Tribunal?

There are, it is true, some small town lawyers who deny the very existence of any international law; and indeed, as I have said, the rules of the law of nations may not satisfy the . . . test of being imposed by a sovereign. But the legal regulation of international relations rests upon quite different juridical foundations. It depends upon consent, but upon a consent which, once given, cannot be withdrawn by unilateral action. In the international field the source of law is not the command of a sovereign but the treaty agreement binding upon every state which has adhered to it. And it is indeed true, and the recognition of its truth today by all the great powers of the world is vital to our future peace—it is indeed true that, as M. Litvinov once said, and as Great Britain fully accepts:

> "Absolute sovereignty and entire liberty of action only belong to such states as have not undertaken international obligations. Immediately a state accepts international obligations it limits its sovereignty."

. . . It is a salutary principle, a principle of law, that politicians who embark upon a particular policy—as here—of aggressive war should not be able to seek immunity behind the intangible personality of the state. It is a salutary legal rule that persons who, in violation of the law, plunge their own and other countries into an aggressive war should do so with a halter around their necks.

To say that those who aid and abet, who counsel and procure a crime are themselves criminals, is a commonplace in our own municipal law. Nor is the principle of individual international responsibility for offenses against the law of nations altogether new. It has been applied not only to pirates. The entire law relating to war crimes, as distinct from the crime of war, is based upon the principle of individual responsibility. The future of international law, and indeed, of the world itself, depends on its application in a much wider sphere, in particular, in that of safeguarding the peace of the world. There must be acknowledged not only, as in the Charter of the United Nations, fundamental human rights, but also, as in the Charter of this Tribunal, fundamental human duties, and of these none is more vital, none is more fundamental, than the duty not to vex the peace of nations in violation of the clearest legal prohibitions and undertakings. If this be an innovation, it is an innovation which we are prepared to defend and to justify, but it is not an innovation which creates a new crime. International law had already, before the Charter was adopted, constituted aggressive war a criminal act. . . .

It may be said that many of the documents which have been referred to were in Hitler's name, and that the orders were Hitler's orders, and that these men were mere instruments of Hitler's will. But they were the instruments without which Hitler's will could not be carried out; and they were more than that. These men were no mere willing tools, although they would be guilty enough if that had been their role. They are the men whose support had built Hitler up into the position of power he occupied; these are the men whose initiative and planning often conceived and certainly made possible the acts of aggression done in Hitler's name; and these are the men who enabled Hitler to build up the Army, the Navy, the Air Force, the war economy, the political philosophy, by which these treacherous attacks were carried out, and by which he was able to lead his fanatical followers into peaceful countries to murder, to loot, and to destroy. They are the men whose cooperation and support made the Nazi Government of Germany possible.

The government of a totalitarian country may be carried on without representatives of the people, but it cannot be carried on without any assistance at all. It is no use having a leader unless there are also people willing and ready to serve their personal greed and ambition by helping and following him. The dictator who is set up in control of the destinies of his country does not depend on himself alone either in acquiring power or in maintaining it. He depends upon the support and the backing which lesser men, themselves lusting to share in dictatorial power, anxious to bask in the adulation of their leader, are prepared to give.

In the criminal courts of our countries, when men are put on their trial for breaches of the municipal laws, it not infrequently happens that of a gang indicted together in the dock, one has the master mind, the leading personality. But it is no excuse for the common thief to say, "I stole because I was told to steal," for the murderer to plead, "I killed because I was asked to kill." And these men are in no different position, for all that it was nations they sought to rob, and whole peoples which they tried to kill. "The warrant of no man excuseth the doing of an illegal act." Political loyalty, military obedience are excellent things, but they neither require nor do they justify the commission of patently wicked acts. There comes a point where a man must refuse to answer to his leader if he is also to answer to his conscience. Even the common soldier, serving in the ranks of his army, is not called upon to obey illegal orders. But these men were no common soldiers: They were the men whose skill and cunning, whose labor and activity made it possible for the German Reich to tear up existing treaties, to enter into new ones and to flout them, to reduce international negotiations and diplomacy to a hollow mockery, to destroy all respect for and effect in international law and, finally, to march against the peoples of the world to secure that domination in which, as arrogant members of their self-styled master race, they professed to believe. . . .

24

FRANÇOIS DE MENTHON

Opening Address

January 17, 1946

France, invaded twice in 30 years in the course of wars, both of which were launched by German imperialism, bore almost alone in May and June 1940 the weight of armaments accumulated by Nazi Germany over a period of years in a spirit of aggression. Although temporarily crushed by superiority in numbers, material, and preparation, my country never gave up the battle for

International Military Tribunal, *Trial of the Major War Criminals before the International Military Tribunal, Nuremberg, 14 November 1945–1 October 1946,* 42 vols. Nuremberg: International Military Tribunal, 1947, 5:368–70, 373–75, 377–79.

freedom and was at no time absent from the field. The engagements undertaken and the will for national independence would have sufficed to keep France behind General De Gaulle in the camp of the democratic nations. If, however, our fight for freedom slowly took the shape of a popular uprising, at the call of the men of the Resistance, belonging to all social classes, to all creeds and to all political parties, it was because, while our soil and our souls were crushed by the Nazi invader, our people refused not only to submit to wretchedness and slavery, but even more they refused to accept the Hitlerian dogmas which were in absolute contradiction to their traditions, their aspirations, and their human calling.

France, which was systematically plundered and ruined; France, so many of whose sons were tortured and murdered in the jails of the Gestapo or in concentration camps; France, which was subjected to the still more horrible grip of demoralization and return to barbarism diabolically imposed by Nazi Germany, asks you, above all in the name of the heroic martyrs of the Resistance, who are among the greatest heroes of our national legend, that justice be done.

France, so often in history the spokesman and the champion of human liberty, of human values, of human progress, through my voice today also becomes the interpreter of the martyred peoples of western Europe, Norway, Denmark, the Netherlands, Belgium, Luxembourg, peoples more than all others devoted to peace, peoples who are among the noblest of humanity by their aspirations and their worship of the values of civilization, peoples who have shared our sufferings and have refused, like us, to give up liberty and to sacrifice their souls before the assault of Nazi barbarism. France here becomes their interpreter to demand that real justice be done.

The craving for justice of the tortured peoples is the basic foundation of France's appearance before Your High Tribunal. It is not the only one, nor perhaps the most important one. More than toward the past, our eyes are turned toward the future.

We believe that there can be no lasting peace and no certain progress for humanity, which still today is torn asunder, suffering, and anguished, except through the co-operation of all peoples and through the progressive establishment of a real international society. . . .

But in order that we may have the hope of founding progressively an international society, through the free co-operation of all peoples, founded on this morality and on this international law, it is necessary that, after having premeditated, prepared, and launched a war of aggression which has caused the death of millions of men and the ruin of a great number of nations, after having thereupon piled up the most odious crimes in the course of the war years, Nazi Germany shall be declared guilty and her rulers and those chiefly responsible punished as such. Without this sentence and without this punishment the people would no longer have any faith in justice. When you have declared that crime is always a crime, whether committed by one national entity against another or by one individual against another, you will thereby have affirmed that there is only one standard of morality, which applies to international relations as well as to individual relations, and that on this morality are built prescriptions of law recognized by the international community; you will then have truly begun to establish an international justice.

This work of justice is equally indispensable for the future of the German people. These people have been for many years intoxicated by Nazism; certain of their eternal and deep seated aspirations, under this regime, have found a monstrous expression; their entire responsibility is involved, not only by their general acceptance but by the effective participation of a great number of them in the crimes committed. Their re-education is indispensable. This represents a difficult enterprise and one of long duration. The efforts which the free peoples will have to make in order to reintegrate Germany into an international community cannot succeed in the end if this re-education is not carried out effectively. The initial condemnation of Nazi Germany by your High Tribunal will be a first lesson for these people and will constitute the best starting point for the work of the revision of values and of re-education which must be its great concern during the coming years. . . .

I propose today to prove to you that all this organized and vast criminality springs from what I may be allowed to call a crime against the spirit, I mean a doctrine which, denying all spiritual, rational, or moral values by which the nations have tried, for thousands of years, to improve human conditions, aims to plunge humanity back into barbarism, no longer the natural and spontaneous barbarism of primitive nations, but into a diabolical barbarism, conscious of itself and utilizing for its ends all material means put at the disposal of mankind by contemporary science.

This sin against the spirit is the original sin of National Socialism from which all crimes spring.

This monstrous doctrine is that of racialism: The German race, composed in theory of Aryans, would be a fundamental and natural concept. Germans as individuals do not exist and cannot justify their existence, except insofar as they belong to the race or Volkstum, to the popular mass which represents and amalgamates all Germans. Race is the matrix of the German people; proceeding therefrom this people lives and develops as an organism. The German may consider himself only as a healthy and vigorous member of this body, fulfilling within the collectivity a definite technical function; his activity and his usefulness are the exact gauge and justification of his liberty. This national body must be "moulded" to prepare it for a permanent struggle.

The ideas and the bodily symbols of racialism form an integral part of its political system. This is what is called authoritative or dictatorial biology.

The expression "blood" which appears so often in the writings of the Nazi theorists denotes this stream of real life, of red sap which flows through the circulatory system of every race and of all genuine culture as it flows through the human body. To be Aryan is to feel this current passing through oneself, this current which galvanizes and vivifies the whole nation. Blood is this region of spontaneous and unconscious life which reveals to each individual the tendencies of the race. The intellectual life must never, in extolling itself, separate us from this elemental basis of the sacred community. Let the individual go into himself and he will receive by direct revelation "the commandments of the blood." Dreams, rites, and myths can lead to this revelation. In other words the modern German can and must bear in himself the call of the old Germany and find again its purity and its youthful primitiveness. . . .

National Socialism is the ultimate result of a long evolution of doctrines; the exploitation by a group of men of one of the most profound and most tragic aspects of the German soul. But the crime committed by Hitler and his companions will be precisely that of unleashing and exploiting to its extreme limit the latent force of barbarity, which existed before him in the German people. . . .

In the middle of the 20th century Germany goes back, of her own free will, beyond Christianity and civilization to the primitive barbarity of ancient Germany. She makes a deliberate break with all universal conceptions of modern nations. The National Socialist doctrine, which raised inhumanity to the level of a principle, constitutes, in fact, a doctrine of disintegration of modern society.

This doctrine necessarily brought Germany to a war of aggression and to the systematic use of criminality in the waging of war.

The absolute primacy of the German race, the negation of any international law whatsoever, the cult of strength, the exacerbation of community mysticism made Germany consider recourse to war, in the interests of the German race, logical and justified. . . .

Whether we consider a Crime against Peace or War Crimes, we are therefore not faced by an accidental or an occasional criminality which events could explain without justifying it. We are, in fact, faced by systematic criminality, which derives directly and of necessity from a monstrous doctrine put into practice with deliberate intent by the masters of Nazi Germany. . . .

25

ROMAN A. RUDENKO

Opening Address

February 8, 1946

In its attempt to conceal its imperialistic aims the Hitlerite clique hysterically shrieked, as usual, about a danger alleged to be forthcoming from the U.S.S.R. and proclaimed that the predatory war which it started against the Soviet Union with aggressive purposes was a "preventive" war.

A pitiful effort!

What "preventive" war can we speak of, when documents prove that long in advance Germany worked out and prepared a plan for an attack on the U.S.S.R., formulated the predatory aims of this

International Military Tribunal, *Trial of the Major War Criminals before the International Military Tribunal, Nuremberg, 14 November 1945–1 October 1946*, 42 vols. Nuremberg: International Military Tribunal, 1947, 7:169–70.

attack, earmarked the territories of the Soviet Union which she intended to seize, established the methods for pillaging of these territories and for the extermination of their population, mobilized her army in good time, and moved to the borders of the U.S.S.R. 170 fully equipped divisions only waiting for the signal to advance?

The fact of aggression committed by fascist Germany against the U.S.S.R., as well as the original documents of the Hitlerite Government which now have been made public, definitely show to the whole world and to history how untrue and laughable was the assertion of the Hitlerite propaganda about the "preventive" character of the war against the U.S.S.R.

Much as the fascist wolf might disguise himself in a sheep's skin, he cannot hide his teeth! . . .

Having prepared and carried out the perfidious assault against the freedom-loving nations, fascist Germany turned the war into a system of militarized banditry. The murder of war prisoners, extermination of civilian populations, plunder of occupied territories, and other war crimes were committed as part of a totalitarian lightning war program projected by the fascists. In particular the terrorism practiced by the fascists on the temporarily occupied Soviet territories reached fabulous proportions and was carried out with an outspoken cruelty. . . .

The Soviet Prosecution has at its disposal numerous documents, collected by the Extraordinary State Commission for the Soviet Union for the prosecution and investigation of crimes committed by the German fascist aggressors and their accomplices, which constitute irrefutable evidence of countless crimes perpetrated by German authorities.

We have at our disposal a document, known as the "Appendix Number 2 to the Operational Order Number 8 of the Chief of the Sipo and SD," dated Berlin, 17 June 1941, and signed by Heydrich, who at that time held the office of Himmler's deputy. This document was worked out in collaboration with the High Command of the German Armed Forces. The appendices to Order Number 8, as well as Orders Number 9 and 14 and the appendices thereto, make it evident that the systematic extermination of Soviet people in fascist concentration camps in the territories of U.S.S.R. and other countries occupied by the fascist aggressors was carried out under the form of "filtration," "cleansing measures," "purges," "extraordinary measures," "special treatment," "liquidation," "execution," and so on. . . .

26

G. N. ALEXANDROV

Cross-Examination of Fritz Sauckel

May 31, 1946

GENERAL ALEXANDROV: [*Turning to the defendant.*] Tell me, do you consider such methods of warfare, the mass driving into slavery of millions of people from the occupied territories, to be in accordance with the laws and customs of war and human morality in general?

SAUCKEL: I do not consider slavery and deportation admissible. Please allow me to add the following explanation to this clear reply. Personally, I was firmly convinced that it is no crime . . .

ALEXANDROV: Please do not evade the question.

SAUCKEL: I am not evading the question, but I may and I have the right to give an explanation of my reply; I have already given the answer.

ALEXANDROV: Give a direct answer.

SAUCKEL: It is necessary for my defense . . .

ALEXANDROV: I do not think it is necessary. Answer directly: Do you consider these methods criminal or do you not?

THE PRESIDENT: One moment, General, you asked the defendant whether he considered it honorable. Let him answer it in his own way. It is not a question whether a thing is honorable. He is entitled to answer it freely. . . .

ALEXANDROV: . . . Tell me, for what purpose, for what kind of work were the foreign laborers employed who had been imported into Germany? Is it correct to state that they were primarily employed in the armament and munitions industries?

SAUCKEL: Workers were brought to Germany for employment in the armament industry. The armament industry is a very wide term, and is not identical with the manufacture of arms and munitions. The armament industry includes all products—from matches to cannons—that have anything to do with supply for the army. It is, therefore, necessary, within this

International Military Tribunal, *Trial of the Major War Criminals before the International Military Tribunal, Nuremberg, 14 November 1945–1 October 1946*, 42 vols. Nuremberg: International Military Tribunal, 1947, 15:137–39.

broad, far-reaching term, to limit or isolate the manufacture of arms and munitions.

Moreover, workers were brought to Germany for all other branches of civil economy essential to the war effort, such as agriculture, mining, skilled trades, and so forth. We made three distinctions: War economy, which meant the entire German economy in wartime; armament economy meant . . .

THE PRESIDENT: Well, Defendant, we do not want a lecture upon that, you know. All you were asked was whether they were brought there for work in the armament industry.

SAUCKEL: A part of them.

ALEXANDROV: I should like you to answer whether the workers brought to Germany were primarily employed in Germany's war industries and for military purposes? Is that right or not? I mean in the broad sense of the word.

SAUCKEL: In the broad sense of the word, yes, including the entire economy in wartime.

ALEXANDROV: Then the utilization of imported manpower was subordinated entirely and fully to the conduct of the war of aggression by Germany? Do you admit that?

SAUCKEL: That is stretching the idea too far. My own views, according to which I acted and could only act at the time, excluded the word "aggressive."

ALEXANDROV: Please answer briefly if it appears to go too far. Tell me do you admit it or do you not?

SAUCKEL: I have already answered. . . .

27

FRANCIS BIDDLE

A Rebuke for the Soviet Prosecutors

The Russian prosecutor immediately filed a petition for a rehearing of the question. It was the only petition for reargument we received. Its language was intemperate: the court, Rudenko claimed, had misconstrued the Charter, violated its duty, and was

Francis Biddle, *In Brief Authority*. Garden City, NY: Doubleday, 1962, 415–16.

grossly in error. The petition followed Nikitchenko's argument and indicated his co-operation.

The occasion warranted action. At our conference the next afternoon I asked my *confrères* to permit me to speak on a matter of personal privilege not on the agenda, but of the most vital importance to all of us. For it concerned the integrity of the members of the Tribunal, their honor, and their competence.

The brethren were by now giving me their attention.

One of the prosecutors—I looked at General Nikitchenko—had filed a slanderous, arrogant, and unwarranted attack on the Tribunal, a body that would go down to history as the most important court in the world. I did not know what the practice would be in other countries. In mine the author of such an outrage would be cited for contempt. Perhaps in this very extreme case we should send him to prison immediately—there could be no defense.

"What do you think, General? Have you read General Rudenko's petition? What do you propose should be done?"

General Nikitchenko was taken off base. He mumbled that he had read the petition, but rather hurriedly. He had nothing to propose. The French were amused—they guessed what I was up to. The British were surprised—they had not been consulted.

I produced an opinion, which Herbert Wechsler and I had drafted with a good deal of care the night before. With their permission I would read it. It could be read in open court immediately before General Rudenko was arrested.

I read the opinion. It denied the contention that government reports should be accepted as "irrefutable evidence of the facts found"—a contention "unsupported by the Charter and intrinsically unreasonable in itself." The Soviet prosecutor was in gross error in his construction of the Charter.

After a good deal of discussion, it was agreed that the opinion should be filed but not made public—with the Soviet member's dissent. The president would simply announce in court that the petition was dismissed. Nikitchenko no longer argued that German witnesses should not be called. His whole energy was directed to keeping the opinion from the press. He took seriously my suggestion that Rudenko be held in contempt; and as part of the "compromise" it was understood that no such action would be taken. He was pleased with the result. Two hours after we had adjourned I got a pleasant note from him indicating that we understood each other—would I pay his country a visit after the trial? He evidently had grasped the purpose of my tactic after he had time to think a little about it.

28

HERMANN GÖRING

Testimony on the Nazi Party

March 14, 1946

DR. STAHMER: Did you take part in laying down the Party program?

GÖRING: No. The Party program had been compiled and announced when I heard about the movement for the first time and when I declared my intention of joining.

STAHMER: What is your attitude towards these points of the Party program?

GÖRING: On the whole, positive. It is a matter of course that there is hardly any politically minded man who acknowledges and agrees with every point of the program of a political party.

STAHMER: In addition to these generally known points of the Party program, were there other aims which were kept secret?

GÖRING: No.

STAHMER: Were these aims to be achieved by every means, even by illegal means?

GÖRING: Of course, they were to be achieved by every means. The conception "illegal" should perhaps be clarified. If I aim at a revolution, then it is an illegal action for the state then in existence. If I am successful, then it becomes a fact and thereby legal and law. Until 1923 and the events of 9 November I and all of us had the view that we would achieve our aim, even, if necessary, in a revolutionary manner. After this proved a failure, the Führer, after his return from the fortress, decided that we should in the future proceed legally by means of a political fight, as the other parties had done, and the Führer prohibited any illegal action in order to avoid any setback in the activity of the Party.[1] . . .

---

[1]Göring refers to the Beer Hall Putsch, an attempted coup d'état by Hitler and his followers in Munich in November 1923. The attempt failed, and the Nazis suffered repression for a time—including Hitler's imprisonment in the "fortress" of Landsberg for nine months, during which time he dictated his autobiographical *Mein Kampf* to Rudolf Hess, his loyal follower.

International Military Tribunal, *Trial of the Major War Criminals before the International Military Tribunal, Nuremberg, 14 November 1945–1 October 1946*, 42 vols. Nuremberg: International Military Tribunal, 1947, 9:262–65.

STAHMER: What did you understand by the term "master race"?

GÖRING: I myself understood nothing by it. In none of my speeches, in none of my writings, will you find that term. It is my view that if you are a master you have no need to emphasize it.

STAHMER: What do you understand by the concept "living space"?

GÖRING: That conception is a very controversial one. I can fully understand that powers who together—I refer only to the four signatory powers—call more than three-quarters of the world their own, explain this idea differently. But for us, where 144 people live in 1 square kilometer, the words "living space" meant the proper relation between a population and its nourishment, its growth, and its standard of living. . . .

STAHMER: What is your attitude to the Leadership Principle?

GÖRING: I upheld this principle and I still uphold it positively and consciously. One must not make the mistake of forgetting that the political structure in different countries has different origins, different developments. Something which suits one country extremely well would perhaps fail completely in another. Germany, through the long centuries of monarchy, has always had a leadership principle. Democracy appeared in Germany at a time when Germany was very badly off and had reached rock-bottom. I explained yesterday the total lack of unity that existed in Germany—the number of parties, the continuous unrest caused by elections. A complete distortion of the concepts of authority and responsibility had arisen, and in the reverse direction. Authority lay with the masses and responsibility was with the leader, instead of the other way about. I am of the opinion that for Germany, particularly at that moment of its lowest ebb, when it was necessary for all forces to be welded together in a positive fashion, the Leadership Principle—that is, authority from above downwards and responsibility from below upwards—was the only possibility. Naturally I realize the fact that here, too, a principle, while thoroughly sound in itself, can lead to extremes. I should like to mention some parallels. The position of the Catholic Church rests now, as before, on the clear leadership principle of its hierarchy. And I think I can also say that Russia, too, without the leadership principle, could not have survived the great burden which was imposed on her by this war. . . .

STAHMER: Was the National Socialist Government recognized by foreign powers?

GÖRING: Our government was recognized from the first day of its existence and remained recognized until the end, that is, except where hostilities severed diplomatic connections with several states.

STAHMER: Did diplomatic representatives of foreign countries visit your Party rallies in Nuremberg?

GÖRING: The diplomatic representatives were invited to the Party rallies, these being the greatest event and the greatest demonstration of the movement; and they all attended, even if not the full number of them every year. But one I remember very well.

STAHMER: Until what year?

GÖRING: Until the last Party rally, 1938.

STAHMER: To what extent after the seizure of power was property of political opponents confiscated?

GÖRING: Laws were issued which decreed confiscation of the property of people hostile to the State, that is, the property of parties we declared to be hostile to the State. The party property of the Communist Party and its associated units, and the property of the Social Democratic Party was partly confiscated—but not, and I want to emphasize that, the private property of the members or even of the leaders of these parties. On the contrary, a number of leading Social Democrats who had been ministers or civil servants were still paid their full pension. In fact, later on it was increased.

STAHMER: How do you explain the actions against the trade unions? How do you explain the actions against free workers' associations?

GÖRING: First of all, the trade unions: Trade unions in Germany were for the most part, or the most important of them, very closely connected with the Social Democratic Party, and also to an increasing extent, due to the influence and the activity of the Communists, with the Communist Party. They were in fact, if not formally so, organs, indeed very active organs, of these parties, and here I am not talking about the masses of the members of the trade unions, but about the leaders of the trade unions. In addition there was also a smaller Christian trade union, an organ of the Center Party.

These trade unions, because of their leaders and the close connection of these leaders with those parties which we regarded as our opponents, agreed with our opponents to such an extent that they did not in any way fit into our new State. Consequently the organization of trade unions was dissolved, and for the workers the organization of the German Labor Front was created. This did not result in the destruction of the liberty of the German worker, in my opinion; on the contrary, I am convinced that we were the ones to give the German workers real freedom, for it consisted first of all in the fact that we made his right to have work secure, and laid particular stress on his position in the State.

We did, of course, do away with two things which perhaps must be regarded as two characteristics of a freedom which I do not understand: strikes on one side and lockouts on the other. These could not be made consistent with the right to have work nor with the duties which every citizen has towards the greatness of his nation. These two disquieting elements, which also contributed to the great number of unemployed, we removed and replaced with an enormous labor program.

Creation of work was another essential point of our social program and has also been adopted by others, though under a different name.

I do not propose to elaborate on this social program. It was, however, the first time that the worker had a right to a vacation, a paid vacation, this I only add as an aside. Great recreation centers were created for the workers. Enormous sums were invested in new housing projects for workers. The whole standard of living for the worker was raised. Up to that time the worker had been used and exploited. He hardly had any property of his own because, during years of unemployment, he had to sell everything or pawn it. Thus, without going into detail, I should like to say in conclusion that we did not enslave free workers, but rather we liberated the worker from the misery of unemployment. . . .

29

ROBERT H. JACKSON

Cross-Examination of Hermann Göring

March 18, 1946

MR. JUSTICE JACKSON: You are perhaps aware that you are the only living man who can expound to us the true purposes of the Nazi Party and the inner workings of its leadership?

GÖRING: I am perfectly aware of that.

JACKSON: You, from the very beginning, together with those who were associated with you, intended to overthrow, and later did overthrow, the Weimar Republic?

GÖRING: That was, as far as I am concerned, my firm intention.

JACKSON: And, upon coming to power, you immediately abolished parliamentary government in Germany?

GÖRING: We found it to be no longer necessary. Also I should like to emphasize the fact that we were moreover the strongest parliamentary party, and had the majority. But you are correct, when you say that parliamentary procedure was done away with, because the various parties were disbanded and forbidden.

JACKSON: You established the Leadership Principle, which you have described as a system under which authority existed only at the top, and is passed downwards and is imposed on the people below; is that correct?

GÖRING: In order to avoid any misunderstanding, I should like once more to explain the idea briefly, as I understand it. In German parliamentary procedure in the past responsibility rested with the highest officials, who were responsible for carrying out the anonymous wishes of the majorities, and it was they who exercised the authority. In the Leadership Principle we sought to reverse the direction, that is, the authority existed at the top and passed downwards, while the responsibility began at the bottom and passed upwards.

International Military Tribunal, *Trial of the Major War Criminals before the International Military Tribunal, Nuremberg, 14 November 1945–1 October 1946*, 42 vols. Nuremberg: International Military Tribunal, 1947, 9:417–21, 507–8.

JACKSON: In other words, you did not believe in and did not permit government, as we call it, by consent of the governed, in which the people, through their representatives, were the source of power and authority?

GÖRING: That is not entirely correct. We repeatedly called on the people to express unequivocally and clearly what they thought of our system, only it was in a different way from that previously adopted and from the system in practice in other countries. We chose the way of a so-called plebiscite. We also took the point of view that even a government founded on the Leadership Principle could maintain itself only if it was based in some way on the confidence of the people. If it no longer had such confidence, then it would have to rule with bayonets, and the Führer was always of the opinion that that was impossible in the long run—to rule against the will of the people.

JACKSON: But you did not permit the election of those who should act with authority by the people, but they were designated from the top downward continuously, were they not?

GÖRING: Quite right. The people were merely to acknowledge the authority of the Führer, or, let us say, to declare themselves in agreement with the Führer. If they gave the Führer their confidence, then it was their concern to exercise the other functions. Thus, not the individual persons were to be selected according to the will of the people, but solely the leadership itself.

JACKSON: Now, was this Leadership Principle supported and adopted by you in Germany because you believed that no people are capable of self-government, or because you believed that some may be, not the German people; or that no matter whether some of us are capable of using our own system, it should not be allowed in Germany?

GÖRING: I beg your pardon, I did not quite understand the question, but I could perhaps answer it as follows:

I consider the Leadership Principle necessary because the system which previously existed, and which we called parliamentary or democratic, had brought Germany to the verge of ruin. I might perhaps in this connection remind you that your own President Roosevelt, as far as I can recall—I do not want to quote it word for word—declared, "Certain peoples in Europe have forsaken democracy, not because they did not wish for democracy as such, but because democracy had brought forth men who were too weak to give their people work and bread, and to satisfy them. For this reason the peoples have abandoned this system and the men belonging to it." . . .

JACKSON: The principles of the authoritarian government which you set up required, as I understand you, that there be tolerated no opposition by political parties which might defeat or obstruct the policy of the Nazi Party?

GÖRING: You have understood this quite correctly. By that time we had lived long enough with opposition and we had had enough of it. Through opposition we had been completely ruined. It was now time to have done with it and to start building up.

JACKSON: After you came to power, you regarded it necessary, in order to maintain power, to suppress all opposition parties?

GÖRING: We found it necessary not to permit any more opposition, yes.

JACKSON: And you also held it necessary that you should suppress all individual opposition lest it should develop into a party of opposition?

GÖRING: Insofar as opposition seriously hampered our work of building up, this opposition of individual persons was, of course, not tolerated. Insofar as it was simply a matter of harmless talk, it was considered to be of no consequence.

JACKSON: Now, in order to make sure that you suppressed the parties, and individuals also, you found it necessary to have a secret political police to detect opposition?

GÖRING: I have already stated that I considered that necessary, just as previously the political police had existed, but on a firmer basis and larger scale.

JACKSON: And upon coming to power you also considered it immediately necessary to establish concentration camps to take care of your incorrigible opponents?

GÖRING: I have already stated that the reason for the concentration camps was not because it could be said, "Here are a number of people who are opposed to us and they must be taken into protective custody." Rather they were set up as a lightning measure against the functionaries of the Communist Party who were attacking us in the thousands, and who, since they were taken into protective custody, were not put in prison. But it was necessary, as I said, to erect a camp for them—one, two, or three camps.

JACKSON: But you are explaining, as the high authority of this system, to men who do not understand it very well, and I want to know what was necessary to run the kind of system that you set up in Germany. The concentration camp was one of the things you found immediately necessary upon coming into power, was it not? And you set them up as a matter of necessity, as you saw it?

GÖRING: That was faultily translated—it went too fast. But I believe I have understood the sense of your remarks. You asked me if I considered it necessary to establish concentration camps immediately in order to eliminate opposition. Is that correct?

JACKSON: Your answer is "yes," I take it?

GÖRING: Yes.

JACKSON: Was it also necessary, in operating this system, that you must not have persons entitled to public trials in independent courts? And you immediately issued an order that your political police would not be subject to court review or to court orders, did you not?

GÖRING: You must differentiate between the two categories; those who had committed some act of treason against the new state, or those who might be proved to have committed such an act, were naturally turned over to the courts. The others, however, of whom one might expect such acts, but who had not yet committed them, were taken into protective custody, and these were the people who were taken to concentration camps. I am now speaking of what happened at the beginning. Later things changed a great deal. Likewise, if for political reasons—to answer your question—someone was taken into protective custody, that is, purely for reasons of state, this could not be reviewed or stopped by any court. Later, when some people were also taken into protective custody for nonpolitical reasons, people who had opposed the system in some other way, I once, as Prussian Prime Minister and Reich Minister of the Interior, I remember . . .

JACKSON: Let's omit that. I have not asked for that. If you will just answer my question, we shall save a great deal of time. Your counsel will be permitted to bring out any explanations you want to make. . . . Well, those preparations were preparations for armed occupation of the Rhineland, were they not?

GÖRING: No, that is altogether wrong. If Germany had become involved in a war, no matter from which side, let us assume from the East, then mobilization measures would have had to be carried out for security reasons throughout the Reich, in this event even in the demilitarized Rhineland; but not for the purpose of occupation, of liberating the Rhineland.

JACKSON: You mean the preparations were not military preparations?

GÖRING: Those were general preparations for mobilization, such as every country makes, and not for the purpose of the occupation of the Rhineland.

JACKSON: But were of a character which had to be kept entirely secret from foreign powers?

GÖRING: I do not think I can recall reading beforehand the publication of the mobilization preparations of the United States.

JACKSON: Well, I respectfully submit to the Tribunal that this witness is not being responsive, and has not been in his examination, and that it is . . .

[*The defendant interposed a few words which were not recorded.*]

It is perfectly futile to spend our time if we cannot have responsive answers to our questions.

[*The defendant interposed a few words which were not recorded.*]

We can strike these things out. I do not want to spend time doing that, but this witness, it seems to me, is adopting, and has adopted, in the witness box and in the dock, an arrogant and contemptuous attitude toward the Tribunal which is giving him the trial which he never gave a living soul, nor dead ones either.

I respectfully submit that the witness be instructed to make notes, if he wishes, of his explanations, but that he be required to answer my questions and reserve his explanations for his counsel to bring out.

THE PRESIDENT: I have already laid down the general rule, which is binding upon this defendant as upon other witnesses.

Perhaps we had better adjourn now at this state.

30

ROBERT H. JACKSON

Appeal to the Bench

March 19, 1946

MR. JUSTICE JACKSON: If the Tribunal please, the last question which I asked last night referring to mobilization preparations in the Rhineland, as shown in the official transcript, was this:

International Military Tribunal, *Trial of the Major War Criminals before the International Military Tribunal, Nuremberg, 14 November 1945–1 October 1946*, 42 vols. Nuremberg: International Military Tribunal, 1947, 9:509–12.

"But of a character which had to be kept entirely secret from foreign powers?" The answer was: "I do not believe I can recall the publication of the preparations of the United States for mobilization."

Now, representing the United States of America, I am confronted with these choices—to ignore that remark and allow it to stand for people who do not understand our system; or to develop, at considerable expense of time, its falsity; or to answer it in rebuttal. The difficulty arises from this, Your Honor, that if the witness is permitted to volunteer statements in cross-examination there is no opportunity to make objection until they are placed on the record. Of course, if such an answer had been indicated by a question of counsel, as I respectfully submit would be the orderly procedure, there would have been objection; the Tribunal would have been in a position to discharge its duty under the Charter and I would have been in a position to have shortened the case by not having that remark placed.

The Charter in Article 18 provides that the Tribunal shall rule out irrelevant issues and statements of any kind whatsoever. We are squarely confronted with that question; we cannot discharge those duties if the defendant is to volunteer these statements without questions which bring them up. I respectfully submit that, if the ruling of the Tribunal that the defendant may volunteer questions of this kind is to prevail, the control of these proceedings is put in the hands of this defendant, and the United States has been substantially denied its right of cross-examination under the Charter, because cross-examination cannot be effective under this kind of procedure. Since we cannot anticipate, we cannot meet . . .

THE PRESIDENT: I quite agree with you that any reference to the United States' secrecy with reference to mobilization is entirely irrelevant, and that the answer ought not to have been made, but the only rule which the Tribunal can lay down as a general rule is the rule—already laid down—that the witness must answer if possible "yes" or "no," and that he may make such explanations as may be necessary after answering questions directly in that way, and that such explanations must be brief and not be speeches. As far as this particular answer goes, I think it is entirely irrelevant.

JACKSON: I must, of course, bow to the ruling of the Tribunal, but it is to the second part, I quite recall the admonition of the

Court that there shall be answers "yes" or "no." This witness, of course, pays not the slightest attention to that, and I must say I cannot blame him; he is pursuing his interests. But we have no way of anticipating, and here we are confronted with this statement in the record, because when these statements are volunteered they are in the record before the Tribunal can rule upon them and I have no opportunity to make objections, and the Tribunal have no opportunity to rule. And it puts, as I said before, the control of these proceedings in the hands of the defendant, if he first makes the charges and then puts it up to us to ignore them or answer them by long cross-examination in rebuttal; and I think the specific charge made against the United States of America from the witness stand presents that.

Your Honor now advises the United States that it is an improper answer, but it is in the record and we must deal with it. I respectfully submit that unless we have . . .

THE PRESIDENT: What exactly is the motion you are making? Are you asking the Tribunal to strike the answer out of the record?

JACKSON: Well, no; in a Trial of this kind, where propaganda is one of the purposes of the defendant, striking out does no good after the answer is made, and Göring knows that as well as I. The charge has been made against the United States and it is in the record. I am now moving that this witness be instructed that he must answer my questions "yes" or "no" if they permit an answer, and that the explanation be brought out by his counsel in a fashion that will permit us to make objections, if they are irrelevant, and to obtain rulings of the Tribunal, so that the Tribunal can discharge its functions of ruling out irrelevant issues and statements of any kind whatsoever. We must not let the Trial degenerate into a bickering contest between counsel and the witness. That is not what the United States would expect me to participate in. I respectfully suggest that if he can draw any kind of challenge . . .

THE PRESIDENT: Are you submitting to the Tribunal that the witness has to answer every question "yes" or "no" and wait until he is re-examined for the purpose of making any explanations at all?

JACKSON: I think that is the rule of cross-examination under ordinary circumstances. The witness, if the question permits it, must answer, and if there are relevant explanations they should be reserved until later.

Now let me come back to the specific problem I have right here this morning. Here is an answer given which the Tribunal now rules is irrelevant. But we have no opportunity to object to it. The Tribunal had no opportunity to rule upon it. The witness asks, "Did you ever hear of the United States publishing its plan of mobilization?" Of course, we would have objected. The difficulty is that the Tribunal loses control of these proceedings if the defendant, in a case of this kind where we all know propaganda is one of the purposes of the defendant, is permitted to put his propaganda in, and then we have to meet it afterwards. I really feel that the United States is deprived of the opportunity of the technique of cross-examination if this is the procedure.

THE PRESIDENT: Surely it is making too much of a sentence the witness has said, whether the United States makes its orders for mobilization public or not. Surely that is not a matter of very great importance. Every country keeps certain things secret. Certainly it would be much wiser to ignore a statement of that sort. But as to the general rule, the Tribunal will now consider the matter. I have already laid down what I believe to be the rule, and I think with the assent of the Tribunal, but I will ascertain . . .

JACKSON: Let me say that I agree with Your Honor that as far as the United States is concerned we are not worried by anything the witness can say about it—and we expected plenty. The point is, do we answer these things or leave them, apart from the control of the Trial? And it does seem to me that this is the beginning of this Trial's getting out of hand, if I may say so, if we do not have control of this situation. I trust the Tribunal will pardon my earnestness in presenting this. I think it is a very vital thing.

THE PRESIDENT: I have never heard it suggested that the Counsel for the Prosecution have to answer every irrelevant observation made in cross-examination.

JACKSON: That would be true in a private litigation, but I trust the Court is not unaware that outside of this courtroom is a great social question of the revival of Nazism and that one of the purposes of the Defendant Göring—I think he would be the first to admit—is to revive and perpetuate it by propaganda from this Trial now in process. . . .

THE PRESIDENT: Mr. Justice Jackson, the Tribunal considers that the rule which it has laid down is the only possible rule and that the witness must be confined strictly to answering the question directly where the question admits of a direct answer, and that he must not make his explanation before he gives a direct answer; but, after having given a direct answer to any question which admits of a direct answer, he may make a short explanation; and that he is not to be confined simply to making direct answers "yes" or "no," and leaving the explanation until his counsel puts it to him in his re-examination.

As to this particular observation of the defendant, the defendant ought not to have referred to the United States, but it is a matter which I think you might well ignore.

JACKSON: I shall bow to the ruling, of course.

31

Motion Adopted by All Defense Counsel
November 19, 1945

A distinction is being made between just and unjust wars and it is asked that the Community of States call to account the State which wages an unjust war and deny it, should it be victorious, the fruits of its outrage. More than that, it is demanded that not only should the guilty State be condemned and its liability be established, but that furthermore those men who are responsible for unleashing the unjust war be tried and sentenced by an International Tribunal. In that respect one goes now-a-days further than even the strictest jurists since the early middle ages. This thought is at the basis of the first three counts of the Indictment which have been put forward in this Trial, to wit, the Indictment for Crimes against Peace. Humanity insists that this idea should in the future be more than a demand, that it should be valid international law.

However, today it is not as yet valid international law. Neither in the statute of the League of Nations, world organization against war, nor in the Kellogg-Briand Pact, nor in any other of the

International Military Tribunal, *Trial of the Major War Criminals before the International Military Tribunal, Nuremberg, 14 November 1945–1 October 1946,* 42 vols. Nuremberg: International Military Tribunal, 1947, 1:168–70.

treaties which were concluded after 1918 in that first upsurge of attempts to ban aggressive warfare, has this idea been realized. But above all the practice of the League of Nations has, up to the very recent past, been quite unambiguous in that regard. On several occasions the League had to decide upon the lawfulness or unlawfulness of action by force of one member against another member, but it always condemned such action by force merely as a violation of international law by the State, and never thought of bringing up for trial the statesmen, generals, and industrialists of the state which recurred to force. And when the new organization for world peace [the United Nations] was set up last summer in San Francisco, no new legal maxim was created under which an international tribunal would inflict punishment upon those who unleashed an unjust war. The present Trial can, therefore, as far as Crimes against Peace [is concerned,] not invoke existing international law, [but rather proceed] pursuant to a new penal law, a penal law enacted only after the crime. This is repugnant to a principle of jurisprudence sacred to the civilized world, the partial violation of which by Hitler's Germany has been vehemently discountenanced outside and inside the Reich. This principle is to the effect that only he can be punished who offended against a law in existence at the time of the commission of the act and imposing a penalty. This maxim is one of the great fundamental principles of the political systems of the Signatories of the Charter for this Tribunal themselves, to wit, of England since the Middle Ages, of the United States since their creation, of France since its great revolution, and the Soviet Union. . . .

Finally, the Defense consider it their duty to point out at this juncture another peculiarity of this Trial which departs from the commonly recognized principles of modern jurisprudence. The Judges have been appointed exclusively by States which were the one party in this war. This one party to the proceeding is all in one: creator of the statute of the Tribunal and of the rules of law, prosecutor and judge. It used to be until now the common legal conception that this should not be so; just as the United States of America, as the champion for the institution of international arbitration and jurisdiction, always demanded that neutrals, or neutrals and representatives of all parties, should be called to the Bench. This principle has been realized in an exemplary manner in the case of the Permanent Court of International Justice at The Hague. . . .

5

Crimes against Peace

32

SIDNEY ALDERMAN

Address to the Tribunal
November 23, 1945

After all, everything else in this case, however dramatic, however sordid, however shocking and revolting to the common instincts of civilized peoples, is incidental to, or subordinate to, the aggressive war aspect of the case.

All the dramatic story of what went on in Germany in the early phases of the conspiracy — the ideologies used, the techniques of terror used, the suppressions of human freedom employed in the seizure of power, and even the concentration camps and the Crimes against Humanity, the persecutions, tortures, and murders committed — all these things would have little juridical international significance except for the fact that they were the preparation for the commission of aggressions against peaceful neighboring peoples.

Even the aspects of the case involving War Crimes in the strict sense are aspects which are merely the inevitable, proximate result of the wars of aggression launched and waged by these conspirators, and of the kind of warfare they waged — that is — total war, the natural result of the totalitarian party-dominated state

International Military Tribunal, *Trial of the Major War Criminals before the International Military Tribunal, Nuremberg, 14 November 1945–1 October 1946*, 42 vols. Nuremberg: International Military Tribunal, 1947, 2:242, 244, 247.

that waged it, and atrocious war, the natural result of the atrocious doctrines, designs, and purposes of these war-makers. . . .

It is familiar law in my country that if two or more persons set out to rob a bank, in accordance with a criminal scheme to that end, and in the course of carrying out their scheme one of the conspirators commits the crime of murder, all of the participants in the planning and execution of the bank robbery are guilty of murder, whether or not they had any other personal participation in the killing. This is a simple rule of law declared in the Charter. All the parties to a Common Plan or Conspiracy are the agents of each other and each is responsible as principal for the acts of all the others as his agents. . . .

These documents fill in the inside story underlying the historical record which we all already knew. This evidence which we will offer constitutes an illustrative spot check on history—on the history of the recent times as the world knows it. The evidence to be offered is not a substitute for history. We hope the Tribunal will find it to be an authentication of history. The evidence which we have drawn from captured documents establishes the validity of the recent history of the past 12 years—a history of many aggressions by the Nazi conspirators accused in this case.

As I offer to the Tribunal document after document, I ask the Court to see in those documents definite additions to history, the addition of new elements long suspected and now proved. . . .

33

HARTLEY SHAWCROSS

On Aggressive War and the Evolution of the Law of Nations

December 4, 1945

For 50 years or more, the people of the world, striving perhaps after that ideal of which the poet speaks:

International Military Tribunal, *Trial of the Major War Criminals before the International Military Tribunal, Nuremberg, 14 November 1945–1 October 1946*, 42 vols. Nuremberg: International Military Tribunal, 1947, 3:94, 96–97.

"When the war drums throb no longer
And the battle flags are furled,
In the parliament of man,
The federation of the world" —[1]

sought to create an operative system of rules based upon the consent of nations to stabilize international relations, to avoid war taking place at all and to mitigate the results of such wars as took place. . . .

The statesmen of the world deliberately set out to make war of aggression an international crime. These are no new terms invented by the victors to embody in this Charter. They have figured, and they have figured prominently, in numerous treaties, in governmental pronouncements, and in the declarations of statesmen in the period preceding the second World War. . . .

These repeated declarations, these repeated condemnations of wars of aggression testified to the fact that with the establishment of the League of Nations, with the legal developments which followed it, the place of war in international law had undergone a profound change. War was ceasing to be the unrestricted prerogative of sovereign states. . . .

The right of war was further circumscribed by a series of treaties, numbering—it is an astonishing figure but it is right—nearly a thousand, of arbitration and conciliation embracing practically all the nations of the world. . . .

---

[1]Alfred, Lord Tennyson, "Locksley Hall," lines 116–17.

34

HERMANN GÖRING

Testimony Denying a Nazi Conspiracy to Wage War
March 14, 1946

The occupation of the Rhineland was not, as has been asserted here, a long-prepared affair. What had been discussed previously

---

International Military Tribunal, *Trial of the Major War Criminals before the International Military Tribunal, Nuremberg, 14 November 1945–1 October 1946*, 42 vols. Nuremberg: International Military Tribunal, 1947, 9:285.

did not deal with the occupation of the Rhineland, but with the question of mobilization measures in the Rhineland in case of an attack on Germany.

The Rhineland occupation came about for two reasons. The balance which was created through the Locarno Pact[1] had been disturbed in western Europe, because a new factor had arisen in France's system of allies, namely Russia, who even at that time had an extraordinarily large armed force. In addition, there was the Russian-Czechoslovakian mutual assistance pact. Thus, the conditions upon which the Locarno Pact had been based no longer existed, according to our way of thinking. So, there was now such a threat to Germany, or the possibility of such a threat, that it would have been a neglect of duty and honor on the part of the Government if it had not done everything to ensure, here also, the security of the Reich. The Government therefore — as a sovereign state — made use of its sovereign right and freed itself from the dishonorable obligation not to place a part of the Reich under its protection, and it did place this important part of the Reich under its protection by building strong fortifications.

The construction of such strong fortifications, such expensive fortifications and such extensive fortifications, is justified only if that frontier is regarded as final and definitive. If I had intended to extend the frontier in the near future, it would never have been possible to go through with an undertaking so expensive and such a burden to the whole nation as was the construction of the West Wall.[2] This was done — and I want to emphasize this particularly — from the very beginning only in the interest of defense and as a defensive measure. It made the western border of the Reich secure against that threat which, because of the recent shift of power, and the new combination of powers such as the Franco-Russian mutual assistance pact, had become a threat to Germany. The actual occupation, the decision to occupy the Rhineland, was made at very short notice. The troops which marched into the Rhineland were of such small numbers — and that is an historical fact — that they provided merely a token occu-

[1]The Locarno Treaties were a series of agreements in 1925 between France and Germany and their neighbors that seemed to stabilize the international order in Europe.
[2]The West Wall, referred to by the Allies as the "Siegfried Line," designated the pre-war defensive fortifications intended to protect Germany against a French attack.

pation. The Luftwaffe itself could not, for the time being, enter the Rhine territory on the left at all, since there was no adequate ground organization. It entered the so-called demilitarized territory on the right of the Rhine, Dusseldorf and other cities. In other words, it was not as if the Rhineland were suddenly occupied with a great wave of troops; but, as I said before, it was merely that a few battalions and a few batteries marched in as a symbol that the Rhineland was now again under the full sovereignty of the sovereign German Reich and would in the future be protected accordingly.

35

HERMANN GÖRING

Testimony on the Hossbach Memorandum
March 14, 1946

This document has already been shown to me here, and I am fairly familiar with the contents. This document played an important role in the Indictment, since it appears under the heading "Testament of the Führer." This word "testament" is, in fact, used in one place by Hossbach.

As far as the technical aspect of this record is concerned, I want to say the following: Hossbach was the adjutant of the Führer, the chief adjutant. As such, he was present at the meeting and took notes. Five days later, as I have ascertained, he prepared this record on the basis of his notes. This is, therefore, a record which contains all the mistakes which easily occur in a record, which is not taken down on the spot by alternating stenographers, and which under certain circumstances contains the subjective opinions of the recorder or his own interpretations.

It contains a number of points, as I said at the time, which correspond exactly to what the Führer had repeatedly said; but there

International Military Tribunal, *Trial of the Major War Criminals before the International Military Tribunal, Nuremberg, 14 November 1945–1 October 1946*, 42 vols. Nuremberg: International Military Tribunal, 1947, 9:306–7.

are other points and expressions which I may say do not seem like the Führer's words.

During the last months I have seen too many records and interrogations which in part had nothing to do with it nor with the interpretation which had been given to it; for that reason I must here too point out the sources of mistakes.

As far as the word "testament" is concerned, the use of this word contradicts the Führer's views completely. If anybody at all knows anything about these views, it is I. . . .

Now, what did he aim at in this discussion? The Minister of War, the Commander-in-Chief of the Army, the Commander-in-Chief of the Navy and the Luftwaffe and the then Reich Foreign Minister were called together. Shortly before the Führer had informed me, as I was there earlier, that he was going to call this meeting mainly in order, as he called it, to put pressure on General Von Fritsch, since he was dissatisfied with the rearmament of the Army. He said it would not do any harm if Herr Von Blomberg would also exercise a certain amount of pressure on Von Fritsch.

I asked why Von Neurath was to be present. He said he did not want the thing to look too military, that as far as the commanders-in-chief were concerned it was not so important, but that he wanted to make it very clear to Commander-in-Chief Fritsch that the foreign political situation required a forced speed in armament and that for that reason he had asked the Foreign Minister, who knew nothing about the details, to come along.

The statements were then made in the way the Führer preferred on such occasions. He went to great lengths to picture things within a large political framework and he talked about the whole world situation from all angles; and for anybody who knew him as well as I did the purpose which he pursued was obvious. He was quite clearly aiming at saying that he had great plans, that the political situation was such and such, and the whole thing ended in the direction of a stronger armament program. I should like to say that, if the Führer, a couple of hours later, had talked to another group, for instance, diplomats of the Foreign Office, or Party functionaries, then he probably would have represented matters quite differently.

Nevertheless, some of these statements naturally do reflect the basic attitude of the Führer, but with the best intentions I cannot attach the same measure of significance to the document as is being attached to it here.

36

ALFRED SEIDL

Questioning of Joachim von Ribbentrop on the Nazi-Soviet Pact

April 1, 1946

DR. SEIDL: . . . Witness, in the affidavit of Gaus, a pact is mentioned whereby the two powers agree to act in mutual agreement with regard to the final settlement of the questions concerning Poland. Had such an agreement already been reached on 23 August 1939?

VON RIBBENTROP: Yes, that is true. At that time the serious German-Polish crisis was acute, and it goes without saying that this question was thoroughly discussed. I should like to empha-size that there was not the slightest doubt in either Stalin's or Hitler's mind that, if the negotiations with Poland came to naught, the territories that had been taken from the two great powers by force of arms could also be retaken by force of arms. In keeping with this understanding, the eastern territories were occupied by Soviet troops and the western territories by German troops after victory. There is no doubt that Stalin can never accuse Germany of an aggression or of an aggressive war for her action in Poland. If it is considered an aggression, then both sides are guilty of it.

SEIDL: Was the demarcation line in this secret agreement described merely in writing or was it drawn on a map attached to the agreement?

VON RIBBENTROP: The line of demarcation was roughly drawn on a map. It ran along the Rivers Rysia, Bug, Narew, and San. These rivers I remember. That was the line of demarcation that was to be adhered to in case of an armed conflict with Poland.

SEIDL: Is it correct that on the basis of that agreement, not Germany but Soviet Russia received the greater part of Poland?

VON RIBBENTROP: I do not know the exact proportions, but, at any rate, the agreement was that the territories east of these rivers

---

International Military Tribunal, *Trial of the Major War Criminals before the International Military Tribunal, Nuremberg, 14 November 1945–1 October 1946*, 42 vols. Nuremberg: International Military Tribunal, 1947, 10:313–15.

were to go to Soviet Russia and the territories west of these rivers were to be occupied by German troops, while the organization of this territory as intended by Germany was still an open question and had not yet been discussed by Hitler and myself. Then, later the Government General was formed when the regions lost by Germany after World War I were incorporated into Germany.

SEIDL: Now, something else. You stated last Friday that you wanted Russia to join in the Tripartite Pact.[1] Why did that fail?

VON RIBBENTROP: That failed because of Russian demands. The Russian demands concerned—I should perhaps say first that I had agreed with M. Molotov in Berlin to conduct further negotiations through diplomatic channels. I wanted to influence the Führer regarding the demands already made by Molotov in Berlin in order that some sort of an agreement or compromise might be arrived at.

Then Schulenburg sent us a report from Moscow with the Russian demands. In this report was, first of all, the renewed demand for Finland. To this the Führer, as is well known, told Molotov that he did not wish that after the winter campaign of 1940 another war should break out in the North. Now the demand for Finland was raised again, and we assumed that it would mean the occupation of Finland. It was difficult since it was a demand which the Führer had already turned down.

Another demand of the Russians was that of the Balkans and Bulgaria. Russia, as is well known, wanted bases there and wished to enter into close relations with Bulgaria. The Bulgarian Government, with whom we got in touch, did not want this. Moreover, this Russian penetration of the Balkans was for both the Führer and Mussolini a difficult question because of our economic interests there: grain, oil, and so on. But above all it was the will of the Bulgarian Government themselves, which was against this penetration.

Then, thirdly, there was the demand of the Russians for outlets to the sea and military bases on the Dardanelles; and then the request which Molotov had already expressed to me in Berlin, to secure somehow at least an interest in the outlets of the Baltic Sea. M. Molotov himself told me at that time that Russia naturally was also very much interested in the Skagerrak and Kattegat.[2] . . .

---

[1]The Tripartite Pact was a ten-year agreement signed in September 1940 bringing Germany, Italy, and Japan together in a wartime alliance.

[2]Skagerrak and Kattegat are arms of the North Sea between Denmark and Norway and Denmark and Sweden, respectively. Ribbentrop's point was an obvious indication of Soviet imperial ambitions.

37

ALFRED SEIDL

Questioning of Ernst von Weizsäcker
on the Secret Protocol

May 31, 1946

DR. SEIDL: I have before me a text and Ambassador Gaus harbors
no doubt at all that the agreements in question are correctly set
out in this text. I shall have it put to you.

THE PRESIDENT: One moment, what document are you putting to
him?

SEIDL: The secret addenda to the protocol of 23 August 1939.

THE PRESIDENT: Is that not the document—what is this document
that you are presenting to the witness? There is a document
which you have already presented to the Tribunal and which
has been ruled out. Is that the same document?

SEIDL: It is the document which I submitted to the Tribunal in my
documentary evidence and which was refused by the Tribunal,
presumably because I refused to divulge the origin and source
of this document. But the Tribunal granted me permission to
produce a new sworn affidavit by Ambassador Gaus on the subject in question. . . .

GEN. RUDENKO: Your Honors! I would like to protest against these
questions for two reasons.

First of all, we are examining the matter of the crimes of
the major German war criminals. We are not investigating
the foreign policies of other states. Secondly, the document
which defense counsel Seidl is attempting to put to the witness has been rejected by the Tribunal, since it is—in
substance — a forged document and cannot have any probative value whatsoever. . . .

MR. DODD: Mr. President, I certainly join General Rudenko
in objecting to the use of this document. We now know that
it comes from some anonymous source. We do not know the

International Military Tribunal, *Trial of the Major War Criminals before the International
Military Tribunal, Nuremberg, 14 November 1945–1 October 1946*, 42 vols, Nuremberg:
International Military Tribunal, 1947, 14:283–86.

source at all, and anyway it is not established that this witness does not remember himself what this purported agreement amounted to. I do not know why he can not ask him, if that is what he wants to do.

THE PRESIDENT: Dr. Seidl, you may ask the witness what his recollection is of the treaty without putting the document to him. Ask him what he remembers of the treaty, or the protocol.

SEIDL: Witness, please describe the contents of the agreement insofar as you can remember them.

VON WEIZSÄCKER: It is about a very incisive, a very far-reaching secret addendum to the nonaggression pact concluded at that time. The scope of this document was very extensive since it concerned the partition of the spheres of influence and drew a demarcation line between areas which, under given conditions, belonged to the sphere of Soviet Russia and those which would fall in the German sphere of interest. Finland, Estonia, Latvia, Eastern Poland and, as far as I can remember, certain areas of Romania were to be included in the sphere of the Soviet Union. Anything west of this area fell into the German sphere of interest. It is true that this secret agreement did not maintain its original form. Later on, either in September or October of the same year, a certain change, an amendment was made. As far as I can recall the essential difference in the two documents consisted in the fact that Lithuania, or—at least—the greater part of Lithuania, fell into the sphere of interest of the Soviet Union, while in the Polish territory the line of demarcation between the two spheres of interest was moved very considerably westwards.

I believe that I have herewith given you the gist of the secret agreement and of the subsequent addendum.

SEIDL: Is it true that in case of a subsequent territorial reorganization, a line of demarcation was agreed upon in the territory of the Polish State?

VON WEIZSÄCKER: I cannot tell you exactly whether the expression "line of demarcation" was contained in this protocol or whether "line of separation of spheres of interest" was the actual term.

SEIDL: But a line was drawn.

VON WEIZSÄCKER: Precisely the line which I have just mentioned, and I believe I can recall that this line, once the agreement became effective, was adhered to as a general rule with possible slight fluctuations.

SEIDL: Can you recall—this is my last question—if this secret addendum of 23 August 1939 also contained an agreement on the future destiny of Poland?

VON WEIZSÄCKER: This secret agreement included a complete redirection of Poland's destiny. It may very well have been that explicitly or implicitly such a redirection had been provided for in the agreement. I would not, however, like to commit myself as to the exact wording.

SEIDL: Mr. President, I have no further questions.

38

ERICH RAEDER

Testimony on the German Attack on Norway
May 17, 1946

DR. SIEMERS: . . . The British prosecutor, Major Elwyn Jones, considers the attack against Norway a special case in the series of aggressive wars waged by the Nazi conspirators. . . . When was the first conversation about this matter between you and Hitler?

RAEDER: The first conversation between Hitler and myself concerning the question of Norway was on 10 October 1939, and that was at my request. The reason for this was that we had received reports at various times during the last week of September through our intelligence service of the offices of Admiral Canaris that the British intended to occupy bases in Norway. . . .

During the last days of September I had a telephone conversation with Admiral Carls who was the commander of Navy Group North and was therefore in charge of operations in the Skagerrak, the Kattegat and in the North Sea. This man had

International Military Tribunal, *Trial of the Major War Criminals before the International Military Tribunal, Nuremberg, 14 November 1945–1 October 1946*, 42 vols. Nuremberg: International Military Tribunal, 1947, 14:85–89, 96, 98.

obviously received similar reports. He informed me that he had composed a private letter addressed to me, in which he dealt with the question of the danger of Norway's being occupied by British forces and in which he was in a general way dealing with the question as to what disadvantages such a step would have for us, and whether we should have to forestall such an attempt, and also what advantages or disadvantages the occupation of Norway—that is, of the Norwegian coast and the Norwegian bases—by our forces would have.

Up until that point I had not concerned myself with the Norwegian question at all, except for the fact I had received these reports. The arrival of this letter at the end of September or the beginning of October, it must have been about then, impelled me to show it to the Chief of Staff of the SKL and to instruct him to deal with all dispatch with the question of the occupation of Norwegian bases by England, and the other questions which Admiral Carls had dealt with, and to have the questions discussed in the SKL. The advantages and disadvantages of an expansion of the war towards the North had to be considered, not only of an expansion on our part but, above all, an expansion on the part of England; what value, what advantage would accrue to us if we acted first; what disadvantages would result if we had to defend the Norwegian coast? . . .

. . . I would like to say, by way of introduction, that it was entirely clear to me that if we undertook to occupy these bases we would violate neutrality. But I also knew of the agreement which existed between the German and Norwegian Governments of 2 September regarding neutrality. . . .

SIEMERS: . . . Please comment on this document.

RAEDER: . . . If the British occupied bases in Norway, especially in the South of Norway, they would be able to dominate the entrance to the Baltic Sea from those points, and also flank our naval operations from the Helgoland Bight and from the Elbe, Jade and Weser. The second outlet which we had was also gravely imperiled, affecting the operations of battleships as well as the courses of our merchantmen.

In addition to that, from their air bases in Norway, they might endanger our air operations, the operations of our pilots for reconnaissance in the North Sea or for attacks against England.

Furthermore, from Norway they could exert strong pressure on Sweden, and that pressure would have been felt in this respect, that the supplies of ore from Sweden would have been hindered or stopped by purely political pressure. Finally, the export of ore from Narvik to Germany could have been stopped entirely, and it is known how much Germany depended on supplies of ore from Sweden and Norway. They might even have gone so far—and we learned about this subsequently that such plans were discussed—as to attack and destroy the ore deposits at Lulea, or to seize them.

All of these dangers might become decisive factors in the outcome of the war. Aside from the fact that I told Hitler that the best thing for us would be to have strict neutrality on the part of Norway, I also called his attention to the dangers which would result to us from an occupation of the Norwegian coast and Norwegian bases, for there would have been lively naval operations near the Norwegian coast in which the British, even after our occupation of bases, would try to hamper our ore traffic from Narvik. A struggle might ensue which we, with our inadequate supply of surface vessels, would be unable to cope with in the long run.

Therefore, at that time I did not make any proposal that we should occupy Norway or that we should obtain bases in Norway. I only did my duty in telling the Supreme Commander of the Wehrmacht about this grave danger which was threatening us, and against which we might have to use emergency measures for our defense. . . .

SIEMERS: Why had Reichsmarschall Göring not been consulted?

RAEDER: I cannot explain that at all. I had no authority to speak about it and I cannot say why he was not consulted.

SIEMERS: It is in the nature of conspiracy that the second man in the Reich would be informed about it from the beginning. Has he not ever spoken to you about that matter?

RAEDER: No, not that I remember, but that shows how little, especially in the Führer's entourage, one can speak of a conspiracy. The Foreign Minister, Von Ribbentrop, also was not present during any of the Quisling conferences or receptions and I had no authority to speak to him about these matters. . . .

. . . I should like to add, as I emphasized before, that being fully conscious of my responsibility I always tried to show the Führer both sides of the picture and that the Führer would have

to be guided by my documentary proof when deciding, to take
or refrain from taking that tremendous step. But that does not
mean to say that because I pointed out to my Supreme Commander of the Armed Forces that particular danger, I in any
way decline to accept responsibility. Of course, I am in some
measure responsible for the whole thing. Moreover, I have
been accused because in a letter submitted here under C-155 I
had told my officers' corps that I was proud of the way in which
this extraordinarily dangerous enterprise had been executed. I
should like to confirm this, because I believe I was entitled to
be proud that the Navy had carried out that operation with such
limited means and in the face of the entire British fleet; I still
stick to that. . . .

39

HARTLEY SHAWCROSS

Evidence on the German Attack on the Soviet Union
December 4, 1945

On the 22d of June 1941 German Armed Forces invaded Russia,
without warning, without declaration of war. It was, of course, a
breach of the usual series of treaties; they meant no more in this
case than they had meant in the other cases. It was a violation
of the Pact of Paris; it was a flagrant contradiction of the Treaty
of Non-Aggression which Germany and Russia had signed on the
23rd of August a year before.

Hitler himself said, in referring to that agreement, that "agreements were only to be kept as long as they served a purpose." . . .

On the 12th of November 1940 Hitler issued a directive, signed
by the Defendant Jodl, in which it was stated that the political task

International Military Tribunal, *Trial of the Major War Criminals before the International Military Tribunal, Nuremberg, 14 November 1945–1 October 1946*, 42 vols. Nuremberg: International Military Tribunal, 1947, 3:140–43.

to determine the attitude of Russia had begun, but that without reference to the result of preparations against the East, which had been ordered orally.

It is not to be supposed that the U.S.S.R. would have taken part in any conversations at that time if it had been realized that on the very day orders were being given for preparations to be made for the invasion of Russia, and that the order for the operation, which was called "Plan Barbarossa," was in active preparation. On the 18th of December the order was issued, and I quote:

> "The German Armed Forces have to be ready to defeat Soviet Russia in a swift campaign before the end of the war against Great Britain."

And later, in the same instruction—and I quote again:

> "All orders which shall be issued by the High Commanders in accordance with this instruction have to be clothed in such terms that they may be taken as measures of precaution in case Russia should change her present attitude towards ourselves."

Germany kept up the pretense of friendliness and, on the 10th of January 1941, well after the Plan Barbarossa for the invasion of Russia had been decided upon, Germany signed the German-Russian Frontier Treaty. Less than a month later, on the 3rd of February of 1941, Hitler held a conference, attended by the Defendants Keitel and Jodl, at which it was provided that the whole operation against Russia was to be camouflaged as if it was part of the preparation for the "Plan Seelöwe," as the plan for the invasion of England was described.

By March of 1941 plans were sufficiently advanced to include provision for dividing the Russian territory into nine separate states to be administered under Reich Commissars, under the general control of the Defendant Rosenberg; and at the same time detailed plans for the economic exploitation of the country were made under the supervision of the Defendant Göring, to whom the responsibility in this matter—and it is a serious one—had been delegated by Hitler. . . .

On the 22d of June, at 3:30 in the morning, the German armies marched again. As Hitler said in his proclamation to them, "I have decided to give the fate of the German people and of the Reich and of Europe again into the hands of our soldiers." . . .

40

WILHELM KEITEL

Testimony on Hitler's Plan to Attack the Soviet Union

April 4, 1946

DR. NELTE: When did Hitler for the first time talk to you about the possibility of a conflict, of an armed conflict with the Soviet Union?

KEITEL: As far as I recollect, that was at the beginning of August 1940, on the occasion of a discussion of the situation at Berchtesgaden, or rather at his house, the Berghof. That was the first time that the possibility of an armed conflict with the Soviet Union was discussed.

NELTE: What were the reasons which Hitler gave at that time which might possibly lead to a war?

KEITEL: I think I can refer to what Reich Marshal Göring has said on this subject.

According to our notions, there were considerable troop concentrations in Bessarabia and Bukovina. The Foreign Minister, too, had mentioned figures which I cannot recall, and there was the anxiety which had been repeatedly voiced by Hitler at that time that developments might result in the Romanian theater which would endanger our source of petroleum, the fuel supply for the conduct of the war, which for the most part came from Romania. Apart from that, I think he talked about strong or manifest troop concentrations in the Baltic provinces. . . .

NELTE: What were your personal views at that time regarding the problem which arose out of the conference with Hitler?

KEITEL: When I became conscious of the fact that the matter had been given really serious thought I was very surprised, and I considered it most unfortunate. I seriously considered what could be done to influence Hitler by using military considerations.

International Military Tribunal, *Trial of the Major War Criminals before the International Military Tribunal, Nuremberg, 14 November 1945–1 October 1946*, 42 vols. Nuremberg: International Military Tribunal, 1947, 10:524–29.

At that time, as has been briefly discussed here by the Foreign Minister, I wrote a personal memorandum containing my thoughts on the subject, I should like to say, independently of the experts working in the General Staff and the Wehrmacht Operations Staff and wanted to present this memorandum to Hitler. I decided on that method because, as a rule, one could never get beyond the second sentence of a discussion with Hitler. He took the word out of one's mouth and afterwards one never was able to say what one wanted to say. . . .

NELTE: Did you give that memorandum to Hitler?

KEITEL: Yes. Some time later at the Berghof, after a report of the situation had been given, I handed him that memorandum when we were alone. I think he told me at the time that he was going to study it. He took it, and did not give me a chance to make any explanations.

NELTE: Considering its importance did you later on find an opportunity to refer to it again?

KEITEL: Yes. At first nothing at all happened, so that after some time I reminded him of it and asked him to discuss the problem with me. This he did, and the matter was dealt with very briefly by his saying that the military and strategic considerations put forward by me were in no way convincing. He, Hitler, considered these ideas erroneous, and turned them down. In that connection I can perhaps mention very briefly that I was again very much upset and there was another crisis when I asked to be relieved of my post, and that another man be put in my office and that I be sent to the front. That once more led to a sharp controversy as has already been described by the Reich Marshal when he said that Hitler took the attitude that he would not tolerate that a general whose views he did not agree with should ask to be relieved of his post because of this disagreement. I think he said that he had every right to turn down such suggestions and ideas if he considered them wrong. I had not the right to take any action.

NELTE: Did he return that memorandum to you?

KEITEL: No, I do not think I got it back. I have always assumed that it was found among the captured Schmundt files, which apparently is not the case. I did not get it back; he kept it.

41

ALFRED JODL

Testimony on Soviet Preparations to Attack Germany

June 5, 1946

DR. EXNER: Now, when did you first hear of the Führer's fears that Russia might prove hostile to us?

JODL: For the first time, on 29 July 1940, at the Berghof near Berchtesgaden.

EXNER: In what connection?

JODL: The Führer kept me back alone after a discussion on the situation and said to me, most unexpectedly, that he was worried that Russia might occupy still more territory in Romania before the winter and that the Romanian oil region, which was the *conditio sine qua non* for our war strategy, would thus be taken from us. He asked me whether we could not deploy our troops immediately, so that we would be ready by autumn to oppose with strong forces any such Russian intention. These are almost the exact words which he used, and all other versions are false. . . .

EXNER: Well, when was the Führer's order issued to prepare for attack?

JODL: The first order for deliberation concerning an attack, or for the discussion of any aggressive operation at all, was issued in writing by the Armed Forces Operations Staff and submitted to the Führer on 12 November. . . .

EXNER: Tell me, in these statements, which Hitler made to you, was there ever any mention made of such things as the extension of the "Lebensraum," and of the food basis as a reason for a war of conquest, and so on?

JODL: In my presence the Führer never even hinted at any other reason than a purely strategic and operational one. For months on end, one might say, he incessantly repeated:

International Military Tribunal, *Trial of the Major War Criminals before the International Military Tribunal, Nuremberg, 14 November 1945–1 October 1946*, 42 vols. Nuremberg: International Military Tribunal, 1947, 15:390–95.

"No further doubt is possible. England is hoping for this final sword-thrust against us on the continent, else she would have stopped the war after Dunkirk. Private or secret agreements have certainly already been made. The Russian deployment is unmistakable. One day we shall suddenly become the victim of cold-blooded political extortion, or we shall be attacked."

But otherwise, though one might talk about it for weeks on end, no word was mentioned to me of any other than purely strategical reasons of this kind. . . .

EXNER: Did Hitler attempt to clear up the political situation by diplomatic means?

JODL: He attempted to do so by the well-known conference with Molotov; and I must say that I placed great hopes on this conference, for the military situation for us soldiers was as follows: With a definitely neutral Russia in our rear—a Russia which in addition sent us supplies—we could not lose the war. An invasion, such as took place on 6 June 1944, would have been entirely out of the question if we had had at our disposal all the forces we had used and lost in this immense struggle in Russia. And it never for a single moment entered my mind that a statesman, who after all was also a strategist, would needlessly let such an opportunity go. And it is a fact that he struggled for months with himself about this decision, being certainly influenced by the many contrary ideas suggested to him by the Reich Marshal, the Commander-in-Chief of the Navy, as well as the Minister for Foreign Affairs.

EXNER: On the basis of the reports which you received, what did the further military situation on both sides look like?

JODL: The Intelligence Service was put to work as from January 1941. The divisions on our borders and also along the Romanian frontier grew rapidly. On 3 February 1941 the Chief of the General Staff of the Army informed the Führer of the operations which he himself intended to carry out. At the same time he presented a map showing the Russian troop deployment. This map indicated—and this has been proved by documents—that there were 100 infantry divisions, 25 cavalry divisions. . . .

EXNER: Then, in your opinion, the Führer waged a preventive war. Did later experiences prove that this was a military necessity?

JODL: It was undeniably a purely preventive war. What we found out later on was the certainty of enormous Russian military preparations opposite our frontiers. I will dispense with details, but I can only say that although we succeeded in a tactical surprise as to the day and the hour, it was no strategic surprise. Russia was fully prepared for war.

EXNER: As an example, could you perhaps tell the Tribunal the number of new airfields which were discovered in the Russian-Polish area?

JODL: I recall approximately that there had been about 20 airfields in eastern Poland, and that in the meantime these had been increased to more than a hundred.

EXNER: Quite briefly, under these conditions what would have been the result of Russia's having forestalled us?

JODL: I do not want to go into the strategic principles, into the operations behind the front; but I can state briefly that we were never strong enough to defend ourselves in the East, as has been proved by the events since 1942. That may sound grotesque, but in order to occupy this front of over 2,000 kilometers we needed 300 divisions at least; and we never had them. If we had waited until the invasion, and a Russian attack had caught us in a pincer movement, simultaneously, we certainly would have been lost. If, therefore, the political premise was correct, namely that we were threatened by this attack, then from a military point of view also the preventive attack was justified. The political situation was presented to us soldiers in this light, consequently we based our military work accordingly. . . .

6

War Crimes

42

FRANÇOIS DE MENTHON

The Concept of War Crimes

January 17, 1946

These crimes flow directly, like the war itself, from the National Socialist doctrine. This doctrine is indifferent to the moral choice of means to attain a final success, and for this doctrine the aim of war is pillage, destruction, and extermination.

Total war, totalitarian war in its methods and its aims, is dictated by the primacy of the German race and the negation of any other value. The Nazi conception maintains selection as a natural principle. The man who does not belong to the superior race counts for nothing. Human life and even less liberty, personality, the dignity of man, have no importance when an adversary of the German community is involved. It is truly "the return to barbarism" with all its consequences. Logically consistent, National Socialism goes to the length of assuming the right, either to exterminate totally races judged hostile or decadent, or to subjugate or put to use individuals and groups capable of resistance, in the nations. Does not the idea of totalitarian war imply the annihilation of any eventual resistance? All those who, in any way, may be capable of opposing

International Military Tribunal, *Trial of the Major War Criminals before the International Military Tribunal, Nuremberg, 14 November 1945–1 October 1946*, 42 vols. Nuremberg: International Military Tribunal, 1947, 5:390–91.

the New Order and the German hegemony will be liquidated. It will thus become possible to assure an absolute domination over a neighboring people that has been reduced to impotence and to utilize, for the benefit of the Reich, the resources and the human material of those people reduced to slavery.

All the moral conceptions which tended to make war more humane are obviously outdated, and the more so, all international conventions which had undertaken to bring some extenuation of the evils of war.

The conquered peoples must concur, willingly or by force, in the German victory by their material resources, as well as by their labor potential. Means will be found to subject them.

The treatment to which the occupied countries will be subjected is likewise related to this war aim. One could read in *Deutsche Volkskraft* of 13 June 1935 that the totalitarian war will end in a totalitarian victory. "Totalitarian" signifies the entire destruction of the conquered nation and its complete and final disappearance from the historic scene.

Among the conquered peoples distinctions can be made according to whether or not the National Socialists consider them as belonging to the Master Race. For the former, an effort is made to integrate them into the German Reich against their will. For the latter, there is applied a policy of weakening them and bringing about their extinction by every means, from that of appropriation of their property to that of extermination of their persons. In regard to both groups, the Nazi rulers assault not only the property and physical persons, but also the spirits and souls. They seek to align the populations according to the Nazi dogma and behavior, when they wish to integrate them in the German community; they apply themselves at least to rooting out whatever conceptions are irreconcilable with the Nazi universe; they aim to reduce to a mentality and status of slaves, those men whose nationality they wish to eradicate for the benefit of the German race.

Inspired by these general conceptions as to the conduct to be observed in occupied countries, the defendants gave special orders or general directives or deliberately identified themselves with such. Their responsibility is that of perpetrators, co-perpetrators, or accomplices in the War Crimes systematically committed between 1 September 1939 and 8 May 1945 by Germany at war. They deliberately willed, premeditated, and ordered these crimes, or knowingly associated themselves with this policy of organized criminality. . . .

43

CHARLES DUBOST

The German Use of Civilian Hostages
January 24, 1946

I shall describe to you how the General Staff formed its pseudo-law on hostages, a pseudo-law which in France found its final expression in what Stülpnagel and the German administration called the "hostages code." I shall show you, in passing, which of these defendants are the most guilty of this crime.

On the 15th of February 1940 in a secret report addressed to the Defendant Göring, the OKW [German High Command] justifies the taking of hostages, as proved by the excerpt from Document Number 1585-PS which I propose to read to you. This document is dated Berlin, 15 February 1940. It bears the heading: "Supreme Command of the Armed Forces. Secret. To the Reich Minister for Aviation and Supreme Commander of the Air Force."

"Subject: Arrest of Hostages.

"According to the opinion of the OKW, the arrest of hostages is justified in all cases in which the security of the troops and the carrying out of their orders demand it. In most cases it will be necessary to have recourse to it in case of resistance or an untrustworthy attitude on the part of the population of an occupied territory, provided that the troops are in combat or that a situation exists which renders other means of restoring security insufficient. . . .

"In selecting hostages it must be borne in mind that their arrest shall take place only if the refractory sections of the population are anxious for the hostages to remain alive. The hostages shall therefore be chosen from sections of the population from which a hostile attitude may be expected. The arrest of hostages shall be carried out among persons whose fate, we may suppose, will influence the insurgents."

International Military Tribunal, *Trial of the Major War Criminals before the International Military Tribunal, Nuremberg, 14 November 1945–1 October 1946,* 42 vols. Nuremberg: International Military Tribunal, 1947, 6:120–23.

This document is filed by the French Delegation as Exhibit Number RF-267.

To my knowledge, Göring never raised any objection to this thesis. Here is one more paragraph from an order . . . from the Commander-in-Chief of the Army in France, administrative section, signed "Stroccius," 12 September 1940. Three months after the beginning of the occupation, the hostages are defined therein as follows:

"Hostages are inhabitants of a country who guarantee with their lives the impeccable attitude of the population. The responsibility for their fate is thus placed in the hands of their compatriots. Therefore, the population must be publicly threatened that the hostages will be held responsible for hostile acts of individuals. Only French citizens may be taken as hostages. The hostages can be held responsible only for actions committed after their arrest and after the public proclamation."

This ordinance cancels 5 directives prior to 12 September 1940. This question was the subject of numerous texts, and two General Staff ordinances, dated . . . 2 November 1940 and 13 February 1941:

"If acts of violence are committed by the inhabitants of the country against members of the occupation forces, if offices and installations of the Armed Forces are damaged or destroyed, or if any other attacks are directed against the security of German units and service establishments, and if, under the circumstances, the population of the place of the crime or of the immediate neighborhood can be considered as jointly responsible for those acts of sabotage, measures of prevention and expiation may be ordered by which the civil population is to be deterred in future from committing, encouraging, or tolerating acts of that kind. The population is to be treated as jointly responsible for individual acts of sabotage, if by its attitude in general towards the German Armed Forces, it has favored hostile or unfriendly acts of individuals, or if by its passive resistance against the investigation of previous acts of sabotage, it has encouraged hostile elements to similar acts, or otherwise created a favorable atmosphere for opposition to the German occupation. All measures must be taken in a way that it is possible to carry out. Threats that cannot be realized give the impression of weakness." . . .

Keitel, on the 16th of September 1941, signed a general order which has already been read and filed by my American colleagues . . . and which I shall begin to explain. This order concerns all the occupied territories of the East and the West, as established by the list of addresses which includes all the military commanders of the countries then occupied by Germany: France, Belgium, Norway, Holland, Denmark, eastern territories, Ukraine, Serbia, Salonika, southern Greece, Crete. This order was in effect for the duration of the war. We have a text of 1944 which refers to it. This order of Keitel, Chief of the OKW, is dictated by a violent spirit of anti-Communist repression. It aims at all kinds of repression of the civilian population.

This order, which concerns even the commanders whose troops are stationed in the West, points out to them that in all cases in which attacks are made against the German Army:

> "It is necessary to establish that we are dealing with a mass movement uniformly directed by Moscow to which may also be imputed the seemingly unimportant sporadic incidents which have occurred in regions which have hitherto remained quiet."

Consequently Keitel orders, among other things, that 50 to 100 Communists are to be put to death for each German soldier killed. . . .

44

MARIE CLAUDE VAILLANT-COUTURIER

Testimony on the Gassing at Auschwitz

January 28, 1946

MME. VAILLANT-COUTURIER: We saw the unsealing of the cars and the soldiers letting men, women, and children out of them. We then witnessed heart-rending scenes; old couples forced to part

International Military Tribunal, *Trial of the Major War Criminals before the International Military Tribunal, Nuremberg, 14 November 1945–1 October 1946*, 42 vols. Nuremberg: International Military Tribunal, 1947, 6:215–18.

from each other, mothers made to abandon their young daughters, since the latter were sent to the camp, whereas mothers and children were sent to the gas chambers. All these people were unaware of the fate awaiting them. They were merely upset at being separated, but they did not know that they were going to their death. To render their welcome more pleasant at this time—June–July 1944—an orchestra composed of internees, all young and pretty girls dressed in little white blouses and navy blue skirts, played during the selection, at the arrival of the trains, gay tunes such as "The Merry Widow," the "Barcarolle" from "The Tales of Hoffman," and so forth. They were then informed that this was a labor camp and since they were not brought into the camp they saw only the small platform surrounded by flowering plants. Naturally, they could not realize what was in store for them. Those selected for the gas chamber, that is, the old people, mothers, and children, were escorted to a red-brick building.

M. DUBOST: These were not given an identification number?

VAILLANT-COUTURIER: No.

DUBOST: They were not tattooed?

VAILLANT-COUTURIER: No. They were not even counted.

DUBOST: You were tattooed?

VAILLANT-COUTURIER: Yes, look. [*The witness showed her arm.*] They were taken to a red brick building, which bore the letters "Baden," that is to say "Baths." There, to begin with, they were made to undress and given a towel before they went into the so-called shower room. Later on, at the time of the large convoys from Hungary, they had no more time left to play-act or to pretend; they were brutally undressed, and I know these details as I knew a little Jewess from France who lived with her family at the "Republique" district.

DUBOST: In Paris?

VAILLANT-COUTURIER: In Paris. She was called "little Marie" and she was the only one, the sole survivor of a family of nine. Her mother and her seven brothers and sisters had been gassed on arrival. When I met her she was employed to undress the babies before they were taken into the gas chamber. Once the people were undressed they took them into a room which was somewhat like a shower room, and gas capsules were thrown through an opening in the ceiling. An SS man would watch the effect produced through a porthole. At the end of 5 or 7 minutes, when the gas had completed its work, he gave the signal to open the doors;

and men with gas masks—they too were internees—went into the room and removed the corpses. They told us that the internees must have suffered before dying, because they were closely clinging to one another and it was very difficult to separate them.

After that a special squad would come to pull out gold teeth and dentures; and again, when the bodies had been reduced to ashes, they would sift them in an attempt to recover the gold.

At Auschwitz there were eight crematories but, as from 1944, these proved insufficient. The SS had large pits dug by the internees, where they put branches, sprinkled with gasoline, which they set on fire. Then they threw the corpses into the pits. From our block we could see after about three-quarters of an hour or an hour after the arrival of a convoy, large flames coming from the crematory, and the sky was lighted up by the burning pits.

One night we were awakened by terrifying cries. And we discovered, on the following day, from the men working in the Sonderkommando—the "Gas Kommando"—that on the preceding day, the gas supply having run out, they had thrown the children into the furnaces alive.

DUBOST: Can you tell us about the selections that were made at the beginning of winter?

VAILLANT-COUTURIER: . . . During Christmas 1944 — no, 1943, Christmas 1943 — when we were in quarantine, we saw, since we lived opposite Block 25, women brought to Block 25 stripped naked. Uncovered trucks were then driven up and on them the naked women were piled, as many as the trucks could hold. Each time a truck started, the infamous Hessler . . . ran after the truck and with his bludgeon repeatedly struck the naked women going to their death. They knew they were going to the gas chamber and tried to escape. They were massacred. They attempted to jump from the truck and we, from our own block, watched the trucks pass by and heard the grievous wailing of all those women who knew they were going to be gassed. Many of them could very well have lived on, since they were suffering only from scabies and were, perhaps, a little too undernourished. . . .

Since the Jewesses were sent to Auschwitz with their entire families and since they had been told that this was a sort of ghetto and were advised to bring all their goods and chattels along, they consequently brought considerable riches with them. As for the Jewesses from Salonika, I remember that on their arrival they were given picture postcards bearing the post office address of "Waldsee," a place which did not exist; and a printed text to be sent to their families, stating, "We are doing very well here; we have work and we are well treated. We await your arrival." I myself saw the cards in question; and the Schreiberinnen, that is, the secretaries of the block, were instructed to distribute them among the internees in order to post them to their families. I know that whole families arrived as a result of these postcards.

45

HANNS MARX

Cross-Examination of Marie Claude Vaillant-Couturier

January 28, 1946

DR. HANNS MARX: How do you explain that you yourself came through these experiences so well and are now in such a good state of health?

MME. VAILLANT-COUTURIER: First of all, I was liberated a year ago; and in a year one has time to recover. Secondly, I was 10 months in quarantine for typhus and I had the great luck not to die of exanthematic typhus, although I had it and was ill for $3^1/_2$ months. Also, in the last months at Ravensbrück, as I knew German, I worked on the Revier roll call,[1] which explains why I did not have to work quite so hard or to suffer from the inclemencies of the weather. On the other hand, out of 230 of us

---

[1]The Revier was the infirmary of the women's camp of Ravensbrück. Working on administrative tasks sheltered Vaillant-Couturier from some of the worst conditions at that camp. On Ravensbrück and Revier, see Germaine Tillion, *Ravensbrück,* trans. Gerald Satterwhite (New York: Doubleday, 1975).

International Military Tribunal, *Trial of the Major War Criminals before the International Military Tribunal, Nuremberg, 14 November 1945–1 October 1946,* 42 vols. Nuremberg: International Military Tribunal, 1947, 6:228–30.

only 49 from my convoy returned alive; and we were only 52 at the end of 4 months. I had the great fortune to return.

MARX: Yes. Does your statement contain what you yourself observed or is it concerned with information from other sources as well?

VAILLANT-COUTURIER: Whenever such was the case I mentioned it in my declaration. I have never quoted anything which has not previously been verified at the sources and by several persons, but the major part of my evidence is based on personal experience.

MARX: How can you explain your very precise statistical knowledge, for instance, that 700,000 Jews arrived from Hungary?

VAILLANT-COUTURIER: I told you that I have worked in the offices; and where Auschwitz was concerned, I was a friend of the secretary (the Oberaufseherin), whose name and address I gave to the Tribunal.

MARX: It has been stated that only 350,000 Jews came from Hungary, according to the testimony of the Chief of the Gestapo, Eichmann.

VAILLANT-COUTURIER: I am not going to argue with the Gestapo. I have good reasons to know that what the Gestapo states is not always true.

MARX: How were you treated personally? Were you treated well?

VAILLANT-COUTURIER: Like the others.

MARX: Like the others? You said before that the German people must have known of the happenings in Auschwitz. What are your grounds for this statement?

VAILLANT-COUTURIER: I have already told you: To begin with there was the fact that, when we left, the Lorraine soldiers of the Wehrmacht who were taking us to Auschwitz said to us, "If you knew where you were going, you would not be in such a hurry to get there." Then there was the fact that the German women who came out of quarantine to go to work in German factories knew of these events, and they all said that they would speak about them outside.

Further, the fact that in all the factories where the Häftlinge (the internees) worked they were in contact with the German civilians, as also were the Aufseherinnen, who were in touch with their friends and families and often told them what they had seen.

MARX: One more question. Up to 1942 you were able to observe the behavior of the German soldiers in Paris. Did not these

German soldiers behave well throughout and did they not pay for what they took?

VAILLANT-COUTURIER: I have not the least idea whether they paid or not for what they requisitioned. As for their good behavior, too many of my friends were shot or massacred for me not to differ with you.

MARX: I have no further question to put to this witness.

46

ROMAN A. RUDENKO

The German Destruction of the Soviet Union
February 8, 1946

The German armies and occupational authorities, carrying out the orders of the criminal Hitlerite Government and of the High Command of the Armed Forces, destroyed and looted Soviet towns and villages and industrial establishments and collective farms seized by them; destroyed works of art, demolished, stole, and removed to Germany machinery, stocks of raw and other materials and finished goods, art and historic treasures, and carried out the general plundering of the urban and rural population. In the occupied territories of the Soviet Union 88 million persons lived before the war; gross industrial production amounted to 46 million rubles (at the fixed Government prices of 1926–27); there were 109 million head of livestock, including 31 million head of horned cattle and 12 million horses; 71 million hectares of cultivated land, and 122,000 kilometers of railway lines.

The German fascist invaders completely or partially destroyed or burned 1,710 cities and more than 70,000 villages and hamlets; they burned or destroyed over 6 million buildings and rendered some 25 million persons homeless. Among the damaged cities which suffered most were the big industrial and cultural centers of Stalingrad, Sevastopol, Leningrad, Kiev, Minsk, Odessa, Smolensk, Novgorod, Pskov, Orel, Kharkov, Voronezh, Rostov-on-Don, and many others.

International Military Tribunal, *Trial of the Major War Criminals before the International Military Tribunal, Nuremberg, 14 November 1945–1 October 1946*, 42 vols. Nuremberg: International Military Tribunal, 1947, 7:189–90.

The Germano-fascist invaders destroyed 31,850 industrial establishments employing some 4 million workers; they destroyed or removed from the country 239,000 electric motors and 175,000 metal cutting machines.

The Germans destroyed 65,000 kilometers of railway tracks, 4,100 railway stations, 36,000 post and telegraph offices, telephone exchanges, and other installations for communications.

The Germans destroyed or devastated 40,000 hospitals and other medical institutions, 84,000 schools, technical colleges, universities, institutes for scientific research, and 43,000 public libraries.

The Hitlerites destroyed and looted 98,000 collective farms, 1,876 state farms, and 2,890 machine and tractor stations; they slaughtered, seized or drove into Germany 7 million horses, 17 million head of horned cattle, 20 million pigs, 27 million sheep and goats, and 110 million head of poultry.

The total damage caused to the Soviet Union by the criminal acts of the Hitlerite armies has been estimated at 679,000 million rubles at the Government prices of 1941. . .

47

ROMAN A. RUDENKO

The Mistreatment and Murder of Soviet Prisoners of War

February 8, 1946

Numerous facts of murders, tortures, and maltreatment to which prisoners of war were subjected have been definitely established. They were tortured with red-hot irons, their eyes were gouged out, their extremities severed, *et cetera*. The systematic atrocities and short-shrift justice against captured officers and men of

International Military Tribunal, *Trial of the Major War Criminals before the International Military Tribunal, Nuremberg, 14 November 1945–1 October 1946*, 42 vols. Nuremberg: International Military Tribunal, 1947, 7:175, 179–80.

the Red Army were not chance episodes or the results of criminal activities of individual officers of the German Army and of German officials. The Hitlerite Government and the High Command of the German Army ruthlessly exterminated prisoners of war. Numerous documents, orders, and decrees of the fascist Government and orders of the German Supreme Command testify to this fact.

As early as March 1941 — as the German Lieutenant General Österreich testified during his interrogation — a secret conference took place at the headquarters of the High Command in Berlin, where measures were planned for the organization of camps for Russian prisoners of war and rules laid down for their treatment. According to Österreich's evidence these rules and measures for Soviet prisoners of war were essentially a plan for their extermination.

Many Soviet prisoners of war were shot or hanged while others perished from hunger and infectious diseases, from cold, and from torture systematically employed by the Germans according to a plan which was developed beforehand and had as its object the mass extermination of Soviet persons. . . .

The wild fascist fanatics stabbed and shot on the spot defenseless, sick, and wounded Red Army soldiers who were in the camps; they raped hospital nurses and medical aid women, and brutally murdered members of the medical personnel. A special count of the victims of these executions was conducted on instructions of the German Government and the Supreme Command. . . .

Among brutalities against Soviet prisoners of war must be included branding with special identification marks, which was laid down by a special order of the German Supreme Command, dated 20 July 1942. This order provides for the following methods of branding: "The tightly drawn skin is to be cut superficially with a heated lancet dipped in india ink."

The Hague Convention of 1907, regarding prisoners of war, prescribed not only humane treatment for prisoners of war, but also respect for their patriotic feelings and forbids their being used to fight against their own fatherland.

Article 3 of the Convention, which refers to the laws and customs of war, forbids the combatants to force enemy subjects to participate in military operations directed against their own country, even in cases where these subjects had been in their service before the outbreak of war. The Hitlerites trod underfoot even this elementary principle of international law. By beatings and threats of shooting they forced prisoners to work as drivers of carts, motor vehicles, and transports carrying ammunition and other equipment to the front, as supply bearers to the firing line, as auxiliaries in antiaircraft artillery, *et cetera.*

In the Leningrad district, in the Yelny region of the Smolensk district, in the Gomel district of Bielorussia, in the Poltava district, and in other places, cases were recorded where the German command, under threat of shooting, drove captured Red Army soldiers forward in front of their advancing columns during attacks.

The mass extermination of Soviet prisoners of war, established by special investigations of the Extraordinary State Commission of the Soviet Union, is also confirmed by the documents of the German police and of the Supreme Command captured by the Soviet and Allied armies on German territory. In these documents it is stated that many Soviet prisoners of war died of hunger, typhus, and other diseases. The camp commandants forbade the civil population to give food to the prisoners and doomed them to death by starvation.

In many cases prisoners of war who were unable to keep in line on the march because of starvation and exhaustion were shot in full view of the civil population and their bodies left unburied. In many camps no arrangements of any sort were made for living quarters for the prisoners of war. They lay in the open in rain and snow. They were not even given tools to dig themselves pits or burrows in the ground. One could hear the arguments of the Hitlerites: "The more prisoners who die, the better for us."

On the basis of the above exposition, I declare, on behalf of the Soviet Government and People, that the responsibility for the bloody butchery perpetrated on Soviet prisoners of war in violation of all the universally accepted rules and customs of war, rests with the criminal Hitlerite Government and German Supreme Command, the representatives of which are now sitting on the defendants' benches. . . .

48

TELFORD TAYLOR

Questioning of Erich von dem Bach-Zelewski

January 7, 1946

COL. TAYLOR: Until what date did you remain Higher SS and Police Leader for central Russia?

VON DEM BACH-ZELEWSKI: I was Higher SS and Police Leader for central Russia until the end of 1942, with occasional interruptions when I was at the front and with one interval of about 6 months when I had an illness. At the end of 1942 I was appointed Chief of Anti-Partisan Combat Units.

TAYLOR: Was this position of Chief of Anti-Partisan Combat Units created specially for you?

VON DEM BACH-ZELEWSKI: Yes.

TAYLOR: To whom were you directly subordinate in this new capacity?

VON DEM BACH-ZELEWSKI: Heinrich Himmler.

TAYLOR: Were your functions in this new capacity restricted to any particular part of the Eastern Front?

VON DEM BACH-ZELEWSKI: No. My sphere of activity comprised the entire Eastern zone.

TAYLOR: What was the general nature of your duties as Chief of Anti-Partisan Combat Units?

VON DEM BACH-ZELEWSKI: First of all, I had to establish an intelligence center at Himmler's headquarters to which all reports in connection with partisan activities were dispatched, where they were evaluated, and then forwarded to the competent authorities.

TAYLOR: In the course of your duties did you confer with the commanders of army groups and armies on the Eastern Front?

VON DEM BACH-ZELEWSKI: With the commanders of the army groups, not of the armies, and with the district commanders of the Wehrmacht. . . .

International Military Tribunal, *Trial of the Major War Criminals before the International Military Tribunal, Nuremberg, 14 November 1945–1 October 1946,* 42 vols. Nuremberg: International Military Tribunal, 1947, 4:478–80.

TAYLOR: What proportion of Wehrmacht troops was used in anti-partisan operations as compared to Police and SS troops?

VON DEM BACH-ZELEWSKI: Since the number of Police and SS troops was very small, anti-partisan operations were undertaken mainly by Wehrmacht formations.

TAYLOR: Were the anti-partisan troops usually commanded by Wehrmacht officers or by SS officers?

VON DEM BACH-ZELEWSKI: It varied, depending mostly on the individual area; in the operational areas Wehrmacht officers nearly always commanded, but an order existed to the effect that the formation, be it Wehrmacht, Waffen-SS or Police, which supplied the most troops for a particular operation, had command of it.

TAYLOR: Did the highest military leaders issue instructions that anti-partisan operations were to be conducted with severity?

VON DEM BACH-ZELEWSKI: Yes.

TAYLOR: Did the highest military authorities issue any detailed instructions as to the methods to be used in anti-partisan operations?

VON DEM BACH-ZELEWSKI: No.

TAYLOR: What was the result, in the occupied territories, of this lack of detailed directives from above?

VON DEM BACH-ZELEWSKI: This lack of detailed directives resulted in a wild state of anarchy in all anti-partisan operations.

TAYLOR: In your opinion, were the measures taken in anti-partisan operations far more severe than the circumstances warranted, or were they not?

VON DEM BACH-ZELEWSKI: Since there were no definite orders and the lower commanders were forced to act independently, the operations varied according to the character of the officer in command and the quality of the troops. I am of the opinion that the operations often not only failed in their purpose but even overshot their mark.

TAYLOR: Did these measures result in the unnecessary killing of large numbers of the civilian population?

VON DEM BACH-ZELEWSKI: Yes.

TAYLOR: Did you report these excessive measures to the commanders of the army groups and other Wehrmacht officers with whom you worked?

VON DEM BACH-ZELEWSKI: This state of affairs was generally known. There was no necessity to make a special report about it, since every operation had immediately to be reported in all detail, and was known to every responsible leader. . . .

49

YURI POKROVSKY

Examination of Erich von dem Bach-Zelewski

January 7, 1946

COL. POKROVSKY: Do you know of any order prescribing the seizure of hostages and the burning of villages as a reprisal for abetting the partisans?

VON DEM BACH-ZELEWSKI: No. I do not think that written orders to that effect were ever issued, and it is precisely this lack of any orders which I considered a mistake. It should, for instance, have been definitely stated how many people could be executed as a reprisal for the killing of one, or of 10 German soldiers.

POKROVSKY: Am I to understand that if certain commanders burned villages as a punitive measure against the local population, they, the commanders, would be acting on their own initiative?

VON DEM BACH-ZELEWSKI: Yes. These steps would be taken by a commander on his own initiative. Nor could his superior officers do anything against it, since orders emanating from the highest authorities definitely stated that if excesses were committed against the civilian population in the partisan areas, no disciplinary or juridical measures could be taken.

POKROVSKY: And can we assume that the same applied to the seizure of hostages?

VON DEM BACH-ZELEWSKI: Well, I think that the question of hostages did not arise at all in the anti-partisan struggle. The hostage system was more common in the West. At any rate the term "hostage" was not used in anti-partisan warfare. . . .

POKROVSKY: If I understood you correctly, you replied to a question of my colleague, the American Prosecutor, by saying that

International Military Tribunal, *Trial of the Major War Criminals before the International Military Tribunal, Nuremberg, 14 November 1945–1 October 1946,* 42 vols. Nuremberg: International Military Tribunal, 1947, 4:484–85.

the struggle against the partisan movement was a pretext for destroying the Slav and Jewish population?

VON DEM BACH-ZELEWSKI: Yes.

POKROVSKY: Was the Wehrmacht Command aware of the methods adopted for fighting the partisan movement and for destroying the Jewish population?

VON DEM BACH-ZELEWSKI: The methods were known generally, and hence to the military leaders as well. I do not, of course, know whether they were aware of the plan mentioned by Himmler. . . .

POKROVSKY: You have told us that the Germans intended to destroy the Slav population in order to reduce the number of Slavs to 30 million. Where did you get this figure and this order?

VON DEM BACH-ZELEWSKI: I must correct that: Not to reduce to 30 million, but by 30 million. Himmler mentioned this figure in his speech at the Weselsburg.

POKROVSKY: Do you confirm the fact that actually all the measures carried out by the German commanders and by the Wehrmacht in the occupied Russian territories were directed to the sole purpose of reducing the number of Slavs and Jews by 30 million?

VON DEM BACH-ZELEWSKI: The meaning of that is not quite clear to me. Did the Wehrmacht know that the Slav population was to be diminished by 30 million? Would you please repeat the question, it wasn't quite clear?

POKROVSKY: I asked: Can you actually and truthfully confirm that the measures taken by the Wehrmacht Command in the district administrative areas then occupied by the Germans were directed to the purpose of diminishing the Slavs and Jews by 30 million? Do you now understand the question?

VON DEM BACH-ZELEWSKI: I believe that these methods would definitely have resulted in the extermination of 30 million if they had been continued, and if developments of that time had not completely changed the situation.

POKROVSKY: I have no further questions to put to the witness.

50

ROBERT H. JACKSON

Cross-Examination of Albert Speer

June 21, 1946

Mr. Justice Jackson: Now, let me ask you to be shown Document D-335. This is a report from the files of Krupp, dated at Essen on 12 June 1944, directed to the "Gau Camp Physician, Herr Dr. Jäger," and signed by Stinnesbeck:

"In the middle of May I took over the medical supervision of the PW [prisoner of war] Camp 1420 in the Nörggerathstrasse. The camp contains 644 French PW's.

"During the air raid on 27 April of this year the camp was largely destroyed and at the moment conditions are intolerable.

"315 prisoners are still accommodated in the camp. 170 of these are no longer in huts, but in the tunnel in Grunerstrasse on the Essen-Mülheim railway line. This tunnel is damp and is not suitable for continued accommodation of human beings. The rest of the prisoners are accommodated in 10 different factories in Krupp's works.

"Medical attention is given by a French military doctor who takes great pains with his fellow countrymen. Sick people from Krupp's factories must be brought to the sick parade too. This parade is held in the lavatory of a burned-out public house outside the camp. The sleeping accommodations of the four French medical orderlies is in what was the urinal room. There is a double tier wooden bed available for sick bay patients. In general, treatment takes place in the open. In rainy weather it has to be held in this small room. These are insufferable conditions! There are no chairs, tables, cupboards, or water. The keeping of a register of sick is impossible.

"Bandages and medical supplies are very scarce, although people badly hurt in the works are often brought here for first aid and have to be bandaged before being taken to the hospital.

International Military Tribunal, *Trial of the Major War Criminals before the International Military Tribunal, Nuremberg, 14 November 1945–1 October 1946,* 42 vols. Nuremberg: International Military Tribunal, 1947, 16:548–50.

There are many strong complaints about food, too, which the guard personnel confirm as being justified.

"Illness and less manpower must be reckoned with under these circumstances.

"The construction of huts for the accommodation of the prisoners and the building of sick quarters for the proper treatment of the sick persons is urgently necessary.

"Please take the necessary steps.

"(Signed) Stinnesbeck."

SPEER: That is a document which shows what conditions can be after severe air raids. The conditions were the same in these cases for Germans and foreign workers. There were no beds, no cupboards, and so forth. That was because the camp in which these things had been provided had been burned down. That the food supply was often inadequate in the Ruhr district during this period was due to the fact that attacks from the air were centered on communication lines, so that food transports could not be brought into the Ruhr to the necessary extent. These were temporary conditions which we were able to improve when the air raids ceased for a time. When conditions became even worse after September or October of 1944, or rather after November of 1944, we made every effort to give food supplies the priority for the first time over armament needs, so that in view of these difficulties the workers would be fed first of all, while armaments had to stand back somewhat.

JACKSON: Well, then you did make it your business to get food and to see to the conditions of these workers? Do I understand that you did it, that you took steps?

SPEER: It is true that I did so, and I am glad that I did, even if I am to be reproached for it. For it is a universal human obligation when one hears of such conditions to try to alleviate them, even if it is somebody else's responsibility. But the witness Riecke testified here that the whole of the food question was under the direction of the Food Ministry.

JACKSON: And it was an essential part of production, was it not, to keep workers in proper condition to produce? That is elementary, is it not?

SPEER: No. That is wrongly formulated.

JACKSON: Well, you formulate it for me as to what the relation is between the nourishment of workers and the amount of production produced.

SPEER: I said yesterday that the responsibility for labor conditions was divided up between the Food Ministry, the Health Office in the Reich Ministry of the Interior, the Labor Trustee in the office of the Plenipotentiary General for the Allocation of Labor, and so on. There was no comprehensive authority in my hands. In the Reich, because of the way in which our state machine was built up, we lacked a comprehensive agency in the form of a Reich Chancellor, who would have gathered all these departments together and held joint discussions. But I, as the man responsible for production, had no responsibility in these matters. However, when I heard complaints from factory heads or from my deputies, I did everything to remove the cause of the complaints.

51

KARL DÖNITZ

Testimony about His Relationship with Hitler
May 9, 1946

FLOTTENRICHTER KRANZBÜHLER: You know, Admiral, that the Prosecution draws very far-reaching conclusions from your acceptance of this appointment as Commander-in-Chief of the Navy, especially with reference to the conspiracy. The Prosecution contends that through your acceptance of this position you ratified the previous happenings, all the endeavors of the Party since 1920 or 1922, and the entire German policy, domestic and foreign, at least since 1933. Were you aware of the significance of this foreign policy? Did you take this into consideration at all?

DÖNITZ: The idea never entered my head. Nor do I believe that there is a soldier who, when he receives a military command,

International Military Tribunal, *Trial of the Major War Criminals before the International Military Tribunal, Nuremberg, 14 November 1945–1 October 1946*, 42 vols. Nuremberg: International Military Tribunal, 1947, 13:298–301.

would entertain such thoughts or be conscious of such considerations. My appointment as Commander-in-Chief of the Navy represented for me an order which I of course had to obey, just as I had to obey every other military order, unless for reasons of health I was not able to do so. Since I was in good health and believed that I could be of use to the Navy, I naturally also accepted this command with inner conviction. Anything else would have been desertion or disobedience.

KRANZBÜHLER: Then as Commander-in-Chief of the Navy you came into very close contact with Adolf Hitler. You also know just what conclusions the Prosecution draws from this relationship. Please tell me just what this relationship was and on what it was based?

DÖNITZ: In order to be brief, I might perhaps explain the matter as follows:

This relationship was based on three ties. First of all, I accepted and agreed to the national and social ideas of National Socialism: the national ideas which found expression in the honor and dignity of the nation, its freedom, and its equality among nations and its security; and the social tenets which had perhaps as their basis: no class struggle, but human and social respect of each person regardless of his class, profession, or economic position, and on the other hand, subordination of each and every one to the interests of the common weal. Naturally I regarded Adolf Hitler's high authority with admiration and joyfully acknowledged it, when in times of peace he succeeded so quickly and without bloodshed in realizing his national and social objectives.

My second tie was my oath. Adolf Hitler had, in a legal and lawful way, become the Supreme Commander of the Wehrmacht, to whom the Wehrmacht had sworn its oath of allegiance. That this oath was sacred to me is self-evident and I believe that decency in this world will everywhere be on the side of him who keeps his oath.

The third tie was my personal relationship: Before I became Commander-in-Chief of the Navy, I believe Hitler had no definite conception of me and my person. He had seen me too few times and always in large circles. How my relationship to him would shape itself was therefore a completely open question when I became Commander-in-Chief of the Navy. My start in this connection was very unfavorable. It was made difficult, first, by the imminent and then the actual collapse of U-boat warfare and, secondly, by my refusal, just as Grossadmiral Raeder had already refused, to scrap the large ships, which in Hitler's opinion had no fighting value in view of the oppressive superiority of the foe. I, like Grossadmiral Raeder, had opposed the scrapping of these ships, and only after a quarrel did he finally agree. But, despite that, I noticed very soon that in Navy matters he had confidence in me and in other respects as well treated me with decided respect.

Adolf Hitler always saw in me only the first soldier of the Navy. He never asked for my advice in military matters which did not concern the Navy, either in regard to the Army or the Air Force, nor did I ever express my opinion about matters concerning the Army or the Air Force, because basically I did not have sufficient knowledge of these matters. Of course, he never consulted me on political matters of a domestic or foreign nature. . . .

KRANZBÜHLER: According to the table submitted, between 1943 and 1945 you were called sometimes once and sometimes twice a month to the Führer's headquarters. Please describe to the Tribunal just what happened, as far as you were concerned, on a day like that at the Führer's headquarters—what you had to do there.

DÖNITZ: Until 2 or 3 months before the collapse, when the Führer was in Berlin, I flew to his headquarters about every 2 or 3 weeks, but only if I had some concrete Navy matter for which I needed his decision. On those occasions I participated in the noontime discussion of the general military situation, that is, the report which the Führer's staff made to him about what had taken place on the fighting fronts within the last 24 hours. At these military discussions the Army and Air Force situation was of primary importance, and I spoke only when my Naval expert was reporting the naval situation and he needed me to supplement his report. Then at a given moment, which was fixed by the Adjutant's Office, I gave my military report which was the purpose of my journey. When rendering this report only those were present whom these matters concerned, that is, when it was a question of reinforcements, *et cetera,* Field Marshal Keitel or General oberst Jodl were generally present.

When I came to his headquarters every 2 or 3 weeks—later in 1944 there was sometimes an interval of 6 weeks—the Führer invited me to lunch. These invitations ceased completely after 20 July 1944, the day of the attempted assassination.[1]

I never received from the Führer an order which in any way violated the ethics of war. Neither I nor anyone in the Navy—and this is my conviction—knew anything about the mass extermination of people, which I learned about here from the Indictment, or, as far as the concentration camps are concerned, after the capitulation in May 1945.

In Hitler I saw a powerful personality who had extraordinary intelligence and energy and a practically universal knowledge, from whom power seemed to emanate and who was possessed of a remarkable power of suggestion. On the other hand, I purposely very seldom went to his headquarters, for I had the feeling that I would best preserve my power of initiative that way and, secondly, because after several days, say 2 or 3 days at his headquarters, I had the feeling that I had to disengage myself from his power of suggestion. I am telling you this because, in this connection I was doubtless more fortunate than his staff who were constantly exposed to his powerful personality with its power of suggestion. . . .

[1]On July 20, 1944, several high-ranking generals and other opponents of Hitler plotted to assassinate the Führer, hoping to pave the way for a negotiated peace with the Allies that would spare Germany further destruction. The attempt failed, and Hitler took bloody retribution. A "people's court" tried and convicted about two hundred people, most of whom were immediately executed.

52

WILHELM KEITEL

Testimony on War Crimes
April 6 and 7, 1946

GEN. RUDENKO: What military training and military rank did Hitler possess?

International Military Tribunal, *Trial of the Major War Criminals before the International Military Tribunal, Nuremberg, 14 November 1945–1 October 1946,* 42 vols. Nuremberg: International Military Tribunal, 1947, 10:600, 613–14, 617–18, 624–26.

KEITEL: Only a few years ago I found out from Hitler himself that after the end of World War I, he had been a lieutenant in a Bavarian infantry regiment. During the war he was a private, then private first class and maybe corporal during the last period.

RUDENKO: Should we not, therefore, conclude that you, with your thorough military training and great experience, could have had an opportunity of influencing Hitler, very considerably, in solving questions of a strategic and military nature, as well as other matters pertaining to the Armed Forces?

KEITEL: No. I have to declare in that respect that, to a degree which is almost incomprehensible to the layman and the professional officer, Hitler had studied general staff publications, military literature, essays on tactics, operations, and strategy and that he had a knowledge in the military fields which can only be called amazing. May I give an example of that which can be confirmed by the other officers of the Wehrmacht. Hitler was so well informed concerning organization, armament, leadership, and equipment of all armies, and what is more remarkable, of all navies of the globe, that it was impossible to prove any error on his part; and I have to add that also during the war, while I was at his headquarters and in his close proximity, Hitler studied at night all the big general staff books by Moltke, Schlieffen, and Clausewitz and from them acquired his vast knowledge by himself. Therefore we had the impression: Only a genius can do that. . . .

RUDENKO: . . . I now pass on to the subject of atrocities and of your attitude towards these crimes. . . .

I shall first of all refer to a document entitled, "Directive on the Introduction of Military Jurisdiction in Region Barbarossa and on the Adoption of Special Military Measures." Do you remember that document? It was drawn up on 13 May 1941 more than a month before the outbreak of war against the Soviet Union. Do you remember that in that document, drawn up before the war, instructions were given that suspect elements should immediately be brought before an officer and that he would decide whether they were to be shot? Do you remember that directive? Did you sign the document?

KEITEL: Yes, I have never denied that. But I have given the necessary explanations as to how the document came into being and who was its originator. . . .

RUDENKO: Although you declare that you have already elucidated the matter to your counsel, I am nevertheless obliged to put

this question to you in a slightly different form: Did you consider that an officer had a right to shoot people without trial or
investigation?

KEITEL: In the German Army there have always been courts-martial
for our own soldiers as well as for our enemies, which could
always be set up, consisting of one officer and one or two soldiers all three of whom would act as judges. That is what we call
a court-martial (Standgericht); the only requisite is always that
an officer must preside at this court. But as a matter of principle
I have to repeat the statement which I have made yesterday . . .

RUDENKO: One moment! Please reply to this question. Did not
this document do away with judicial proceedings in the case of
so-called suspects, at the same time leaving to an officer of the
German Army the right to shoot them? Is that correct?

KEITEL: In the case of German soldiers it was correct and was permitted. There is a military tribunal with judicial officers and
there is a court-martial which consists of soldiers. These have
the right to pass and to execute an appropriate sentence against
any soldier of the German Army in court-martial proceedings.

THE PRESIDENT: You are not answering the question. The question
is, what right does this document give, not what the orders in
the German Army are.

RUDENKO: Can you reply to the following question? Did this document do away with judicial proceedings and did it give the
German officer the right to shoot suspects, as stated herein?

KEITEL: That was an order which was given to me by Hitler. He
had given me that order and I put my name under it. What that
means, I explained in detail yesterday.

RUDENKO: You, a Field Marshal, signed that decree. You considered that the decree was irregular; you understood what the
consequences of that decree were likely to be. Then why did
you sign it?

KEITEL: I cannot say any more than that I put my name to it and
I thereby, personally, assumed in my position a degree of
responsibility.

RUDENKO: And one more question. This decree was dated 13 May
1941, almost a month before the outbreak of war. So you had
planned the murder of human beings beforehand?

KEITEL: That I do not understand. It is correct that this order
was issued about 4 weeks before the beginning of the campaign Barbarossa, and another 4 weeks earlier it had been

communicated to the generals in a statement by Hitler. They knew that weeks before. . . .

RUDENKO: Defendant Keitel, I am asking you about the directive concerning the so-called communist insurrectionary movement in the occupied territories. Yesterday your counsel showed you this directive. It is an order of 16 September 1941. . . . I shall remind you of one passage from this order. It states:

"In order to nip in the bud any conspiracy, the strongest measures should be taken at the first sign of trouble in order to maintain the authority of the occupying power and to prevent the conspiracy from spreading . . .";

and furthermore:

". . . one must bear in mind that in the countries affected human life has absolutely no value and that a deterrent effect can be achieved only through the application of extraordinarily, harsh measures."

You remember this basic idea of the order, that human life absolutely does not amount to anything. Do you remember this statement, the basic statement of the order, that "human life has absolutely no value"? Do you remember this sentence?

KEITEL: Yes.

RUDENKO: You signed the order containing this statement?

KEITEL: Yes.

RUDENKO: Do you consider that necessity demanded this extremely evil order?

KEITEL: I explained some of the reasons for this order yesterday and I pointed out that these instructions were addressed in the first place to the Commander-in-Chief of the Wehrmacht offices in the Southeast; that is, the Balkan regions, where extensive partisan warfare and a war between the leaders had assumed enormous proportions, and secondly, because the same phenomena had been observed and established on the same or similar scale in certain defined areas of the occupied Soviet territory.

RUDENKO: Does this mean that you consider this order to have been entirely correct?

KEITEL: I have already explained in detail, in replying to questions, my fundamental standpoint with regard to all orders concerning the treatment of the population. I signed the order and by doing so I assumed responsibility within the scope of my official jurisdiction.

THE PRESIDENT: The Tribunal considers that you are not answering the question. The question was perfectly capable of an answer "yes" or "no" and an explanation afterwards. It is not an answer to the question to say that you have already explained to your counsel.

RUDENKO: I ask you once more, do you consider this order, this particular order—and I emphasize, in which it is stated that "human life has absolutely no value"—do you consider this order correct?

KEITEL: It does not contain these words; but I knew from years of experience that in the Southeastern territories and in certain parts of the Soviet territory, human life was not respected to the same degree. . . .

RUDENKO: I am asking you, Defendant Keitel, known as Field Marshal and one who, before this Tribunal, has repeatedly referred to yourself as a soldier, whether you, in your own bloodthirsty decision of September 1941, confirmed and sanctioned the murder of the unarmed soldiers whom you had captured? Is that right?

KEITEL: I signed both decrees and I, therefore, bear the responsibility within the sphere of my office; I assume the responsibility.

RUDENKO: That is quite clear. In this connection I would like to ask you, since you have repeatedly mentioned it before the Tribunal, about the duty of a soldier. I want to ask you: Is it in accordance with the concept of a "soldier's duty" and the "honor of an officer" to promulgate such orders for reprisals on prisoners of war and on peaceful citizens?

KEITEL: Yes, as far as the reprisals of August and September are concerned, in view of what happened to German prisoners of war whom we found in the field of battle, and in Lvov where we found them murdered by the hundreds.

RUDENKO: I have a few last questions to ask you: You informed the Tribunal that the generals of the German Army were only blindly carrying out Hitler's orders?

KEITEL: I have stated that I do not know if any generals raised objections or who they were, and I said that it did not happen in my presence when Hitler proclaimed the principles of the ideological war and ordered them to be put into practice.

RUDENKO: And do you know that the generals, on their own initiative, promulgated orders on atrocities and on the violation of the laws and customs of war, and that these orders were approved by Hitler?

KEITEL: I know that high authorities in the Army issued orders altering, modifying, and even cancelling in part; for instance, as regards jurisdiction, the March decree and other measures, because they also discussed it with me.

RUDENKO: You do not understand me. I did not ask about modifications, but whether the generals, on their own initiative, ever promulgated orders inciting to the violation of the laws and customs of war.

KEITEL: I do not know of that. I do not know what order you are referring to, General. At the moment I cannot say that I know that. . . . I have always thought of myself as a soldier; not as a political soldier or politician.

RUDENKO: Should we not conclude, after all that has been said here, that you were a Hitler General, not because duty called you but on account of your own convictions?

KEITEL: I have stated here that I was a loyal and obedient soldier of my Führer. And I do not think that there are generals in Russia who do not give Marshal Stalin implicit obedience.

RUDENKO: I have exhausted all my questions.

53

HERMANN GÖRING

Testimony on the Applicability of the Hague Convention of 1907

March 15, 1946

DR. STAHMER: In your military and economic measures in the occupied territories, did you take into consideration whether these measures were in keeping with the Hague Convention on land warfare?

GÖRING: I scanned through the regulations for land warfare of the Hague Convention for the first time just before the outbreak of the Polish conflict. As I read them at that time I regretted that I

International Military Tribunal, *Trial of the Major War Criminals before the International Military Tribunal, Nuremberg, 14 November 1945–1 October 1946,* 42 vols. Nuremberg: International Military Tribunal, 1947, 9:362–64.

had not studied them much more thoroughly at an earlier date. If so I would have told the Führer that, in view of these Hague Convention regulations for land warfare, set down paragraph for paragraph, a modern war could not be waged under any circumstances. One would perforce come into conflict with conditions laid down in 1906 or 1907, because of the technological expansion of modern war. Either they would have to be cancelled, or else modern new viewpoints corresponding to technical developments would have to be introduced. My reasoning is as follows:

The regulations on land warfare of the Hague Convention, as they now existed, I had in my opinion studied quite correctly and logically as regulations for land warfare in 1907. But from 1939 to 1945 there was no longer merely land warfare but also air warfare, which had not been taken into consideration here and which in part created an entirely new situation, and changed the regulations on land warfare of the Hague Convention in many respects. But that is not so much the decisive point; rather, modern and total war develops, as I see it, along three lines: the war of weapons on land, at sea, and in the air; economic war, which has become an integral part of every modern war; and, third, propaganda war, which is also an essential part of this warfare.

If one recognizes these principles on the basis of logic, certain deviations will then result which, according to the letter, may be a violation of logic, but not according to the spirit. If the regulations on land warfare of the Hague Convention provide that weapons of the opponent are to be regarded as booty, as a matter of course, then I must say that today in a modern war the weapons of the opponent under certain circumstances have value only as scrap, but that economic goods however, raw materials, high grade steel, aluminum, copper, lead, and tin, seem and are much more essential as war booty than obsolete weapons which I might take from an opponent. But beyond that it is not only a matter of raw materials, no matter whose property they are. The regulations on land warfare of the Hague Convention provided at one point—I do not remember it now — that those things which are necessary can be confiscated, but against compensation, of course. That is also not the decisive factor, as one can readily believe. Decisive is, however, the fact that in this modern war, and in an economic war, which forms the basis for any further conduct of war, supplies, first of all food, must be regarded as absolutely necessary for war and must be made available for use in war, and beyond that raw materials for industry. Moreover production plants and machinery are also part of economic warfare. If they have until now served the opponent—be they industries directly or indirectly contributing to armaments and the conduct of war—they must now also serve whoever has come into the possession of these means of production through military decision, even if only temporarily, during an armistice in occupied territories. In this connection the labor question naturally also plays a far greater role in economic war than it did in those former wars which served as examples in the regulations on land warfare of the Hague Convention. In 1907 the most recent wars, the Russo-Japanese War, and perhaps the English Boer War, which were, however, conducted under entirely different circumstances—wars which practically lay only one decade behind at that time—could serve as an example of warfare. A war at that time between one army and another, in which the population was more or less not involved, cannot be compared with today's total war, in which everyone, even the child, is drawn into the experience of war through the introduction of air warfare.

According to my opinion, manpower and thereby the workers and their use at the moment, are also an integral part of economic war. By that it is not meant that a worker should be so exploited that he suffers physical injury, but only that his labor should be fully used. . . .

The question of the deportation of workers had therefore also to be regarded from this point of view of security. We were obliged to feed, as far as possible, the entire occupied territory. We also had to dispose of manpower and, at the same time had to consider the removal especially of those who had no work in their own country and represented a danger in the growth of the underground resistance arising against us.

If these age groups were drafted into Germany for work, it was because of basic considerations of security, in order that they should not be left idle in their own country—and thus be made available for the work and the struggle against us—but should be used to our advantage in economic war.

Thirdly—I want to mention these things just very briefly—in conclusion, the war of propaganda. At one point in the Indictment it is also mentioned that we requisitioned radios, which is, to be sure, a matter of course. For the great importance in propaganda warfare enemy propaganda had, which extended by way of radio far into the hinterland, no one has felt more strongly than Germany. All the great dangers of underground movements, partisan war, the resistance movements and sabotage, and everything connected with it, and finally also in this war, this embitterment and this atmosphere, have been called forth to the extreme by this mutual fight over the radio.

Also whatever happened in the way of atrocities and similar acts, which should not be tolerated, are in the last analysis, if one thinks about it calmly, to be attributed primarily to the war of propaganda.

Therefore the regulations on land warfare of the Hague Convention are in my opinion not an instrument which can be used as a basis for a modern war, because they do not take into consideration the essential principles of this war; the war in the air, the economic war, and the war of propaganda.

And at this point I should like to say the same words which one of our greatest, most important, and toughest opponents, the British Prime Minister, Winston Churchill, used: "In the struggle for life and death there is in the end no legality."

54

ROBERT H. JACKSON

On the Guilt of the Leader and His Followers

July 26, 1946

But their guilt cannot exculpate the defendants. Hitler did not carry all responsibility to the grave with him. All the guilt is not wrapped in Himmler's shroud. It was these dead men whom these living chose to be their partners in this great conspiratorial brotherhood, and the crimes that they did together they must pay for one by one.

It may well be said that Hitler's final crime was against the land he had ruled. He was a mad messiah who started the war without cause and prolonged it without reason. If he could not rule he cared not what happened to Germany. As Fritzsche has told us from the stand, Hitler tried to use the defeat of Germany for the

International Military Tribunal, *Trial of the Major War Criminals before the International Military Tribunal, Nuremberg, 14 November 1945–1 October 1946,* 42 vols. Nuremberg: International Military Tribunal, 1947, 19:429–31.

self-destruction of the German people. He continued to fight when he knew it could not be won, and continuance meant only ruin. . . .

Hitler ordered everyone else to fight to the last and then retreated into death by his own hand. But he left life as he lived it, a deceiver; he left the official report that he had died in battle. This was the man whom these defendants exalted to a Führer. It was they who conspired to get him absolute authority over all of Germany. And in the end he and the system they created for him brought the ruin of them all. . . .

But let me for a moment turn devil's advocate. I admit that Hitler was the chief villain. But for the defendants to put all blame on him is neither manly nor true. We know that even the head of the state has the same limits to his senses and to the hours of his days as do lesser men. He must rely on others to be his eyes and ears as to most that goes on in a great empire. Other legs must run his errands; other hands must execute his plans. On whom did Hitler rely for such things more than upon these men in the dock? Who led him to believe he had an invincible air armada if not Göring? Who kept disagreeable facts from him? Did not Göring forbid Field Marshal Milch to warn Hitler that in his opinion Germany was not equal to the war upon Russia? Did not Göring, according to Speer, relieve General Galland of his air force command for speaking of the weaknesses and bungling of the air forces? Who led Hitler, utterly untraveled himself, to believe in the indecision and timidity of democratic peoples if not Ribbentrop, Von Neurath, and Von Papen? Who fed his illusion of German invincibility if not Keitel, Jodl, Raeder, and Dönitz? Who kept his hatred of the Jews inflamed more than Streicher and Rosenberg? Who would Hitler say deceived him about conditions in concentration camps if not Kaltenbrunner, even as he would deceive us? These men had access to Hitler and often could control the information that reached him and on which he must base his policy and his orders. They were the Praetorian Guard, and while they were under Caesar's orders, Caesar was always in their hands.

If these dead men could take the witness stand and answer what has been said against them, we might have a less distorted picture of the parts played by these defendants. Imagine the stir that would occur in the dock if it should behold Adolf Hitler advancing to the witness box, or Himmler with an armful of dossiers, or Goebbels, or Bormann with the reports of his Party spies, or the murdered Rohm or Canaris. The ghoulish defense that the world is entitled to retribution only from the cadavers is an argument worthy of the crimes at which it is directed. . . .

7

Crimes against Humanity

55

FRANÇOIS DE MENTHON

On Crimes against the Human Status
January 17, 1946

The human status expresses itself, we say, in major statutes, every one of which comprises a complex apparatus of very different provisions. But these statutes are inspired in the laws of civilized countries by a conception essential to the nature of man. This conception is defined in two complementary ideas: The dignity of the human being considered in each and every person individually, on the one hand; and on the other hand, the permanence of the human being considered within the whole of humanity. Every juridical organization of the human being in a state of civilization proceeds from this essential, two-fold conception of the individual, in each and in all, the individual and the universal. . . .

As a consequence of such a doctrine, the upsetting of the human status appears not only to be a means to which one has recourse in the presence of temporary opportunities, such as those arising from war, but also as an aim both necessary and desirable. The Nazis propose to classify mankind in three main categories: That of their adversaries, or persons whom they consider inadaptable

---

International Military Tribunal, *Trial of the Major War Criminals before the International Military Tribunal, Nuremberg, 14 November 1945–1 October 1946,* 42 vols. Nuremberg: International Military Tribunal, 1947, 5:407–9.

to their peculiar constructions—this category can be bullied in all sorts of ways and even destroyed; that of superior men which they claim is distinguishable by their blood or by some arbitrary means; that of inferior men, who do not deserve destruction and whose vital power should be used in a regime of slavery for the well-being of the "overlords."

The Nazi leaders proposed to apply this conception everywhere they could in territories more and more extended, to populations ever more numerous; and in addition they demonstrated the frightful ambition to succeed in imposing it on intelligent people, to convince their victims and to demand from them, in addition to so many sacrifices, an act of faith. The Nazi war is a war of fanatic religion in which one can exterminate infidels and equally as well impose conversion upon them. It should further be noted that the Nazis aggravated the excesses of those horrible times, for in a religious war converted adversaries were received like brothers, whereas the Nazis never gave their pitiable victims the chance of saving themselves, even by the most complete recantation. . . .

56

WILLIAM F. WALSH

On the Warsaw Ghetto Uprising

December 14, 1945

MAJOR WALSH: I would now like to discuss annihilation within the ghettos. Justice Jackson in his opening address to the Tribunal made reference to Document 1061-PS, "The Warsaw Ghetto Is No More," marked Exhibit USA-275.

This finest example of ornate German craftsmanship, leather bound, profusely illustrated, typed on heavy bond paper, is the almost unbelievable recital of a proud accomplishment by Major General of the Police Stroop, who signed the report with a bold

International Military Tribunal, *Trial of the Major War Criminals before the International Military Tribunal, Nuremberg, 14 November 1945–1 October 1946*, 42 vols. Nuremberg: International Military Tribunal, 1947, 3:553–58.

hand. General Stroop in this report first pays tribute to the bravery and heroism of the German forces who participated in the ruthless and merciless action against a helpless, defenseless group of Jews, numbering, to be exact, 56,065, including, of course, the infants and the women. In this document he proceeds to relate the day-by-day account of the ultimate accomplishment of his mission—to destroy and to obliterate the Warsaw ghetto.

According to this report, the ghetto, which was established in Warsaw in November 1940, was inhabited by about 400,000 Jews; and prior to the action for the destruction of this ghetto, some 316,000 had already been deported. The Court will note that this report is approximately 75 pages in length, and the Prosecution believes that the contents are of such striking evidentiary value that no part should be omitted from the permanent records of the Tribunal and that the Tribunal should consider the entire report in judging the guilt of these defendants. . . .

THE PRESIDENT: You are going to read the passages that you think necessary?

WALSH: Yes . . . I would like to read the boastful but nonetheless vivid account of some of this ruthless action within the Warsaw ghetto . . . :

"The resistance put up by the Jews and bandits could be broken only by the relentless and energetic use of our shock-troops by day and night. On 23 April 1943 the Reichsführer SS issued through the Higher SS and Police Leader East at Kraków his order to complete the combing out of the Warsaw ghetto with the greatest severity and relentless tenacity. I therefore decided to destroy the entire Jewish residential area by setting every block on fire, including the blocks of residential buildings near the armament works. One building after the other was systematically evacuated and subsequently destroyed by fire. The Jews then emerged from their hiding places and dugouts in almost every case. Not infrequently the Jews stayed in the burning buildings until, because of the heat and the fear of being burned alive, they preferred to jump down from the upper stories after having thrown mattresses and other upholstered articles into the street from the burning buildings. With their bones broken they still tried to crawl across the street into blocks of buildings which had not yet been set on fire or were only partially in flames. Often the Jews changed their hiding places during the night by moving into the ruins of burnt-out buildings, taking refuge there until they were found by our patrols. Their stay in the sewers also ceased to be pleasant after the first week. Frequently from the street we could hear loud voices coming through the sewer shafts. Then the men of the Waffen-SS, the Police, or the Wehrmacht Engineers courageously climbed down the shafts to bring out the Jews and not infrequently they then stumbled over Jews already dead or were shot at. It was always necessary to use smoke candles to drive out the Jews. Thus one day we opened 183 sewer entrance holes and at a fixed time lowered smoke candles into them, with the result that the bandits fled from what they believed to be gas into the center of the former ghetto, where they could then be pulled out of the sewer holes there. A great number of Jews who could not be counted were exterminated by blowing up sewers and dugouts.

"The longer the resistance lasted, the tougher the men of the Waffen-SS, Police, and Wehrmacht became. They fulfilled their duty indefatigably in faithful comradeship and stood together as models and examples of soldiers. Their duty hours often lasted from early morning until late at night. At night search patrols, with rags wound around their feet, remained at the heels of the Jews and gave them no respite. Not infrequently they caught and killed Jews who used the night hours for supplementing their stores from abandoned dugouts and for contacting neighboring groups or exchanging news with them.

"Considering that the greater part of the men of the Waffen-SS had only been trained for 3 to 4 weeks before being assigned to this action, high credit should be given to the pluck, courage, and devotion to duty which they showed. It must be stated that the Wehrmacht Engineers, too, executed the blowing up of dugouts, sewers, and concrete buildings with indefatigability and great devotion to duty. Officers and men of the Police, a large part of whom had already been at the front, again excelled by their dashing spirit.

"Only through the continuous and untiring work of all involved did we succeed in catching a total of 56,065 Jews whose extermination can be proved. To this should be added the number of Jews who lost their lives in explosions or fires but whose number could not be ascertained."

THE PRESIDENT: Major Walsh, in the section that you are just upon now, ought you not to read the opening paragraphs of this document, which set out the amount of the losses of the German troops?

WALSH: I will do so, Sir. On Page 1 of the translation, I quote. The title: "The Warsaw Ghetto is no more."

"For the Führer and their country the following fell in the battle for the destruction of Jews and bandits in the former Jewish residential area of Warsaw."—Fifteen names are thereafter listed.

"Furthermore, the Polish Police Sergeant Julian Zielenski, born 13 November 1891, 8th Commissariat, fell on 19 April 1943 while fulfilling his duty. They gave their utmost, their life. We shall never forget them.

"The following were wounded. . . ."

Then follow the names of 60 Waffen-SS personnel, 11 watchmen from training camps (probably Lithuanians), 12 Security Police officers in SS units, 5 men of the Polish Police, and 2 soldiers of the Wehrmacht Engineers. . . .

On 24 May 1943 the final figures have been compiled by Major General Stroop. . . :

"Of the total of 56,065 caught, about 7,000 were destroyed in the former Jewish residential area during large-scale operations; 6,929 Jews were destroyed by transporting them to T. II" — which we believe to be Treblinka, Camp Number 2 . . . — "the sum total of Jews destroyed is therefore 13,929. Beyond the number of 56,065 an estimated number of 5,000 to 6,000 Jews were destroyed by being blown up or by perishing in the flames." . . .

[*Still pictures were projected on the screen in the courtroom.*]

WALSH: This first picture [*pointing to a picture on the screen*] is shown on Page 27 of the photographs in Document 1061-PS. It is entitled "The Destruction of a Block of Buildings." The Court will recall those portions of the teletype messages that referred to the setting of fires for the purpose of driving out the Jews. This picture, taken from the record, portrays such a scene. . . .

This picture [*pointing to a picture on the screen*] is taken from Page 36 of the photographs. The Court's attention is invited to the figure of a man in mid-air who appears in the picture about halfway between the center and the upper right-hand corner. He has jumped from one of the upper floors of the burning building. A close examination of this picture by the Court in the original photograph will disclose other figures, in the upper floor windows, who apparently are about to follow him. The teletype message of 22 April reported that entire families jumped from burning buildings and were liquidated at once.

This picture [*pointing to a picture on the screen*] is from Page 39 of the photographs. It is entitled "The Leader of the Large-scale Action." The Nazi-appointed commander of this action was SS Major General Stroop, who probably is the central figure in this picture. I cannot refrain from commenting at this point on the smiling faces of the group shown there, in the midst of the violence and destruction. . . .

57

ABRAM SUZKEVER

Persecution of the Jews of Vilna
February 27, 1946

MR. COUNSELLOR SMIRNOV: Please tell me, Witness, where did the German occupation find you?

SUZKEVER: In the town of Vilna.

SMIRNOV: You stayed in this town for a long time during the German occupation?

SUZKEVER: I stayed there from the first to nearly the last day of the occupation.

SMIRNOV: You witnessed the persecution of the Jews in that city?

SUZKEVER: Yes.

SMIRNOV: I would like you to tell the Court about this.

SUZKEVER: When the Germans seized my city, Vilna, about 80,000 Jews lived in the town. Immediately the so-called Sonderkommando was set up at 12 Vilenskaia Street, under the command of Schweichenberg and Martin Weiss. The man-hunters of the Sonderkommandos, or as the Jews called them, the "Khapun," broke into the Jewish houses at any time of day or night, dragged

International Military Tribunal, *Trial of the Major War Criminals before the International Military Tribunal, Nuremberg, 14 November 1945–1 October 1946,* 42 vols. Nuremberg: International Military Tribunal, 1947, 8:302–8.

away the men, instructing them to take a piece of soap and a towel, and herded them into certain buildings near the village of Ponari, about 8 kilometers from Vilna. From there hardly one returned. When the Jews found out that their kin were not coming back, a large part of the population went into hiding. However, the Germans tracked them with police dogs. Many were found, and any who were averse to going with them were shot on the spot.

I have to say that the Germans declared that they were exterminating the Jewish race as though legally.

On 8 July an order was issued which stated that all Jews should wear a patch on their back; afterwards they were ordered to wear it on their chest. This order was signed by the commandant of the town of Vilna, Zehnpfennig. But 2 days later some other commandant named Neumann issued a new order that they should not wear these patches but must wear the yellow Star of David.

SMIRNOV: And what does this yellow Star of David mean?

SUZKEVER: It was a six-pointed patch worn on the chest and on the back, in order to distinguish the Jews from the other inhabitants of the town. On another day they were ordered to wear a blue band with a white star. The Jews did not know which insignia to wear as very few lived in the town. Those who did not wear this sign were immediately arrested and never seen again. . . .

In the first days of August 1941 a German seized me in the Dokumenskaia Street. I was then going to visit my mother. The German said to me, "Come with me, you will act in the circus." As I went along I saw that another German was driving along an old Jew, the old rabbi of this street, Kassel, and a third German was holding a young boy. When we reached the old synagogue on this street I saw that wood was piled up there in the shape of a pyramid. A German drew out his revolver and told us to take off our clothes. When we were naked, he lit a match and set fire to this stack of wood. Then another German brought out of the synagogue three scrolls of the Torah, gave them to us, and told us to dance around this bonfire and sing Russian songs. Behind us stood the three Germans; with their bayonets they forced us toward the fire and laughed. When we were almost unconscious, they left.

I must say that the mass extermination of the Jewish people in Vilna began at the moment when District Commissar Hans Fincks arrived, as well as the referant, or reporter on the

Jewish problems, Muhrer. On 31 August, under the direction of District Commissioner Fincks and Muhrer . . .

THE PRESIDENT: Which year?

SUZKEVER: 1941.

THE PRESIDENT: Go on.

SUZKEVER: Under the direction of Fincks and Muhrer, the Germans surrounded the old Jewish quarter of Vilna, taking in Rudnitskaia and Jewish Streets, Galonsky Alley, the Shabelsky and Strashouna Streets, where some 8 to 10 thousand Jews were living.

I was ill at the time and asleep. Suddenly I felt the lash of a whip on me. When I jumped up from my bed I saw Schweichenberg standing in front of me. He had a big dog with him. He was beating everybody and shouting that we must all run out into the courtyard. When I was out in the courtyard, I saw there many women, children, and aged persons—all the Jews who lived there. Schweichenberg had the Sonderkommando surround all this crowd and said that they were taking us to the ghetto. But, of course, like all their statements, this was also a lie. We went through the town in columns and were led toward Lutishcheva Prison. All knew that we were going to our death. When we arrived at Lutishcheva Prison, near the so-called Lutishkina market, I saw a whole double line of German soldiers with white sticks standing there to receive us. While we had to pass between them they beat us with sticks. If a Jew fell down, the one next to him was told to pick him up and carry him through the large prison gates which stood open. Near the prison I took to my heels. I swam across the River Vilia and hid in my mother's house. . . .

On 6 September at 6 o'clock in the morning thousands of Germans, led by District Commissar Fincks, by Muhrer, Schweichenberg, Martin Weiss, and others, surrounded the whole town, broke into the Jewish houses, and told the inhabitants to take only that which they could carry off in their hands and get out into the street. Then they were driven off to the ghetto. When they were passing by Wilkomirowskaia Street where I was, I saw the Germans had brought sick Jews from the hospitals. They were all in blue hospital gowns. They were all forced to stand while a German newsreel operator, who was driving in front of the column, filmed this scene.

I must say that not all the Jews were driven into the ghetto. Fincks did this on purpose. He drove the inhabitants of one street to the ghetto and the inhabitants of another street to Ponari. Previously the Germans had set up two ghettos in Vilna. In the first were 29,000 Jews, and in the second some 15,000 Jews. About half the Jewish population of Vilna never reached the ghetto; they were shot on the way. I remember how, when we arrived at the ghetto . . .

SMIRNOV: Just a moment, Witness. Did I understand you correctly, that before the ghetto was set up, half the Jewish population of Vilna was already exterminated?

SUZKEVER: Yes, that is right. When I arrived at the ghetto I saw the following scene: Martin Weiss came in with a young Jewish girl. When we went in farther, he took out his revolver and shot her on the spot. The girl's name was Gitele Tarlo.

SMIRNOV: Tell us, how old was this girl?

SUZKEVER: Eleven. I must state that the Germans organized the ghetto only to exterminate the Jewish population with greater ease. The head of the ghetto was the expert on Jewish questions, Muhrer, and he issued a series of mad orders. For instance, Jews were forbidden to wear watches. The Jews could not pray in the ghetto. When a German passed by, they had to take off their hats but were not allowed to look at him. . . . At the end of December 1941 an order was issued in the ghetto which stated that the Jewish women must not bear children.

SMIRNOV: I would like you to tell us how, or in what form, this order was issued by the German fascists.

SUZKEVER: Muhrer came to the hospital in Street Number 6 and said that an order had come from Berlin to the effect that Jewish women should not bear children and that if the Germans found out that a Jewish woman had given birth, the child would be exterminated.

Towards the end of December in the ghetto my wife gave birth to a child, a boy. I was not in the ghetto at that time, having escaped from one of these so-called "actions." When I came to the ghetto later I found that my wife had had a baby in a ghetto hospital. But I saw the hospital surrounded by Germans and a black car standing before the door. Schweichenberg was standing near the car, and the hunters of the Sonderkommando were dragging sick and old people out of the hospital and throwing them like logs into the truck. Among them I saw the well known Jewish writer and editor, Grodnensky, who was also dragged and dumped into this truck.

In the evening when the Germans had left, I went to the hospital and found my wife in tears. It seems that when she had had her baby, the Jewish doctors of the hospital had already received the order that Jewish women must not give birth; and they had hidden the baby, together with other newborn children, in one of the rooms. But when this commission with Muhrer came to the hospital, they heard the cries of the babies. They broke open the door and entered the room. When my wife heard that the door had been broken, she immediately got up and ran to see what was happening to the child. She saw one German holding the baby and smearing something under its nose. Afterwards he threw it on the bed and laughed. When my wife picked up the child, there was something black under his nose. When I arrived at the hospital, I saw that my baby was dead. He was still warm. . . .

Shortly afterwards the second ghetto was liquidated, and the German newspaper in Vilna announced that the Jews from this district had died of an epidemic. . . .

SMIRNOV: Please, Witness, I am interested in the following question: You said that at the beginning of the German occupation 80,000 Jews lived in Vilna. How many remained after the German occupation?

SUZKEVER: After the occupation about 600 Jews remained in Vilna.

SMIRNOV: Thus, 79,400 persons were exterminated?

SUZKEVER: Yes.

SMIRNOV: Your Honors, I have no further questions to ask of the witness.

THE PRESIDENT: Does any other Chief Prosecutor want to ask any questions?

MAXWELL-FYFE: No questions.

DODD: No questions.

THE PRESIDENT: Does any member of the defendants' counsel wish to ask any questions? No? Then the witness can retire.

58

RUDOLF HÖSS

Testimony on Auschwitz

April 15, 1946

DR. KAUFFMANN: Witness, your statements will have far-reaching significance. You are perhaps the only one who can throw some light upon certain hidden aspects, and who can tell which people gave the orders for the destruction of European Jewry, and can further state how this order was carried out and to what degree the execution was kept a secret.

THE PRESIDENT: Dr. Kauffmann, will you kindly put questions to the witness.

KAUFFMANN: Yes. [*Turning to the witness.*] From 1940 to 1943, you were the Commander of the camp at Auschwitz. Is that true?

HÖSS: Yes.

KAUFFMANN: And during that time, hundreds of thousands of human beings were sent to their death there. Is that correct?

HÖSS: Yes.

KAUFFMANN: Is it true that you, yourself, have made no exact notes regarding the figures of the number of those victims because you were forbidden to make them?

HÖSS: Yes, that is correct.

KAUFFMANN: Is it furthermore correct that exclusively one man by the name of Eichmann had notes about this, the man who had the task of organizing and assembling these people?

HÖSS: Yes.

KAUFFMANN: Is it furthermore true that Eichmann stated to you that in Auschwitz a total sum of more than 2 million Jews had been destroyed?

HÖSS: Yes.

KAUFFMANN: Men, women, and children?

HÖSS: Yes. . . .

International Military Tribunal, *Trial of the Major War Criminals before the International Military Tribunal, Nuremberg, 14 November 1945–1 October 1946,* 42 vols. Nuremberg: International Military Tribunal, 1947, 11:396–401.

KAUFFMANN: What job did you have from 1938 on and where were you then?

HÖSS: In 1938 I went to the concentration camp at Sachsenhausen where, to begin with, I was adjutant to the commander and later on I became the head of the protective custody camp.

KAUFFMANN: When were you commander at Auschwitz?

HÖSS: I was commander at Auschwitz from May 1940 until December 1943.

KAUFFMANN: What was the highest number of human beings, prisoners, ever held at one time at Auschwitz?

HÖSS: The highest number of internees held at one time at Auschwitz was about 140,000 men and women.

KAUFFMANN: Is it true that in 1941 you were ordered to Berlin to see Himmler? Please state briefly what was discussed.

HÖSS: Yes. In the summer of 1941 I was summoned to Berlin to Reichsführer SS Himmler to receive personal orders. He told me something to the effect—I do not remember the exact words—that the Führer had given the order for a final solution of the Jewish question. We, the SS, must carry out that order. If it is not carried out now then the Jews will later on destroy the German people. He had chosen Auschwitz on account of its easy access by rail and also because the extensive site offered space for measures ensuring isolation.

KAUFFMANN: During that conference did Himmler tell you that this planned action had to be treated as a secret Reich matter?

HÖSS: Yes. He stressed that point. He told me that I was not even allowed to say anything about it to my immediate superior Gruppenführer Glücks. This conference concerned the two of us only and I was to observe the strictest secrecy.

KAUFFMANN: What was the position held by Glücks whom you have just mentioned?

HÖSS: Gruppenführer Glücks was, so to speak, the inspector of concentration camps at that time and he was immediately subordinate to the Reichsführer.

KAUFFMANN: Does the expression "secret Reich matter" mean that no one was permitted to make even the slightest allusion to outsiders without endangering his own life?

HÖSS: Yes, "secret Reich matter" means that no one was allowed to speak about these matters with any person and that everyone promised upon his life to keep the utmost secrecy.

KAUFFMANN: Did you happen to break that promise?

Höss: No, not until the end of 1942.

KAUFFMANN: Why do you mention that date? Did you talk to outsiders after that date?

Höss: At the end of 1942 my wife's curiosity was aroused by remarks made by the then Gauleiter of Upper Silesia, regarding happenings in my camp. She asked me whether this was the truth and I admitted that it was. That was my only breach of the promise I had given to the Reichsführer. Otherwise I have never talked about it to anyone else.

KAUFFMANN: When did you meet Eichmann?

Höss: I met Eichmann about 4 weeks after having received that order from the Reichsführer. He came to Auschwitz to discuss the details with me on the carrying out of the given order. As the Reichsführer had told me during our discussion, he had instructed Eichmann to discuss the carrying out of the order with me and I was to receive all further instructions from him.

KAUFFMANN: Will you briefly tell whether it is correct that the camp of Auschwitz was completely isolated, describing the measures taken to insure as far as possible the secrecy of carrying out of the task given to you.

Höss: The Auschwitz camp as such was about 3 kilometers away from the town. About 20,000 acres of the surrounding country had been cleared of all former inhabitants, and the entire area could be entered only by SS men or civilian employees who had special passes. The actual compound called "Birkenau," where later on the extermination camp was constructed, was situated 2 kilometers from the Auschwitz camp. The camp installations themselves, that is to say, the provisional installations used at first were deep in the woods and could from nowhere be detected by the eye. In addition to that, this area had been declared a prohibited area and even members of the SS who did not have a special pass could not enter it. Thus, as far as one could judge, it was impossible for anyone except authorized persons to enter that area.

KAUFFMANN: And then the railway transports arrived. During what period did these transports arrive and about how many people, roughly, were in such a transport?

Höss: During the whole period up until 1944 certain operations were carried out at irregular intervals in the different countries, so that one cannot speak of a continuous flow of incoming transports. It was always a matter of 4 to 6 weeks. During those

4 to 6 weeks two to three trains, containing about 2,000 persons each, arrived daily. These trains were first of all shunted to a siding in the Birkenau region and the locomotives then went back. The guards who had accompanied the transport had to leave the area at once and the persons who had been brought in were taken over by guards belonging to the camp.

They were there examined by two SS medical officers as to their fitness for work. The internees capable of work at once marched to Auschwitz or to the camp at Birkenau and those incapable of work were at first taken to the provisional installations, then later to the newly constructed crematoria.

KAUFFMANN: During an interrogation I had with you the other day you told me that about 60 men were designated to receive these transports, and that these 60 persons, too, had been bound to the same secrecy described before. Do you still maintain that today?

HÖSS: Yes, these 60 men were always on hand to take the internees not capable of work to these provisional installations and later on to the other ones. This group, consisting of about ten leaders and subleaders, as well as doctors and medical personnel, had repeatedly been told, both in writing and verbally, that they were bound to the strictest secrecy as to all that went on in the camps.

KAUFFMANN: Were there any signs that might show an outsider who saw these transports arrive, that they would be destroyed or was that possibility so small because there was in Auschwitz an unusually large number of incoming transports, shipments of goods and so forth?

HÖSS: Yes, an observer who did not make special notes for that purpose could obtain no idea about that because to begin with not only transports arrived which were destined to be destroyed but also other transports arrived continuously, containing new internees who were needed in the camp. Furthermore, transports likewise left the camp in sufficiently large numbers with internees fit for work or exchanged prisoners.

The trains themselves were closed, that is to say, the doors of the freight cars were closed so that it was not possible, from the outside, to get a glimpse of the people inside. In addition to that, up to 100 cars of materials, rations, *et cetera,* were daily rolled into the camp or continuously left the workshops of the camp in which war material was being made.

KAUFFMANN: And after the arrival of the transports were the victims stripped of everything they had? Did they have to undress completely; did they have to surrender their valuables? Is that true?

HÖSS: Yes.

KAUFFMANN: And then they immediately went to their death?

HÖSS: Yes.

KAUFFMANN: I ask you, according to your knowledge, did these people know what was in store for them?

HÖSS: The majority of them did not, for steps were taken to keep them in doubt about it and suspicion would not arise that they were to go to their death. For instance, all doors and all walls bore inscriptions to the effect that they were going to undergo a delousing operation or take a shower. This was made known in several languages to the internees by other internees who had come in with earlier transports and who were being used as auxiliary crews during the whole action.

KAUFFMANN: And then, you told me the other day, that death by gassing set in within a period of 3 to 15 minutes. Is that correct?

HÖSS: Yes.

KAUFFMANN: You also told me that even before death finally set in, the victims fell into a state of unconsciousness?

HÖSS: Yes. From what I was able to find out myself or from what was told me by medical officers, the time necessary for reaching unconsciousness or death varied according to the temperature and the number of people present in the chambers. Loss of consciousness took place within a few seconds or a few minutes.

KAUFFMANN: Did you yourself ever feel pity with the victims, thinking of your own family and children?

HÖSS: Yes.

KAUFFMANN: How was it possible for you to carry out these actions in spite of this?

HÖSS: In view of all these doubts which I had, the only one and decisive argument was the strict order and the reason given for it by the Reichsführer Himmler. . . .

59

HERMANN GÖRING

Testimony on Nazi Policy toward the Jews

March 14, 1946

GÖRING: After Germany's collapse in 1918 Jewry became very powerful in Germany in all spheres of life, especially in the political, general intellectual and cultural, and, most particularly, the economic spheres. The men came back from the front, had nothing to look forward to, and found a large number of Jews who had come in during the war from Poland and the East, holding positions, particularly economic positions. It is known that, under the influence of the war and business concerned with it—demobilization, which offered great possibilities for doing business, inflation, deflation—enormous shifts and transfers took place in the propertied classes.

There were many Jews who did not show the necessary restraint and who stood out more and more in public life, so that they actually invited certain comparisons because of their numbers and the position they controlled in contrast to the German people. In addition there was the fact that particularly those parties which were avoided by nationally minded people also had Jewish leadership out of proportion to the total number of Jews.

That did not apply only to Germany, but also to Austria, which we have always considered a part of Germany. There the entire Social Democratic leadership was almost exclusively in Jewish hands. They played a very considerable part in politics, particularly in the left-wing parties, and they also became very prominent in the press in all political directions.

At that time, there thus ensued a continuous uninterrupted attack on everything national, national concepts and national ideals. I draw attention to all the magazines and articles which dragged through the mud things which were holy to us. I likewise

---

International Military Tribunal, *Trial of the Major War Criminals before the International Military Tribunal, Nuremberg, 14 November 1945–1 October 1946,* 42 vols. Nuremberg: International Military Tribunal, 1947, 9:272–76.

call attention to the distortion which was practiced in the field of art in this direction, to plays which dragged the fighting at the front through the mud and befouled the ideal of the brave soldier. In fact I could submit an enormous pile of such articles, books, plays, and so forth; but this would lead too far afield and I am actually not too well informed on the subject. Because of all this, a defense movement arose which was by no means created by National Socialism but which had existed before, which was already strong during the war and which came even more strongly to the fore after the war, when the influence of Jewry had such effects. . . .

When the movement then drew up its program, which was done by a few simple people—as far as I know, not even Adolf Hitler himself took part in the drafting of the program, at least not yet as a leader—the program included that point which played a prominent part as a defensive point among large sections of the German people. Shortly before that there had been the Räte-Republik in Munich and the murder of hostages, and here, too the leaders were mostly Jews.[1] It can be understood, therefore, that a program drawn up in Munich by simple people quite naturally took this up as a defense point. News also came of a Räte-Republik in Hungary—again consisting mainly of Jews. All this had made a very strong impression. When the program became known, the Party—which was at that time extremely small—was at first not taken seriously and was laughed at. But then, from the very beginning, a concentrated and most bitter attack on the part of the entire Jewish press, or the Jewish-influenced press, was started against the movement. Everywhere Jewry was in the lead in the fight against National Socialism, whether in the press, in politics, in cultural life by making National Socialism contemptible and ridiculous, or in the economic sphere. Whoever was a National Socialist could not get a position; the National Socialist businessman could not get supplies or space for advertisements, and so

[1]In early 1919, in the wake of World War I, authority in the Bavarian capital of Munich dissolved. Workers' and soldiers' councils proclaimed a Räte-Republik, or Soviet Republic, on April 5 and pressed for democratization. A week later, in circumstances of virtual civil war, the Räte-Republik was taken over by Communists led by Eugen Leviné, of Jewish background. The Communists claimed that it was time for the dictatorship of the proletariat. Until early May, when the Räte-Republik was crushed by troops sent from Berlin, Munich was a symbol for many Germans of a wild revolutionary potential activated by Jews, who were carrying on the work of the Russian Revolution.

on. All this naturally resulted in a strong defensive attitude on the part of the Party and led from the very beginning to an intensification of the fight, such as had not originally been the intention of the program. For the program aimed very definitely at one thing above all—that Germany should be led by Germans. And it was desired that the leadership, especially the political shaping of the fate of the German people, should be in the hands of German persons who could raise up the spirit of the German people again in a way that people of a different kind could not. Therefore the main point was at first merely to exclude Jewry from politics, from the leadership of the State. Later on, the cultural field was also included because of the very strong fight which had developed, particularly in this sphere, between Jewry on the one side and National Socialism on the other. . . . The extraordinary intensification which set in later did not really start in until after the events of 1938, and then to a still greater extent in the war years. . . .

STAHMER: In the Indictment it says that the destruction of the Jewish race was part of the planning of aggressive wars.

GÖRING: That has nothing to do with the planning of aggressive wars; also, the destruction of the Jewish race was not planned in advance. . . .

60

TELFORD TAYLOR

*Memorandum on a Separate Trial
for the Murder of European Jewry*

February 6, 1947

1. It has been suggested to me that it would be desirable to have an entire case which would concern itself only with the charge that the Nazis exterminated approximately 6,000,000 European Jews. It is represented that this is by far the most important

Memorandum from Telford Taylor to Mr. Ervin (6 February 1947). Box 22, Folder 6: Flick Case No. 2. Paul H. Gantt Nuremberg Trial Papers, Towson University Archives.

and sinister item in the entire Nazi history, and that this wide-scale slaughter of Jews has nevertheless been submerged in the great variety of other charges which were dealt with in the International Trial. . . .

2. I have come to no conclusion on the wisdom of this proposal: however, I would like to give it some consideration and I would like to have your thoughts and recommendations on this subject.

3. One difficulty which occurs to me at the outset is that of selecting the defendants for such a trial. We are not concerned here with people in the concentration camp or camp commandant level; we are concerned with the central planners and organizers. With the exception of such people as Eichmann whom we have never been able to locate, I am not aware that there are many leading Nazi officials who were primarily concerned with the extermination of Jews, as such. Rather it is my impression that such an extermination was sort of a Standing Operating Procedure in many fields of activity, and that most of the people who played an important role in ordering and planning the Jewish extermination probably committed many other crimes as well. In all events, I would like to have this particular aspect of the question given careful consideration.

61

ALFRED THOMA

Defense of Alfred Rosenberg on the Persecution of the Jews

July 10, 1946

DR. THOMA: Now I come to a new subject: Contrary to the assumption of the Prosecution, Rosenberg was in no instance the instigator of a persecution of Jews, any more than he was one of the leaders and originators of the policy adopted by the Party

International Military Tribunal, *Trial of the Major War Criminals before the International Military Tribunal, Nuremberg, 14 November 1945–1 October 1946,* 42 vols. Nuremberg: International Military Tribunal, 1947, 18:92–95.

and the Reich, as the Prosecution claims. . . . Rosenberg was certainly a convinced anti-Semite and expressed his conviction and the reasons for it both verbally and in writing. However, in his case anti-Semitism was not the most outstanding of his activities. . . . Anti-Semitism was for him a negative element, and his chief and most positive efforts were directed toward the proclamation of a new German intellectual attitude, and a new German culture. Because he found this endangered after 1918, he became an opponent of Jewry. Even such different personalities as Von Papen, Von Neurath, and Raeder now confess to their belief that the penetration of the Jewish element into the whole of public life was so great that a change had to be brought about. It strikes me as very important, however, that the nature of Rosenberg's anti-Semitism was intellectual above all. For example, at the Party Rally of 1933 he explicitly mentioned a "chivalrous solution" of the Jewish question. We never heard Rosenberg use expressions like "We must annihilate the Jews wherever we find them; we shall take measures that will insure success. We must abandon all feelings of sympathy." The Prosecution itself quotes the following as an expression of the program Rosenberg set up for himself . . .

"After the Jews have been ousted as a matter of course from all official positions, the Jewish question will find a decisive solution through the setting up of ghettos."

GENERAL R. A. RUDENKO: Mr. President, rather reluctantly I interrupt counsel for the defense, and I do not like to take the time of the Tribunal, but what I just heard is going beyond any permissible limits. When the defendants sitting in the dock tried to express their Fascist views, this was deemed inappropriate and cut short by the Tribunal.

I think that it is absolutely inadmissible that defense counsel should use this place to promote antihuman propaganda; I cannot understand the contention of the lawyer who alleges the existence of a noble, spiritual anti-Semitism which Rosenberg advocates and that Rosenberg's belief in gathering all Jews in ghettos was chivalrous. Please note that the lawyer is not quoting any Nazi leader but expresses his own opinion, and I protest against the use of the International Military Tribunal for the spreading of Fascist propaganda. I ask the Tribunal to consider this objection of mine and to take appropriate action.

THOMA: May it please the Tribunal—may I make an answer to that?

THE PRESIDENT: Dr. Thoma, we don't think it is necessary to trouble you. The Tribunal thinks—there may be, of course, differences of opinion as to the use of words in the course of your argument, but they see no reason for stopping you in the argument that you are presenting to the Tribunal.

THOMA: Thank you, My Lord.

May it please the Tribunal, after what General Rudenko has said, I should like to make one statement. In my speech I have tried to argue upon the statements of the Prosecution and nothing else. I would like to say something else. The words "chivalrous solution of the Jewish question" were not my expression; I just quoted that as a statement made by Rosenberg a long time before he came into this Court. The Prosecution quotes the following as Rosenberg's statement of a program: "The Jewish question . . ." and so on; I have already read that.

It was not a mere question of chance that Rosenberg did not take part in the boycotting of Jews in 1933, that he was not called upon to work out the laws against the Jews in 1933, 1934, 1935, and so on (expatriation, prohibition of marriages, withdrawal of the right to vote, expulsion from all important positions and offices). Above all, he never took part in the action of 1938 against the Jews, nor in the destruction of synagogues, nor in anti-Semitic demonstrations. Neither was he the instigator in the background who sent out, or ordered, lesser people to commit certain actions. To be sure, Rosenberg was a true follower of Hitler, who took up Hitler's slogans and passed them on. For example, the motto, "The Jewish question will be solved only when the last Jew has left Germany and the European continent," and once the slogan of "Extermination of Jewry."

Exaggerated expressions were always part of the National Socialist weapons of propaganda. A Hitler speech was hardly imaginable without insults to his internal or external political opponents, or without threats of extermination. Every one of Hitler's speeches was echoed a million times by Goebbels down to the last speaker of the Party in a small country inn. The same sentences and words which Hitler had used were repeated, and not only in all the political speeches, but in the German press as well, in all the editorials and essays, until, weeks or months later, a new speech was given which brought about a new echo of a similar kind.

Rosenberg was no exception. He repeated, as everyone did, all of Hitler's slogans, including that of the "solution of the Jewish question," and once also that of the "extermination of Jewry." Apparently, like Hitler's other supporters, he gave as much or as little thought to the fact that in reality none of those phrases were clear but that they had a sinister double meaning and, while they might have meant real expulsion, they might also have implied the physical annihilation and murder of the Jews.

May I remind the Tribunal at this point that Rosenberg, during his testimony, made a reference to a speech of the British Prime Minister in the House of Commons in September 1943, in which speech it was stated that Prussian militarism and National Socialism had to be exterminated root and branch. No German interpreted that literally, and I believe no one interpreted it to mean that German soldiers and the National Socialism had to be exterminated physically.

Aside from the knowledge and will of the German people, and aside from the knowledge and will of the majority of the leadership of the Party—that is to say, known only to Bormann, Himmler, and Eichmann—there was hatched and carried out, from 1941 onward, a mass crime which surpassed all human concepts of reason and morality. The "Jewish question" was developed even further and brought to a so-called "final solution." . . .

I believe I can say that Rosenberg never aimed, either openly or in secret, at the physical extermination of the Jews. His reserve and moderation were certainly no mere tactics. The slipping of anti-Semitism into crime took place without his knowledge or will. The fact in itself that he preached anti-Semitism justifies his punishment as the murderer of Jews as little as one could hold Rousseau and Mirabeau responsible for the subsequent horrors of the French Revolution.

62

WALTHER FUNK

Statement of Remorse

May 6, 1946

FUNK: I did not know before that I had been accused of being a murderer and a thief and I do not know what else. I was sick for 9 or
10 weeks, and from the hospital bed I was brought here during
the night. During those days my interrogations here started
immediately. I must admit that the American officer who interrogated me, Colonel Murrey Gurfein, conducted the interrogation with extreme consideration and forbearance and again and
again called a halt when I was unable to go on. And when I was
reproached with these measures of terror and violence against
the Jews I suffered a spiritual breakdown, because at that moment
it came to my mind with all clearness that the catastrophe took
its course from here on down to the horrible and dreadful things
of which we have heard here and of which I knew, in part at least,
from the time of my captivity. I felt a deep sense of shame and of
personal guilt at that moment, and I feel it also today. But that I
issued directives for the execution of the basic orders and laws
which were made, that is no crime against humanity. In this matter I placed the will of the State before my conscience and my
inner sense of duty because, after all, I was the servant of the
State. I also considered myself obliged to act according to the
will of the Führer, the supreme Head of the State, especially since
these measures were necessary for the protection of the Jews, in
order to save them from absolute lack of legal protection, from
further arbitrary acts and violence. Besides, they were compen-
sated and, as can be seen from the circular letter which you have
just quoted, I gave strict instructions to my officials to carry out
these legal directives in a correct and just way.

It is terribly tragic indeed that I in particular am charged
with these things. I have said already that I took no part in

International Military Tribunal, *Trial of the Major War Criminals before the International
Military Tribunal, Nuremberg, 14 November 1945–1 October 1946,* 42 vols. Nuremberg;
International Military Tribunal, 1947, 13:120.

these excesses against the Jews. From the first moment I disapproved of them and condemned them very strongly, and they affected me personally very profoundly. I did everything, as much as was within my power, to continue helping the Jews. I never thought of an extermination of the Jews, and I did not participate in these things in any way.

63

FRANZ von PAPEN

Explanation for Remaining at His Post
June 19, 1946

MAXWELL-FYFE: Why didn't you after this series of murders which had gone on over a period of 4 years, why didn't you break with these people and stand up like General Yorck or any other people that you may think of from history, stand up for your own views and oppose these murderers? Why didn't you do it?

VON PAPEN: If you ask me, Sir David, why despite everything I remained in the service of the Reich, then I can say only that . . . I did my duty to Germany, if you wish to know. I can understand very well, Sir David, that after all the things we know today, after the millions of murders which have taken place, you consider the German people a nation of criminals, and that you cannot understand that this nation has its patriots as well. I did these things in order to serve my country, and I should like to add, Sir David, that up to the time of the Munich Agreement, and even up to the time of the Polish campaign, even the major powers tried, although they knew everything that was going on in Germany, to work with this Germany.

Why do you wish to reproach a patriotic German with acting likewise, and with hoping likewise, for the same thing for which all the major powers hoped?

International Military Tribunal, *Trial of the Major War Criminals before the International Military Tribunal, Nuremberg, 14 November 1945–1 October 1946,* 42 vols. Nuremberg: International Military Tribunal, 1947, 16:416.

8
LAST WORDS

64

HERMANN GÖRING

Final Statement

August 31, 1946

The Prosecution brings forward individual statements over a period of 25 years, which were made under completely different circumstances and without any consequences arising from them at the time, and quotes them as proof of intent and guilt, statements which can easily be made in the excitement of the moment and of the atmosphere that prevailed at the time. There is probably not one leading personage on the opposing side who did not speak or write similarly in the course of a quarter of a century.

Out of all the happenings of these 25 years, from conferences, speeches, laws, actions, and decisions, the Prosecution proves that everything was desired and intended from the beginning according to a deliberate sequence and an unbroken connection. This is an erroneous conception which is entirely devoid of logic, and which will be rectified some day by history, after the proceedings here have proved the incorrectness of these allegations. . . .

International Military Tribunal, *Trial of the Major War Criminals before the International Military Tribunal, Nuremberg, 14 November 1945–1 October 1946,* 42 vols. Nuremberg: International Military Tribunal, 1947, 22:367–68.

Mr. Jackson stated . . . that one cannot accuse and punish a state, but rather that one must hold the leaders responsible. One seems to forget that Germany was a sovereign state, and that her legislation within the German nation was not subject to the jurisdiction of foreign countries. No state ever gave notice to the Reich at the proper time, pointing out that any activity for National Socialism would be made subject to punishment and persecution. On the other hand, if we, the leaders as individuals, are called to account and condemned — very well; but you cannot punish the German people at the same time. The German people placed their trust in the Führer, and under his authoritarian government they had no influence on events. Without knowledge of the grave crimes which have become known today, the people, loyal, self-sacrificing, and courageous, fought and suffered through the life-and-death struggle which had broken out against their will. The German people are free of guilt.

I did not want a war, nor did I bring it about. I did everything to prevent it by negotiations. After it had broken out, I did everything to assure victory. Since the three greatest powers on earth, together with many other nations, were fighting against us, we finally succumbed to their tremendous superiority.

I stand up for the things that I have done, but I deny most emphatically that my actions were dictated by the desire to subjugate foreign peoples by wars, to murder them, to rob them, or to enslave them, or to commit atrocities or crimes.

The only motive which guided me was my ardent love for my people, its happiness, its freedom, and its life. And for this I call on the Almighty and my German people to witness.

65

RUDOLF HESS

Final Statement

August 31, 1946

HESS: First of all, I should like to make a request to the High Tribunal that I may remain seated because of my state of health.

THE PRESIDENT: Certainly.

HESS: Some of my comrades here can confirm the fact that at the beginning of the proceedings I predicted the following:

(1) That witnesses would appear who, under oath, would make untrue statements while, at the same time, these witnesses could create an absolutely reliable impression and enjoy the best possible reputation.

(2) That it was to be reckoned with that the Court would receive affidavits containing untrue statements.

(3) That the defendants would be astonished and surprised at some German witnesses.

(4) That some of the defendants would act rather strangely: they would make shameless utterances about the Führer; they would incriminate their own people; they would partially incriminate each other, and falsely at that. Perhaps they would even incriminate themselves, and also wrongly.

All of these predictions have come true. . . .

In the years 1936 to 1938 political trials were taking place [in countries outside Germany]. These were characterized by the fact that the defendants accused themselves in an astonishing way. For example, they cited great numbers of crimes which they had committed or which they claimed to have committed. At the end, when death sentences were passed upon them, they clapped in frenzied approval to the astonishment of the world.

But some foreign press correspondents reported that one had the impression that these defendants, through some means

International Military Tribunal, *Trial of the Major War Criminals before the International Military Tribunal, Nuremberg, 14 November 1945–1 October 1946,* 42 vols. Nuremberg: International Military Tribunal, 1947, 22:368–73.

hitherto unknown, had been put into an abnormal state of mind, as a result of which they acted the way they did. . . .

I said before that a certain incident in England caused me to think of the reports of the earlier trials. The reason was that the people around me during my imprisonment acted towards me in a peculiar and incomprehensible way, in a way which led me to conclude that these people somehow were acting in an abnormal state of mind. Some of them—these persons and people around me were changed from time to time. Some of the new ones who came to me in place of those who had been changed had strange eyes. They were glassy and like eyes in a dream. This symptom, however, lasted only a few days and then they made a completely normal impression. They could no longer be distinguished from normal human beings. Not only I alone noticed these strange eyes, but also the physician who attended me at the time, Dr. Johnston, a British Army doctor, a Scotsman.

In the spring of 1942 I had a visitor, a visitor who quite obviously tried to provoke me and acted towards me in a strange way. This visitor also had these strange eyes. Afterwards, Dr. Johnston asked me what I thought of this visitor. He told me—I told him I had the impression that for some reason or other he was not completely normal mentally, whereupon Dr. Johnston did not protest, as I had expected, but agreed with me and asked me whether I had not noticed those strange eyes, these eyes with a dreamy look. Dr. Johnston did not suspect that he himself had exactly the same eyes when he came to me.

The essential point, however, is that in one of the reports of the time, which must still be in the press files on the proceedings—this was in Paris, about the Moscow trial—it said that the defendants had had strange eyes. They had had glazed and dreamy eyes! I have already said that I am convinced that the governments here concerned knew nothing of these happenings. Therefore it would not be in the interest of the British Government either if my statements about what I experienced during my imprisonment were denied publicity in any way, for that would give the impression that something was actually supposed to be concealed here, and that the British Government had actually had a finger in the pie. . . .

Obviously, it would have been of the utmost importance if I had stated under oath what I have to say about the happenings during my own imprisonment in England. However, it was impossible for me to persuade my counsel to declare himself willing to put the proper questions to me. It was likewise impossible for me to get another counsel to agree to put these questions to me. But it is of the utmost importance that what I am saying be said under oath. Therefore I now declare once more: I swear by God the Almighty and Omniscient, that I will speak the pure truth, that I shall leave out nothing and add nothing. I ask the High Tribunal, therefore, to consider everything which I shall say from now on as under oath. Concerning my oath, I should also like to say that I am not a churchgoer; I have no spiritual relationship with the Church, but I am a deeply religious person. I am convinced that my belief in God is stronger than that of most other people. I ask the High Tribunal to give all the more weight to everything which I declare under oath, expressly calling God as my witness. In the spring of 1942 . . .

THE PRESIDENT *[Interposing]:* I must draw the attention of the Defendant Hess to the fact that he has already spoken for 20 minutes, and the Tribunal has indicated to the defendants that it cannot allow them to continue to make statements of great length at this stage of the proceedings.

We have to hear all the defendants. The Tribunal, therefore, hopes that the Defendant Hess will conclude his speech.

HESS: Mr. President, may I point out that I was taking into account the fact that I am the only defendant who, up to now, has not been able to make a statement here. For what I have to say here, I could only have said as a witness if the proper questions had been put to me. But as I have already stated . . .

THE PRESIDENT: I do not propose to argue with the defendants. The Tribunal has made its order that the defendants shall only make short statements. The Defendant Hess had full opportunity to go into the witness box and give his evidence upon oath. He chose not to do so. He is now making a statement, and he will be treated like the other defendants and will be confined to a short statement.

HESS: Therefore, Mr. President, I shall forego making the statements which I had wanted to make in connection with the things I have just said. I ask you to listen to only a few more concluding words, which are of a more general nature and have nothing to do with the things that I have just stated.

The statements which my counsel made in my name before the High Tribunal I permitted to be made for the sake of the future judgment of my people and of history. That is the only thing which matters to me. I do not defend myself against accusers to whom I deny the right to bring charges against me and my fellow-countrymen. I will not discuss accusations which concern things which are purely German matters and therefore of no concern to foreigners. I raise no protest against statements which are aimed at attacking my honor, the honor of the German people. I consider such slanderous attacks by the enemy as a proof of honor.

I was permitted to work for many years of my life under the greatest son whom my people has brought forth in its thousand-year history. Even if I could, I would not want to erase this period of time from my existence. I am happy to know that I have done my duty to my people, my duty as a German, as a National Socialist, as a loyal follower of my Führer. I do not regret anything.

If I were to begin all over again, I would act just as I have acted, even if I knew that in the end I should meet a fiery death at the stake. No matter what human beings may do, I shall some day stand before the judgment seat of the Eternal. I shall answer to Him, and I know He will judge me innocent.

66

ALBERT SPEER

Final Statement

August 31, 1946

Mr. President, may it please the Tribunal: Hitler and the collapse of his system have brought a time of tremendous suffering upon the German people. The useless continuation of this war and the unnecessary destruction make the work of reconstruction more difficult. Privation and misery have come to the German people. After this Trial, the German people will despise and condemn Hitler as the proven author of its misfortune. But the world will

International Military Tribunal, *Trial of the Major War Criminals before the International Military Tribunal, Nuremberg, 14 November 1945–1 October 1946,* 42 vols. Nuremberg: International Military Tribunal, 1947, 22:405–7.

learn from these happenings not only to hate dictatorship as a form of government, but to fear it.

Hitler's dictatorship differed in one fundamental point from all its predecessors in history. His was the first dictatorship in the present period of modern technical development, a dictatorship which made complete use of all technical means in a perfect manner for the domination of its own nation.

Through technical devices such as radio and loudspeaker 80 million people were deprived of independent thought. It was thereby possible to subject them to the will of one man. The telephone, teletype, and radio made it possible, for instance, for orders from the highest sources to be transmitted directly to the lowest-ranking units, where, because of the high authority, they were carried out without criticism. Another result was that numerous offices and headquarters were directly attached to the supreme leadership, from which they received their sinister orders directly. Also, one of the results was a far-reaching supervision of the citizen of the state and the maintenance of a high degree of secrecy for criminal events.

Perhaps to the outsider this machinery of the state may appear like the lines of a telephone exchange — apparently without system. But like the latter, it could be served and dominated by one single will.

Earlier dictators during their work of leadership needed highly-qualified assistants, even at the lowest level, men who could think and act independently. The totalitarian system in the period of modern technical development can dispense with them; the means of communication alone make it possible to mechanize the subordinate leadership. As a result of this there arises a new type: the uncritical recipient of orders.

We had only reached the beginning of the development. The nightmare of many a man that one day nations could be dominated by technical means was all but realized in Hitler's totalitarian system.

Today the danger of being terrorized by technocracy threatens every country in the world. In modern dictatorship this appears to me inevitable. Therefore, the more technical the world becomes, the more necessary is the promotion of individual freedom and the individual's awareness of himself as a counterbalance.

Hitler not only took advantage of technical developments to dominate his own people—he almost succeeded, by means of his technical lead, in subjugating the whole of Europe. It was merely due to a few fundamental shortcomings of organization such as are typical in a dictatorship because of the absence of criticism, that he did not have twice as many tanks, aircraft, and submarines before 1942.

But, if a modern industrial state utilizes its intelligence, its science, its technical developments, and its production for a number of years in order to gain a lead in the sphere of armament, then even with a sparing use of its manpower it can, because of its technical superiority, completely overtake and conquer the world, if other nations should employ their technical abilities during that same period on behalf of the cultural progress of humanity.

The more technical the world becomes, the greater this danger will be, and the more serious will be an established lead in the technical means of warfare.

This war ended with remote-controlled rockets, aircraft traveling at the speed of sound, new types of submarines, torpedoes which find their own target, with atom bombs, and with the prospect of a horrible kind of chemical warfare.

Of necessity the next war will be overshadowed by these new destructive inventions of the human mind.

In 5 or 10 years the technique of warfare will make it possible to fire rockets from continent to continent with uncanny precision. By atomic power it can destroy one million people in the center of New York in a matter of seconds with a rocket operated, perhaps, by only 10 men, invisible, without previous warning, faster than sound, by day and by night. Science is able to spread pestilence among human beings and animals and to destroy crops by insect warfare. Chemistry has developed terrible weapons with which it can inflict unspeakable suffering upon helpless human beings.

Will there ever again be a nation which will use the technical discoveries of this war for the preparation of a new war, while the rest of the world is employing the technical progress of this war for the benefit of humanity, thus attempting to create a slight compensation for its horrors? As a former minister of a highly developed armament system, it is my last duty to say the following:

A new large-scale war will end with the destruction of human culture and civilization. Nothing can prevent unconfined engineering and science from completing the work of destroying human beings, which it has begun in so dreadful a way in this war.

Therefore this Trial must contribute towards preventing such degenerate wars in the future, and towards establishing rules whereby human beings can live together.

Of what importance is my own fate, after everything that has happened, in comparison with this high goal?

During the past centuries the German people have contributed much towards the creation of human civilization. Often they have made these contributions in times when they were just as powerless and helpless as they are today. Worthwhile human beings will not let themselves be driven to despair. They will create new and lasting values, and under the tremendous pressure brought to bear upon everyone today these new works will be of particular greatness.

But if the German people create new cultural values in the unavoidable times of their poverty and weakness, and at the same time in the period of their reconstruction, then they will have in that way made the most valuable contribution to world events which they could make in their position.

It is not the battles of war alone which shape the history of humanity, but also, in a higher sense, the cultural achievements which one day will become the common property of all humanity. A nation which believes in its future will never perish. May God protect Germany and the culture of the West.

67

Judgment: "The Law of the Charter"
September 30–October 1, 1946

The jurisdiction of the Tribunal is defined in the Agreement and Charter, and the crimes coming within the jurisdiction of the Tribunal, for which there shall be individual responsibility, are set out in Article 6. The law of the Charter is decisive, and binding upon the Tribunal.

The making of the Charter was the exercise of the sovereign legislative power by the countries to which the German Reich unconditionally surrendered; and the undoubted right of these

International Military Tribunal, *Trial of the Major War Criminals before the International Military Tribunal, Nuremberg, 14 November 1945–1 October 1946,* 42 vols. Nuremberg: International Military Tribunal, 1947, 1:218–24.

countries to legislate for the occupied territories has been recognized by the civilized world. The Charter is not an arbitrary exercise of power on the part of the victorious Nations, but in the view of the Tribunal, as will be shown, it is the expression of international law existing at the time of its creation; and to that extent is itself a contribution to international law. . . .

The Charter makes the planning or waging of a war of aggression or a war in violation of international treaties a crime; and it is therefore not strictly necessary to consider whether and to what extent aggressive war was a crime before the execution of the London Agreement. But in view of the great importance of the questions of law involved, the Tribunal has heard full argument from the Prosecution and the Defense, and will express its view on the matter.

It was urged on behalf of the defendants that a fundamental principle of all law—international and domestic—is that there can be no punishment of crime without a pre-existing law. *"Nullum crimen sine lege, nulla poena sine lege."* It was submitted that *ex post facto* punishment is abhorrent to the law of all civilized nations, that no sovereign power had made aggressive war a crime at the time that the alleged criminal acts were committed, that no statute had defined aggressive war, that no penalty had been fixed for its commission, and no court had been created to try and punish offenders.

In the first place, it is to be observed that the maxim *nullum crimen sine lege* is not a limitation of sovereignty, but is in general a principle of justice. To assert that it is unjust to punish those who in defiance of treaties and assurances have attacked neighboring states without warning is obviously untrue, for in such circumstances the attacker must know that he is doing wrong, and so far from it being unjust to punish him, it would be unjust if his wrong were allowed to go unpunished. Occupying the positions they did in the Government of Germany, the defendants, or at least some of them must have known of the treaties signed by Germany, outlawing recourse to war for the settlement of international disputes; they must have known that they were acting in defiance of all international law when in complete deliberation they carried out their designs of invasion and aggression. On this view of the case alone, it would appear that the maxim has no application to the present facts.

This view is strongly reinforced by a consideration of the state of international law in 1939, so far as aggressive war is concerned. The General Treaty for the Renunciation of War of 27 August 1928, more generally known as the Pact of Paris or the Kellogg-Briand Pact, was binding on 63 nations, including Germany, Italy, and Japan at the outbreak of war in 1939. . . . The question is, what was the legal effect of this Pact? The nations who signed the Pact or adhered to it unconditionally condemned recourse to war for the future as an instrument of policy, and expressly renounced it. After the signing of the Pact, any nation resorting to war as an instrument of national policy breaks the Pact. In the opinion of the Tribunal, the solemn renunciation of war as an instrument of national policy necessarily involves the proposition that such a war is illegal in international law; and that those who plan and wage such a war, with its inevitable and terrible consequences, are committing a crime in so doing. War for the solution of international controversies undertaken as an instrument of national policy certainly includes a war of aggression, and such a war is therefore outlawed by the Pact. . . . But it is argued that the Pact does not expressly enact that such wars are crimes, or set up courts to try those who make such wars. To that extent the same is true with regard to the laws of war contained in the Hague Convention. The Hague Convention of 1907 prohibited resort to certain methods of waging war. These included the inhumane treatment of prisoners, the employment of poisoned weapons, the improper use of flags of truce, and similar matters. Many of these prohibitions had been enforced long before the date of the Convention; but since 1907 they have certainly been crimes, punishable as offenses against the laws of war; yet the Hague Convention nowhere designates such practices as criminal, nor is any sentence prescribed, nor any mention made of a court to try and punish offenders. For many years past, however, military tribunals have tried and punished individuals guilty of violating the rules of land warfare laid down by this Convention. In the opinion of the Tribunal, those who wage aggressive war are doing that which is equally illegal, and of much greater moment than a breach of one of the rules of the Hague Convention. In interpreting the words of the Pact, it must be remembered that international law is not the product of an international legislature, and that such international agreements as the Pact of Paris have to deal with general principles of law, and not with administrative matters of procedure. The law of war is to be found not only in treaties, but in the customs and practices of states which gradually obtained universal recognition, and from the general principles of justice applied by jurists and practised by military courts. This law is not static, but by continual adaptation follows the needs of a changing world. Indeed, in many cases treaties do no more than express and define for more accurate reference the principles of law already existing. . . .

It was submitted that international law is concerned with the actions of sovereign States, and provides no punishment for individuals; and further, that where the act in question is an act of State, those who carry it out are not personally responsible, but are protected by the doctrine of the sovereignty of the State. In the opinion of the Tribunal, both these submissions must be rejected. That international law imposes duties and liabilities upon individuals as well as upon States has long been recognized. . . .

It was also submitted on behalf of most of these defendants that in doing what they did they were acting under the orders of Hitler, and therefore cannot be held responsible for the acts committed by them in carrying out these orders. The Charter specifically provides in Article 8:

> "The fact that the Defendant acted pursuant to order of his Government or of a superior shall not free him from responsibility, but may be considered in mitigation of punishment."

The provisions of this article are in conformity with the law of all nations. That a soldier was ordered to kill or torture in violation of the international law of war has never been recognized as a defense to such acts of brutality, though, as the Charter here provides, the order may be urged in mitigation of the punishment. The true test, which is found in varying degrees in the criminal law of most nations, is not the existence of the order, but whether moral choice was in fact possible. . . .

68

Judgment: "The Law as to the Common Plan or Conspiracy"

September 30–October 1, 1946

The Prosecution says, in effect, that any significant participation in the affairs of the Nazi Party or Government is evidence of a participation in a conspiracy that is in itself criminal. Conspiracy is not defined in the Charter. But in the opinion of the Tribunal the conspiracy must be clearly outlined in its criminal purpose. It must not be too far removed from the time of decision and of action. The planning, to be criminal, must not rest merely on the declarations of a party program, such as are found in the 25 points of the Nazi Party, announced in 1920, or the political affirmations expressed in *Mein Kampf* in later years. The Tribunal must examine whether a concrete plan to wage war existed, and determine the participants in that concrete plan.

It is not necessary to decide whether a single master conspiracy between the defendants has been established by the evidence. The seizure of power by the Nazi Party, and the subsequent domination by the Nazi State of all spheres of economic and social life must of course be remembered when the later plans for waging war are examined. That plans were made to wage war, as early as 5 November 1937, and probably before that, is apparent. And thereafter, such preparations continued in many directions, and against the peace of many countries. Indeed the threat of war — and war itself if necessary — was an integral part of the Nazi policy. But the evidence establishes with certainty the existence of many separate plans rather than a single conspiracy embracing them all. That Germany was rapidly moving to complete dictatorship from the moment that the Nazis seized power, and progressively in the direction of war, has been overwhelmingly shown in the ordered sequence of aggressive acts and wars already set out in this Judgment.

International Military Tribunal, *Trial of the Major War Criminals before the International Military Tribunal, Nuremberg, 14 November 1945–1 October 1946*, 42 vols. Nuremberg: International Military Tribunal, 1947, 1:225–26.

In the opinion of the Tribunal, the evidence establishes the common planning to prepare and wage war by certain of the defendants. It is immaterial to consider whether a single conspiracy to the extent and over the time set out in the Indictment has been conclusively proved. Continued planning, with aggressive war as the objective, has been established beyond doubt. . . . The argument that such common planning cannot exist where there is complete dictatorship is unsound. A plan in the execution of which a number of persons participate is still a plan, even though conceived by only one of them; and those who execute the plan do not avoid responsibility by showing that they acted under the direction of the man who conceived it. Hitler could not make aggressive war by himself. He had to have the cooperation of statesmen, military leaders, diplomats, and business men. When they, with knowledge of his aims, gave him their cooperation, they made themselves parties to the plan he had initiated. They are not to be deemed innocent because Hitler made use of them, if they knew what they were doing. That they were assigned to their tasks by a dictator does not absolve them from responsibility for their acts. The relation of leader and follower does not preclude responsibility here any more than it does in the comparable tyranny of organized domestic crime.

Count One, however, charges not only the conspiracy to commit aggressive war, but also to commit War Crimes and Crimes against Humanity. But the Charter does not define as a separate crime any conspiracy except the one to commit acts of aggressive war. Article 6 of the Charter provides:

> "Leaders, organizers, instigators, and accomplices participating in the formulation or execution of a Common Plan or Conspiracy to commit any of the foregoing crimes are responsible for all acts performed by any persons in execution of such plan."

In the opinion of the Tribunal these words do not add a new and separate crime to those already listed. The words are designed to establish the responsibility of persons participating in a common plan. The Tribunal will therefore disregard the charges in Count One that the defendants conspired to commit War Crimes and Crimes against Humanity, and will consider only the common plan to prepare, initiate, and wage aggressive war. . . .

69

Judgment: "The Persecution of the Jews"

September 30–October 1, 1946

The persecution of the Jews at the hands of the Nazi Government
has been proved in the greatest detail before the Tribunal. It is a
record of consistent and systematic inhumanity on the greatest
scale. . . .

The Nazi persecution of Jews in Germany before the war,
severe and repressive as it was, cannot compare, however, with
the policy pursued during the war in the occupied territories.
Originally the policy was similar to that which had been in force
inside Germany. Jews were required to register, were forced to
live in ghettos, to wear the yellow star, and were used as slave
laborers. In the summer of 1941, however, plans were made for
the "final solution" of the Jewish question in Europe. This "final
solution" meant the extermination of the Jews, which early in 1939
Hitler had threatened would be one of the consequences of an
outbreak of war, and a special section in the Gestapo under Adolf
Eichmann, as head of Section B 4 of the Gestapo, was formed to
carry out the policy.

The plan for exterminating the Jews was developed shortly
after the attack on the Soviet Union. Einsatzgruppen of the Security Police and SD, formed for the purpose of breaking the resistance of the population of the areas lying behind the German
armies in the East, were given the duty of exterminating the Jews
in those areas. . . .

These atrocities were all part and parcel of the policy inaugurated in 1941, and it is not surprising that there should be evidence
that one or two German officials entered vain protests against the
brutal manner in which the killings were carried out. But the methods employed never conformed to a single pattern. The massacres of Rowno and Dubno, of which the German engineer Graebe

---

International Military Tribunal, *Trial of the Major War Criminals before the International
Military Tribunal, Nuremberg, 14 November 1945–1 October 1946,* 42 vols. Nuremberg:
International Military Tribunal, 1947, 1:247, 249–53.

spoke, were examples of one method; the systematic extermination of Jews in concentration camps, was another. . . .

Evidence was given of the treatment of the inmates before and after their extermination. There was testimony that the hair of women victims was cut off before they were killed, and shipped to Germany, there to be used in the manufacture of mattresses. The clothes, money, and valuables of the inmates were also salvaged and sent to the appropriate agencies for disposition. After the extermination the gold teeth and fillings were taken from the heads of the corpses and sent to the Reichsbank.

After cremation the ashes were used for fertilizer, and in some instances attempts were made to utilize the fat from the bodies of the victims in the commercial manufacture of soap. Special groups traveled through Europe to find Jews and subject them to the "final solution." German missions were sent to such satellite countries as Hungary and Bulgaria, to arrange for the shipment of Jews to extermination camps and it is known that by the end of 1944, 400,000 Jews from Hungary had been murdered at Auschwitz. Evidence has also been given of the evacuation of 110,000 Jews from part of Rumania for "liquidation." Adolf Eichmann, who had been put in charge of this program by Hitler, has estimated that the policy pursued resulted in the killing of 6 million Jews, of which 4 million were killed in the extermination institutions. . . .

70

Judgment: "The Accused Organizations"
September 30–October 1, 1946

Since declarations of criminality which the Tribunal makes will be used by other courts in the trial of persons on account of their membership in the organizations found to be criminal, the Tribunal feels it appropriate to make the following recommendations:

International Military Tribunal, *Trial of the Major War Criminals before the International Military Tribunal, Nuremberg, 14 November 1945–1 October 1946,* 42 vols. Nuremberg: International Military Tribunal, 1947, 1:256–57.

1. That so far as possible throughout the four zones of occupation in Germany the classifications, sanctions, and penalties be standardized. Uniformity of treatment so far as practical should be a basic principle. This does not, of course, mean that discretion in sentencing should not be vested in the court; but the discretion should be within fixed limits appropriate to the nature of the crime.

2. Law No. 10, to which reference has already been made, leaves punishment entirely in the discretion of the trial court even to the extent of inflicting the death penalty.

The De-Nazification Law of 5 March 1946, however, passed for Bavaria, Greater-Hesse, and Württemberg-Baden, provides definite sentences for punishment in each type of offense. The Tribunal recommends that in no case should punishment imposed under Law No. 10 upon any members of an organization or group declared by the Tribunal to be criminal exceed the punishment fixed by the De-Nazification Law. No person should be punished under both laws.

3. The Tribunal recommends to the Control Council that Law No. 10 be amended to prescribe limitations on the punishment which may be imposed for membership in a criminal group or organization so that such punishment shall not exceed the punishment prescribed by the De-Nazification Law. . . .

9

Assessment

71

HENRY L. STIMSON

"Nuremberg: Landmark in Law"

January 1947

The defendants at Nuremberg were leaders of the most highly
organized and extensive wickedness in history. It was not a trick
of the law which brought them to the bar; it was the "massed
angered forces of common humanity." There were three different
courses open to us when the Nazi leaders were captured: release,
summary punishment, or trial. Release was unthinkable; it would
have been taken as an admission that there was here no crime.
Summary punishment was widely recommended. It would have
satisfied the immediate requirement of the emotions, and in its
own roughhewn way it would have been fair enough, for this was
precisely the type of justice that the Nazis themselves had so
often used. But this fact was in reality the best reason for reject-
ing such a solution. The whole moral position of the victorious
Powers must collapse if their judgments could be enforced only
by Nazi methods. Our anger, as righteous anger, must be subject
to the law. We therefore took the third course and tried the captive criminals by a judicial proceeding. We gave to the Nazis what
they had denied their own opponents—the protection of the Law.

Henry L. Stimson, "Nuremberg: Landmark in Law." *Foreign Affairs* 25 (1947): 179–80,
188–89.

The Nuremberg Tribunal was thus in no sense an instrument of vengeance but the reverse. It was, as Mr. Justice Jackson said in opening the case for the prosecution, "one of the most significant tributes that Power has ever paid to Reason."

The function of the law here, as everywhere, has been to insure fair judgment. By preventing abuse and minimizing error, proceedings under law give dignity and method to the ordinary conscience of mankind. For this purpose the law demands three things: that the defendant be charged with a punishable crime; that he have full opportunity for defense; and that he be judged fairly on the evidence by a proper judicial authority. Should it fail to meet any one of these three requirements, a trial would not be justice. Against these standards, therefore, the judgment of Nuremberg must itself be judged. . . .

A single landmark of justice and honor does not make a world of peace. The Nazi leaders are not the only ones who have renounced and denied the principles of western civilization. They are unique only in the degree and violence of their offenses. In every nation which acquiesced even for a time in their offense, there were offenders. There have been still more culpable offenders in nations which joined before or after in the brutal business of aggression. If we claimed for Nuremberg that it was final justice, or that only these criminals were guilty, we might well be criticized as being swayed by vengeance and not justice. But this is not the claim. The American prosecutor has explicitly stated that he looks uneasily and with great regret upon certain brutalities that have occurred since the ending of the war. He speaks for us all when he says that there has been enough bloodletting in Europe. But the sins of others do not make the Nazi leaders less guilty, and the importance of Nuremberg lies not in any claim that by itself it clears the board, but rather in the pattern it has set. The four nations prosecuting, and the 19 others subscribing to the Charter of the International Military Tribunal, have firmly bound themselves to the principle that aggressive war is a personal and punishable crime.

It is this principle upon which we must henceforth rely for our legal protection against the horrors of war. We must never forget that under modern conditions of life, science and technology, all war has become greatly brutalized, and that no one who joins in it, even in self-defense, can escape becoming also in a measure brutalized. Modern war cannot be limited in its destructive methods and in the inevitable debasement of all participants. A fair scrutiny of the last two World Wars makes clear the steady intensification in the inhumanity of the weapons and methods employed by both the aggressors and the victors. In order to defeat Japanese aggression, we were forced, as Admiral Nimitz has stated, to employ a technique of unrestricted submarine warfare not unlike that which 25 years ago was the proximate cause of our entry into World War I. In the use of strategic air power, the Allies took the lives of hundreds of thousands of civilians in Germany, and in Japan the destruction of civilian life wreaked by our B-29s, even before the final blow of the atomic bombs, was at least proportionately great. It is true that our use of this destructive power, particularly of the atomic bomb, was for the purpose of winning a quick victory over aggressors, so as to minimize the loss of life, not only of our troops but of the civilian populations of our enemies as well, and that this purpose in the case of Japan was clearly effected. But even so, we as well as our enemies have contributed to the proof that the central moral problem is war and not its methods, and that a continuance of war will in all probability end with the destruction of our civilization.

International law is still limited by international politics, and we must not pretend that either can live and grow without the other. But in the judgment of Nuremberg there is affirmed the central principle of peace—that the man who makes or plans to make aggressive war is a criminal. A standard has been raised to which Americans, at least, must repair; for it is only as this standard is accepted, supported and enforced that we can move onward to a world of law and peace.

72

FRANCIS BIDDLE

Andrei Vyshinsky's Visit to Nuremberg

1962

Jackson gave Andrei Vyshinsky, the Soviet delegate to the UN, a large dinner at the Grand Hotel with the usual flow of speeches and liquor. I sat next to a smart-looking general in his party, obviously

Francis Biddle, *In Brief Authority*. Garden City, NY: Doubleday, 1962, 427–28.

eager to please. Like most representatives of his country he spoke not a word of French or English. Through an interpreter we discussed Mark Twain — the Russians had recently discovered him — and the general particularly liked *Life on the Mississippi*. The subject was soon exhausted and, experimentally, I asked him what he thought of the Dardanelles[1] — could not the conflict of interests be worked out? The Soviet claim in the Straits might be recognized to some extent; the difficulty was by no means insoluble. He shrugged, smiled faintly, and answered, "We are not permitted to discuss political problems . . ." Vyshinsky rose to his feet, genial, faintly bibulous, expansive. Vodka, he said, was the enemy of man, and should therefore be consumed . . . He wanted to propose a toast. He raised his glass, and we got up; and now he was speaking very fast, so that it was hard to follow the interpreter. "To the German prisoners, may they all be hanged!" The judges, not quite taking in what he said, touched their lips to the champagne. But it did not take long for them to realize what they had done.

Parker came to my room that night to talk about it. It was "awful" he thought. He hadn't understood. He would not be able to sleep, thinking about it.

I tried to brush it off, saying that no one had noticed what we did, it was a triviality that would be forgotten tomorrow — the essential was our approach to the prisoners. So far that had been fair.

"Supposing Drew Pearson gets hold of it?[2] Can't you see the heading: American judges drink to the death sentence of the men whom they are trying . . ."

"Anyway, we're both in the same boat, John," I ventured.

"But you don't seem to care," he ended, shaking his head, looking at me mournfully.

[1]Biddle's reference to the Dardanelles evokes a postwar clash between Soviet and Western interests. After the disappearance of France and Italy as Mediterranean powers at the end of the war, the Soviets attempted to assert themselves in the Mediterranean, following a traditional path of Russian policy and particularly confronting British interests in the region. At the Potsdam conference in July 1945, Churchill opposed Stalin's request for a Soviet naval base at the Dardanelles, the passage between the Sea of Marmara and the Aegean Sea.

[2]Drew Pearson was an American journalist with a huge popular following thanks to his syndicated newspaper column and regular radio broadcasts. The fear that Drew Pearson might get "hold of it" was therefore not an idle one.

73

OTTO KRANZBÜHLER

Challenge to the Nuremberg Procedures

1964

. . . The prosecution, through a multitude of investigators, had searched all the German archives, which had been confiscated, in order to find material in support of the prosecution's case. And the defense counsel had to live on what was left over, so to speak, from the documents which the prosecutor had introduced into evidence against the defendants. For the defense counsel, access to the archives was barred. Thus, they were unable to make the investigations, always necessary for the defense, but particularly necessary in an historical trial. It is easily recognized what this means whenever judging particular sets of facts in the fields of foreign policy or strategy. A further deficiency was that the defense was restricted to using purely German material; and this was a matter of grave importance in an historical trial. It was the ambition of the prosecution to dispose of the Nazi war criminals on the basis of their own documents, and that meant that foreign archives remained strictly barred. The picture unfolded to the court was thus one-sided and incomplete. As an example, I merely wish to refer to the German-Soviet Treaty of August 23, 1939, the political basis of the occupation of Poland, which was not submitted to the court. Its existence was proved to the court by many detours through affidavits, subject to continued objections on the part of the Russian prosecution. This is one small instance, indicating the historical imperfection and thus the deficiency in fact-finding which appears in a trial of this kind.

The rules that were applied in this trial were not, as is generally assumed, rules of international law. The law of nations, at Nuremberg, was applicable only secondarily. This the judges knew very well, and it appeared to restrict some of them. Primarily, the laws created for the purpose of the Nuremberg Trial were

Otto Kranzbühler, "Nuremberg Eighteen Years Afterwards." *De Paul Law Review* 14 (1964–65): 336–38.

as follows: the London Charter, which was based on discussions between the four occupying powers in July and August, 1945, and which was applicable to the International Military Tribunal; and Law No. 10 of the Control Council which reshaped the rules of the London Charter into German occupation law, with some changes, and which applied to the succeeding American war crime trials. The London Charter was created in a manner which was not calculated to increase the authority of the legislator or the judge. We know about it from the very extensive report submitted by American Chief Prosecutor Jackson to the President of the United States.

No attempt was made to come to a really thorough understanding of what was defensible under international law. The Charter obviously was merely intended to bring certain defendants to prosecution and conviction. As an instance I refer to the discussion aimed at introducing the American concept of conspiracy, *i.e.* a common plan or design to commit criminal acts. The Continental participants at the conference had considerable doubts about including this concept, which was unknown to them, in the rules of the London Charter. But when the argument was brought forward that without this concept a man such as Schacht could not be convicted, this was accepted as a sufficient basis for including conspiracy in the London Charter.

In connection with the origin of the Charter, another phenomenon must be considered that greatly weakens the authority of this administration of justice. Since the French Revolution it has been considered a basic requirement of true administration of justice that the separation of powers is strictly observed in legal proceedings. In Nuremberg, in the International Military Tribunal, it appeared that two of the legislators of the London Charter, that is the American, Jackson, and a Britisher, Sir David Maxwell-Fyfe, acted as chief prosecutors, thus as part of the executive power, while two other legislators of the London Charter, a Frenchman, Falco, and a Russian, Nikichenkow, reappeared at Nuremberg in the capacity of judges. By this personal overlapping, the doctrine of separation of powers was grossly neglected and thus the authority of the administration of justice greatly impaired from the very outset. . . .

74

HENRY L. STIMSON

Assessment of the Judgment
January 1947

Not having made a study of the evidence presented in the case with special reference to each defendant, I am not qualified to pass judgment on the verdicts and sentences of the Tribunal against individuals and criminal groups. I have, however, heard no claim that these sentences were too severe. The Tribunal's findings as to the law are on the whole encouraging. The charge of aggressive war was accepted and ably explained. The charge of war crimes was sustained almost without comment. The charge of crimes against humanity was limited by the Tribunal to include only activities pursued in connection with the crime of war. The Tribunal eliminated from its jurisdiction the question of the criminal accountability of those responsible for wholesale persecution before the outbreak of the war in 1939. With this decision I do not here venture to quarrel, but its effect appears to me to involve a reduction of the meaning of crimes against humanity to a point where they become practically synonymous with war crimes.

If there is a weakness in the Tribunal's findings, I believe it lies in its very limited construction of the legal concept of conspiracy. That only eight of the 22 defendants should have been found guilty on the count of conspiracy to commit the various crimes involved in the indictment seems to me surprising. I believe that the Tribunal would have been justified in a broader construction of the law of conspiracy, and under such a construction it might well have found a different verdict in a case like that of Schacht.

In this first great international trial, however, it is perhaps as well that the Tribunal has very rigidly interpreted both the law and the evidence. In this connection we may observe that only in the case of Rudolf Hess, sentenced to life imprisonment, does the punishment of any of the defendants depend solely on the count of aggressive war. All of those who have been hanged were

Henry L. Stimson, "Nuremberg: Landmark in Law." *Foreign Affairs* 25 (1947): 187–88.

convicted of war crimes or crimes against humanity, and all but one were convicted of both. Certainly, then, the charge of aggressive war has not been established in international law at the expense of any innocent lives.

The judgment of the Tribunal is thus, in its findings of guilt, beyond challenge. We may regret that some of the charges were not regarded as proven and some of the defendants not found clearly guilty. But we may take pride in the restraint of a tribunal which has so clearly insisted upon certain proof of guilt. It is far better that a Schacht should go free than that a judge should compromise his conscience.

The Defendants and Their Fates

Martin Bormann (1900–1945). Head of the party chancellery and secretary to Adolf Hitler, Bormann was by the end of the war the closest confidant of the Führer and one of the most powerful men in Nazi Germany. Disappeared in 1945. Tried and sentenced to death in absentia. Formally pronounced dead by a West German court in 1973.

Karl Dönitz (1891–1980). Grand admiral of the German navy, Dönitz commanded the navy's submarine fleet from 1935 and succeeded Raeder as commander in chief of the German navy in 1943. Named head of state by Hitler just before his suicide. Sentenced to ten years' imprisonment. Released in 1956.

Hans Frank (1900–1946). The Nazi Party's leading jurist, Frank was governor general of the Generalgouvernement, responsible for the civil administration of that part of German-occupied Poland not incorporated into the Reich. Hanged.

Wilhelm Frick (1877–1946). Reich minister of the interior from 1933 to 1943, Frick was one of Hitler's closest advisers before the Nazis came to power. From 1943 to the end of the war he was Reich protector of Bohemia and Moravia. Hanged.

Hans Fritzsche (1900–1953). A Nazi propagandist, Fritzsche was head of radio broadcasting in Joseph Goebbels's Reich Ministry of Propaganda from 1942 until the end of the war. Acquitted. Convicted by a German de-Nazification court in 1947, he was released in 1950.

Walther Funk (1890–1960). Schacht's successor as minister of economics, Funk held this post from 1937 to 1945. Sentenced to life imprisonment. Released in 1957 for health reasons.

Hermann Göring (1893–1946). Reichsmarschall and commander of the Luftwaffe, president of the Reichstag, and plenipotentiary of the four-year Plan. Until 1942 he was the most powerful personality in Nazi Germany after Hitler. Sentenced to hang, but committed suicide before his execution.

Rudolf Hess (1894–1987). Deputy leader of the Nazi Party and, after Göring, the third man in Nazi Germany, Hess flew to Scotland on May 10, 1941, in an apparent effort to persuade the British that Germany had no

259

wish to destroy Britain but sought only a free hand to act against the Soviet Union. Sentenced to life imprisonment, Hess committed suicide in Spandau Prison in 1987.

Alfred Jodl (1890–1946). Colonel general of the German army, Jodl was chief of the operations staff of the Armed Forces High Command (OKW) from 1939 to 1945. Hanged.

Ernst Kaltenbrunner (1903–1946). Of Austrian background, Kaltenbrunner rose to become chief of the Reich Security Main Office in January 1943, succeeding Reinhard Heydrich. Hanged.

Wilhelm Keitel (1882–1946). General field marshal and chief of staff of the Armed Forces High Command (OKW) from 1938 to 1945. Hanged.

Robert Ley (1890–1945). Leader of the German Labor Front from 1933 to 1945, Ley was named in the indictment of the accused but committed suicide in his cell in October 1945 and thus never came to trial.

Constantin von Neurath (1873–1956). An aristocratic diplomat of the old school, Neurath was German foreign minister from 1932 to 1938 and subsequently Reich protector of Bohemia and Moravia until 1941. Sentenced to fifteen years' imprisonment. Released in 1954 for health reasons.

Franz von Papen (1879–1969). A leading Catholic politician in the Weimar period, Papen was chancellor in 1932 and Hitler's deputy chancellor in 1933–1934. Thereafter he was the German minister in Vienna and ambassador in Ankara from 1939 to 1945. Acquitted. Sentenced to eight years' imprisonment by a German de-Nazification court, he was released on appeal in 1949.

Erich Raeder (1876–1960). Grand admiral and commander in chief of the German navy from 1935 until his enforced retirement in 1943, precipitated by differences with Hitler over strategy. Sentenced to life imprisonment. Released for health reasons in 1955.

Joachim von Ribbentrop (1893–1946). Without diplomatic or political experience, Ribbentrop became foreign minister of the Reich in 1938 and remained in office until the end of the war. Hanged.

Alfred Rosenberg (1893–1946). Leading Nazi philosopher and wartime minister for the occupied eastern territories. Hanged.

Fritz Sauckel (1894–1946). Of working-class background, Sauckel became plenipotentiary general for labor mobilization from 1942 to 1945 and was in charge of forced labor for the Reich. Hanged.

Hjalmar Schacht (1877–1970). A leading banker and head of the Reichsbank during the Weimar period, Schacht became president of the Reichsbank in 1933 and a year later minister of economics, a post he held until 1937. Arrested in the wake of the July 1944 assassination plot against Hitler, he finished the war in a concentration camp. Acquitted. Sentenced to eight years' imprisonment by a German de-Nazification court, Schacht was acquitted on appeal in 1948 and was cleared of all charges in 1950.

Baldur von Schirach (1907–1974). Named Reich youth leader in 1933, Schirach was gauleiter and governor of Vienna during the Second World War. Sentenced to twenty years' imprisonment. Released from prison in 1966.

Arthur Seyss-Inquart (1892–1946). Of Austrian background, Seyss-Inquart played a key role in the Anschluss with Austria and served as deputy to Hans Frank in Poland. From 1940 to the end of the war he was Reich commissioner in the occupied Netherlands. Hanged.

Albert Speer (1905–1981). Hitler's favorite architect, Speer was Reich minister for armaments and war production from 1942 to 1945. Sentenced to twenty years' imprisonment. Speer was released from Spandau Prison in 1966 and became a best-selling writer on the Third Reich.

Julius Streicher (1885–1946). Gauleiter of Franconia, Streicher was founder and editor of the anti-semitic newspaper *Der Stürmer.* Dismissed from his party positions for corruption in 1940, Streicher was under house arrest for most of the war. Hanged.

Charges, Verdicts, and Sentences

Key: • = indicted and convicted   o = indicted and acquitted   — = not indicted on charge

DEFENDANT	COUNT ONE	COUNT TWO	COUNT THREE	COUNT FOUR	SENTENCE
Hermann Göring	•	•	•	•	to hang
Joachim von Ribbentrop	•	•	•	•	to hang
Wilhelm Keitel	•	•	•	•	to hang
Alfred Jodl	•	•	•	•	to hang
Alfred Rosenberg	•	•	•	•	to hang
Wilhelm Frick	o	•	•	•	to hang
Arthur Seyss-Inquart	o	•	•	•	to hang
Fritz Sauckel	o	o	•	•	to hang
Martin Bormann (absent)	o	—	•	•	to hang
Ernst Kaltenbrunner	o	—	•	•	to hang
Hans Frank	o	—	•	•	to hang
Julius Streicher	o	—	—	•	to hang
Erich Raeder	•	•	•	—	life in prison
Walther Funk	o	•	•	•	life in prison
Rudolf Hess	•	•	o	o	life in prison
Albert Speer	o	o	•	•	20 years
Baldur von Schirach	o	—	—	•	20 years
Constantin von Neurath	•	•	•	•	15 years
Karl Dönitz	o	•	•	—	10 years
Hans Fritzsche	o	—	o	o	acquitted
Franz von Papen	o	o	—	—	acquitted
Hjalmar Schacht	o	o	—	—	acquitted
Total Guilty	8	12	16	16	19
Total Acquitted	14	4	4	2	3

Chronology of Events Related to the Nuremberg Trial (1919–1946)

1919 *March 29* Report of the Commission of Responsibilities, Conference of Paris.

June 28 Treaty of Versailles, formally ending World War I, signed by German representatives.

1920 *May 7* Allies agree to leave to the German government full and entire responsibility for war crimes trials.

1921 *May 23* German Supreme Court (Reichsgericht) in Leipzig begins hearing the first war crimes case.

1928 *August 27* Kellogg-Briand Pact, signed by the representatives of fifteen governments including Germany, Italy, and Japan, condemns "the recourse to war for the solution of international controversies."

1933 *January 30* Adolf Hitler appointed chancellor of Germany.

1937 *November 7* "Hossbach conference": secret meeting in which Hitler announces his aggressive intentions.

1938 *March 12* Anschluss: incorporation of Austria within the German Reich.

1939 *March 16* Hitler signs a decree establishing a "protectorate" of Bohemia and Moravia; Slovakian Premier Tiso places Slovakia under German protection.

August 23 Molotov-Ribbentrop Pact between Nazi Germany and the Soviet Union.

September 1 Germany attacks Poland.

September 17 Soviet Union attacks Poland.

1941 *December 7* Japanese attack the American fleet at Pearl Harbor; the United States enters the war against Japan.

December 11 Germany declares war on the United States.

1942   *January 13*   St. James's Palace declaration on war crimes by representatives of nine governments in exile.

1943   *November 1*   Moscow conference: Roosevelt, Churchill, and Stalin sign the Moscow Declaration.

November 29   Exchange between Churchill, Roosevelt, and Stalin at the Teheran conference.

1944   *September 5*   Henry Morgenthau Jr.'s memorandum to Roosevelt (the Morgenthau Plan).

September 9   Henry Stimson's memorandum opposing the Morgenthau Plan.

September 15   Quebec conference: Roosevelt and Churchill initial the Morgenthau Plan.

November 11   Murray Bernays's memorandum on German war crimes, signed by Cordell Hull, Henry Stimson, and James Forrestal, sent to Roosevelt.

1945   *January 22*   Henry Stimson, Edward Stettinius Jr., and Francis Biddle propose a trial plan to Roosevelt.

April 12   Death of President Roosevelt.

April 30   Hitler and Goebbels commit suicide.

May 2   Truman appoints Robert Jackson American chief prosecutor to prepare charges against those accused of war crimes.

May 3   American representatives present a trial proposal to British, French, and Soviet representatives at San Francisco.

May 9   Field Marshal Keitel signs the unconditional surrender of Germany at Berlin.

June 26   London conference of American, British, Soviet, and French representatives begins.

August 8   Four-power agreement for a trial signed in London, to which is appended a charter of the International Military Tribunal.

October 6   Indictment of the major German war criminals and six German organizations.

October 29   International Military Tribunal holds its first full meeting at Nuremberg.

November 19   Defense counsel petition the Tribunal.

November 20   Nuremberg trial begins.

November 21   Robert Jackson's opening speech.

1946 *March 13* Hermann Göring begins his testimony.

March 18 Jackson begins his cross-examination of Göring.

August 31 Defendants make their final statements to the court.

September 30 Judges begin reading their judgment.

October 1 Judges complete reading of the judgment.

October 15 Göring commits suicide.

October 16 Execution of the condemned defendants.

Questions for Consideration

1. Following the First World War, the victorious Allies pondered how they should judge and punish their defeated opponents, accused of grave war crimes. In March 1919, they released a report on the matter. What were their conclusions? How did the Americans respond to the views of the majority (Documents 1 and 2)?

2. In 1928, fifteen governments signed the Kellogg-Briand Pact, to which some sixty-five states adhered by the time Hitler came to power (Documents 4, 5, 23). What role did this agreement play at the Nuremberg Trial?

3. By the autumn of 1943, the leaders of the United Kingdom, the United States, and the Soviet Union felt that victory was within their grasp. Meeting in Moscow in November, they issued a declaration outlining their policies toward Nazi Germany in respect of war crimes (Document 6). How would you evaluate their thinking on this matter? To what degree were they agreed upon a policy that eventually emerged as a trial before what became the International Military Tribunal?

4. In response to the very harsh vision for postwar Germany in the Roosevelt administration known as the Morgenthau Plan (Document 8), some American policymakers began to elaborate an alternative approach to dealing with accused German war criminals (Documents 9, 10, 11, 12, and 13). Describe the evolution of this policy. How did this view shape the eventual approach of the Allies (Documents 14, 15, 16, and 17)?

5. What were some of the problems faced by representatives of the Allies, meeting in London in the summer of 1945, as they prepared a blueprint for the International Military Tribunal (Documents 15, 16, and 17)?

6. Article 6 of the Charter of the International Military Tribunal defined the "crimes coming within the jurisdiction of the Tribunal for which there [was to] be individual responsibility" (Documents 17, 19, and 23). What was the significance of Article 6(a)? How important was this provision to the various Allies, and what were some of the issues it raised? Why were *Crimes against Humanity* (Article 6(c)) added to

267

this article? Didn't *War Crimes* cover, for example, crimes against the Jews?

7. What explains the inclusion in the Nuremberg Charter of reference to "a Common Plan or Conspiracy to commit any of the groups of crimes" (Documents 14, 17, 19, 23, 68)? Where did the notion of a "common plan and conspiracy" come from? What was the significance of its inclusion?

8. In addition to twenty-two accused individuals, the Nuremberg Tribunal was empowered to hear cases against five specific organizations and to find them as being criminal (Documents 11, 13, 14, 17, 22, 32 and 70). Why was this step taken? What problems did it entail?

9. In his opening address before the Nuremberg Tribunal, the American Chief Prosecutor, Robert Jackson, addressed one of the most persistent charges against the trial, that it was based upon a violation of the legal principle of *nullum crimen sine lege,* namely that it was applying laws that were unknown to the accused and determined after the wrongs committed by them (Documents 14, 22, 54, 67). How did Jackson deal with this charge, and what do you think of the respective arguments of the two sides?

10. Telford Taylor, a prominent member of the American prosecution staff and later the Chief Prosecutor for the Nuremberg Military Tribunals (Nuremberg Subsequent Proceedings), wrote that in retrospect he opposed Article 8 of the Charter (Document 17), providing that obedience to a superior's command to commit a crime should be "considered [only] in mitigation of punishment." In Taylor's view, "if the defendant did not know, and had no basis for knowing, that the order he had obeyed was unlawful, the defendant should not be held liable at all. If he knew that the order called for unlawful acts, the defendant should be found guilty and allowed to rely on duress or other factors only as a matter of mitigation." What do you think of this view and to what extent was it relevant to cases of particular defendants at Nuremberg? Consider testimony and legal arguments presented in Document 2 .

11. At the close of his important book on Nuremberg, *The Anatomy of the Nuremberg Trials,* Telford Taylor raises what he calls "political warts on Nuremberg and the IMT." "The biggest wart," Taylor writes, "was the presence, necessary as it was, of the Soviet judges on the bench." Do you agree? Consider both the general principle of Soviet involvement in the trial and specific instances that arose, from time to time, during the course of the Nuremberg Trial.

12. Can you identify other "warts" at Nuremberg? Were these inescapable, given the circumstances of 1945? Do you think that Nuremberg can be

said to have set a memorable and valuable precedent, notwithstanding the existence of these warts?

13. One of the most persistent arguments against Nuremberg was the accusation of what was called *tu quoque*, the charge that the Allies had no justification for trying the accused because they had also committed the crimes for which the German defendants had to answer. What do you think of this argument? Can you point to specific instances in which this became a problem for the prosecution?

14. How were crimes against the Jews, what we now call the Holocaust, understood at Nuremberg (Documents 18, 19, 22, 24, 25, 56, 57, 58, 59, 60, 61, 62, 69)? What differences can you detect among the presentations of Allied prosecutors? What place was given to these crimes in the overall understanding of Nazi criminality, and how does this picture differ from our perspective, more than seventy years after the events?

15. In his opening address to the Nuremberg Tribunal, the American Chief Prosecutor, Robert H. Jackson, described the hastily improvised nature of the trial: "Less than 8 months ago nearly all our witnesses and documents were in enemy hands. The law had not been codified, no procedures had been established, no tribunal was in existence, no usable courthouse stood here, none of the hundreds of tons of official German documents had been examined, no prosecuting staff had been assembled, nearly all of the present defendants were at large, and the four prosecuting powers had not yet joined in common cause to try them. I should be the last to deny that the case may well suffer from incomplete researches and quite likely will not be the example of professional work which any of the prosecuting nations would normally wish to sponsor" (Document 22). How and why do you think these obstacles were overcome? Might these conditions have affected the conduct of the Nuremberg Trial? In what way? What was the basis, and what were the consequences of the decision, especially by the Americans, to center their case on written evidence?

16. All things considered, do you think that the accused German war criminals received a "fair trial" at Nuremberg? What alternatives were available to the Allies at the time, and to what degree were they prepared to consider different options?

Selected Bibliography

BIBLIOGRAPHICAL AIDS

Lewis, John R. *Uncertain Judgment: A Bibliography of War Crimes Trials.* Santa Barbara: ABC-Clio, 1979.

Robinson, Jacob, and Henry Sachs. *The Holocaust: The Nuremberg Evidence.* Jerusalem: Yad Vashem, 1976.

Tutorow, Norman E., ed. *War Crimes, War Criminals, and Source Book.* New York: Greenwood Press, 1986.

DOCUMENTARY SOURCES

Francis Biddle Papers. Syracuse University.

Carnegie Endowment for International Peace, Division of International Law. *Violation of the Laws and Customs of War: Reports of Majority and Dissenting Reports of American and Japanese Members of the Commission of Responsibilities, Conference of Paris 1919,* pamphlet no. 32. Oxford: Clarendon Press, 1919.

Friedman, Leon, ed. *The Law of War: A Documentary History.* 2 vols. New York: Random House, 1972.

Inter-Allied Information Committee. *Punishment for War Crimes: The Inter-Allied Declaration Signed at St. James's Palace, London, on 13th January 1942 and Relative Documents.* 2 vols. [London]: His Majesty's Stationery Office, [1942].

International Military Tribunal. *Trial of the Major War Criminals before the International Military Tribunal, Nuremberg, 14 November 1945–1 October 1946.* 42 vols. Nuremberg: International Military Tribunal, 1947.

Jackson, Robert H. "Report to the President from Justice Robert H. Jackson, Chief of Counsel for the United States in the Prosecution of Axis War Criminals." *American Journal of International Law* 39 (Supplement, 1945): 178–90.

———. *Report of Robert H. Jackson, United States Representative to the International Conference on Military Trials, London, 1945.* Washington, D.C.: Department of State, 1949.

———. *The Nürnberg Case as Presented by Robert H. Jackson, Chief of Counsel for the United States, together with Other Documents.* New York: Cooper Square Publishers, 1971.

United States Office of Chief Counsel for Prosecution of Axis Criminality. *Nazi Conspiracy and Aggression.* 11 vols., 2 supplements. Washington, D.C.: Government Printing Office, 1946–1948.

CONTEMPORARY LEGAL AND OTHER COMMENTARY

Alderman, Sidney S. "Negotiating on War Crimes Prosecutions, 1945." In Raymond Dennett and Joseph E. Johnson, eds., *Negotiating with the Russians,* 49–98. Boston: World Peace Foundation, 1951.

Anderson, C. Arnold. "The Utility of the Proposed Trial and Punishment of Enemy Leaders." *American Political Science Review* 37 (1943): 1081–1100.

Benton, Wilbourn E., and Georg Grimm, eds. *Nuremberg: German Views of the War Trials.* Dallas: Southern Methodist University Press, 1955.

Berger, Jacob. "The Legal Nature of War Crimes and the Problem of Superior Command." *American Political Science Review* 38 (1944): 1203–8.

Bernays, Murray C. "Legal Basis of the Nuremberg Trials." *Survey Graphic* 35 (January 1946): 4–9.

Brand, James T. "Crimes against Humanity and the Nürnberg Trials." *Oregon Law Review* 28 (1949): 93–119.

Calvocoressi, Peter. *Nuremberg: The Facts, the Law, and the Consequences.* London: Chatto and Windus, 1947.

Donnedieu de Vabres, Henri. "Le Procès de Nuremberg." *Revue de droit pénal et de criminologie* 27 (1946): 480–90.

Glueck, Sheldon. "By What Tribunal Shall War Offenders Be Tried?" *Harvard Law Review* 56 (1943): 1059–89.

———. "The Nurenberg Trial and Aggressive War." *Harvard Law Review* 59 (1945–1946): 396–456.

———. *The Nuremberg Trial and Aggressive War.* New York: Kraus Reprint Corporation, 1946.

Jackson, Robert H. "Nürnberg in Retrospect." *Canadian Bar Review* 27 (August–September 1949): 761–81.

Jaspers, Karl. "The Significance of the Nurnberg Trials for Germany and the World." *Notre Dame Lawyer* 22 (1946): 150–60.

Kelley, Douglas M. *22 Cells at Nuremberg.* New York: Greenberg, 1947.

Kelsen, Hans. "Will the Judgment in the Nuremberg Trial Constitute a Precedent in International Law?" *International Law Quarterly* 1 (Summer 1947): 153–71.

Konovitz, Milton R. "Will Nuremberg Serve Justice?" *Commentary,* January 1946, 9–15.

Kranzbühler, Otto. "Nuremberg Eighteen Years Afterwards." *De Paul Law Review* 14 (1964–1965): 333–47.

Lauterpacht, H. "The So-Called Anglo-American and Continental Schools of Thought in International Law." *British Year Book of International Law* 12 (1931): 31–62.

————. "The Law of Nations and the Punishment of War Crimes. *British Year Book of International Law* 21 (1944): 58–95.

Leventhal, Harold, Sam Harris, John M. Woolsey Jr., and Warren F. Farr. "The Nuremberg Verdict." *Harvard Law Review* 60 (1947): 857–907.

Levy, Albert G. D. "The Law and Procedure of War Crime Trials." *American Political Science Review* 37 (1943): 1052–81.

Lippe, Victor Frh. von der. *Nürnberger Tagebuchnotizen, November 1945 bis Oktober 1946.* Frankfurt am Main: Verlag Fritz Knapp, 1951.

"The Nürnberg Novelty." *Fortune,* December 1945, 140–41.

Phleger, Herman. "Nuremberg — a Fair Trial?" *Atlantic Monthly,* April 1946, 60–65.

Radin, Max. "Justice at Nuremberg." *Foreign Affairs* 24 (1946): 369–84.

Schwelb, Egon. "Crimes against Humanity." *British Year Book of International Law* 23 (1946): 178–226.

Stimson, Henry L. "The Pact of Paris: Three Years of Development." *Foreign Affairs* 11 (supplement, 1932), i–ix.

————. "The Nuremberg Trial: Landmark in Law." *Foreign Affairs* 25 (1947): 179–89.

Taylor, Telford. *Nuremberg Trials: War Crimes and International Law.* New York: Carnegie Endowment for International Peace, 1949.

Trainin, A. N. *Hitlerite Responsibility under Criminal Law.* Edited by A. Y. Vyshinsky, translated by A. Rothstein. London: Hutchinson, [1945].

United Nations War Crimes Commission. *History of the United Nations War Crimes Commission and the Development of the Laws of War.* London: United Nations War Crimes Commission, 1948.

Vambery, Rustem. "Law and Legalism." *Nation,* December 1, 1945, 573–75.

Wechsler, Herbert. "The Issues of the Nuremberg Trial." *Political Science Quarterly* 62 (1947): 11–26.

West, Rebecca. *A Train of Powder.* New York: Viking Press, 1965.

Wright, Lord. "War Crimes under International Law." *Law Quarterly Review* 62 (1946): 40–52.

Wright, Quincy. "Legal Positivism and the Nuremberg Judgement." *American Journal of International Law* 42 (1948): 405–14.

Wyzanski, Charles E. Jr. "Nuremberg — a Fair Trial?" *Atlantic Monthly,* April 1946, 66–70.

————. "Nuremberg in Retrospect." *Atlantic Monthly,* December 1946, 56–59.

OTHER SOURCES

Bass, Gary Jonathan. *Stay the Hand of Vengeance: The Politics of War Crimes Tribunals.* Princeton: Princeton University Press, 2000.

Barrett, John Q. "The Nuremberg Roles of Justice Robert H. Jackson." *Washington University Global Studies Law Review* 6 (2007), 511–25.

Bassiouni, M. Cherif. *Crimes against Humanity in International Criminal Law.* Dordrecht: Martinus Nijhoff Publishers, 1992.

Best, Geoffrey. *Humanity in Warfare: The Modern History of the International Law of Armed Conflicts.* London: Weidenfeld and Nicolson, 1980.

———. *War and Law since 1945.* Oxford: Clarendon Press, 1994.

Biddis, Michael. "The Nuremberg Trial: Two Exercises in Judgment." *Journal of Contemporary History* 16 (1981): 597–615.

———. "Victor's Justice? The Nuremberg Trial." *History Today* 45 (May 1995): 40–46.

Biddle, Francis. *In Brief Authority.* Garden City, N.Y.: Doubleday, 1962.

Bloxham, Donald, *Genocide on Trial: War Crimes Trials and the Formation of Holocaust History and Memory.* Oxford: Oxford University Press, 2001.

———. "The Nuremberg Trials and the Occupation of Germany." *Cardozo Law Review* 27 (2006), 1599–608.

———. " 'The Trial That Never Was': Why There Was No Second International Trial of Major War Criminals at Nuremberg." *History* 87 (2002), 41–60.

Bosch, William J. *Judgment on Nuremberg: American Attitudes toward the Major German War-Crime Trials.* Chapel Hill: University of North Carolina Press, 1970.

Bower, Tom. *The Pledge Betrayed: America and Britain and the Denazification of Postwar Germany.* Garden City, NY: Doubleday, 1982.

Bush, Jonathan. "'The Supreme . . . Crime' and its Origins: The Lost Legislative History of the Crime of Aggressive War." *Columbia Law Review* 102 (2002), 2324–423.

———. "Nuremberg: The Modern Law of War and Its Limitations." *Columbia Law Review* 93 (1993), 2022–86.

———. "The Prehistory of Corporations and Conspiracy in International Criminal Law: What Nuremberg Really Said." *Columbia Law Review* 109 (2009), 1094–242.

Clark, Roger S. "Crimes against Humanity." In George Ginsburgs and V. N. Kudriavtsev, *The Nuremberg Trial and International Law,* 177–212. Dordrecht: Martinus Nijhoff Publishers, 1990.

Conot, Robert E. *Justice at Nuremberg.* New York: Harper and Row, 1983.

Dautricourt, Joseph Y. "Crime against Humanity: European Views on Its Conception and Its Future." *Journal of Criminal Law and Criminology* 40 (1949–1950): 170–75.

Davidson, Eugene. *The Trial of the Germans: An Account of the Twenty-Two Defendants before the International Military Tribunal at Nuremberg.* New York: Collier Books, 1966.

Deák, István. "Misjudgment at Nuremberg." *New York Review of Books,* October 7, 1993, 46–52.

Dinstein, Yoram. *The Defence of 'Obedience to Superior Orders' in International Law.* Leyden: A. W. Sijthoff, 1965.

Dodd, Christopher J. *Letters from Nuremberg: My Father's Narrative of a Quest for Justice.* New York: Crown, 2007.

Dönitz, Karl. *Ten Years and Twenty Days.* Translated by R. H. Stevens. Cleveland: World, 1959.

Douglas, Lawrence. *The Memory of Judgment: Making Law and History in the Trials of the Holocaust.* New Haven: Yale University Press, 2007.

Errera, Roger. "Nuremberg: le droit et l'histoire (1945–1985)." In *L'Allemagne nazie et le génocide juif,* 44–64. Paris: Gallimard/Le Seuil, 1985.

Flanner, Janet. *Janet Flanner's World: Uncollected Writings, 1932–1975.* New York: Harcourt Brace Jovanovich, 1979.

Fox, John P. "The Jewish Factor in British War Crimes Policy in 1942." *English Historical Review* 92 (1977): 82–106.

Fritzsche, Hans. *The Sword in the Scales.* Translated by Diana Pike and Heinrich Fraeker. London: Alan Wingate, 1953.

Gerhart, Eugene C. *America's Advocate: Robert H. Jackson.* Indianapolis: Bobbs-Merrill, 1958.

Gilbert, G. M. *Nuremberg Diary.* New York: Signet, 1947.

Ginsburgs, George. "The Nuremberg Trial: Background." In George Ginsburgs and V. N. Kudriavtsev, *The Nuremberg Trial and International Law,* 9–37. Dordrecht: Martinus Nijhoff Publishers, 1990.

———, and V. N. Kudriavtsev. *The Nuremberg Trial and International Law.* Dordrecht: Martinus Nijhoff Publishers, 1990.

Goldenberg, Sydney L. "Crimes against Humanity — 1945–1970." *Western Ontario Law Review* 10 (1971): 1–55.

Gros, Dominique. "Le 'Statut des Juifs' et les manuels en usage dans les facultés de droit (1940–44): de la description à la légitimation." In Philippe Baurd, ed., *La Violence politique dans les démocraties européennes occidentales,* 139–71. Paris: L'Harmattan, 1993.

Harris, Whitney R. *Tyranny on Trial: The Evidence at Nuremberg.* Dallas: Southern Methodist University Press, 1954.

Heberer, Patricia, and Jürgen Matthäus. *Atrocities on Trial: Historical Perspectives on the Politics of Prosecuting War Crimes.* Lincoln: University of Nebraska Press, 2008.

Heller, Kevin Jon. *The Nuremberg Military Tribunals and the Origins of International Criminal Law.* Oxford: Oxford University Press, 2011.

Hirsch, Francine. "The Soviets at Nuremberg: International Law, Propaganda, and the Making of the Postwar Order." *American Historical Review* 113 (2008): 701–30.

Hyde, H. Montgomery. *Norman Birkett: The Life of Lord Birkett of Ulverston.* London: Hamish Hamilton, 1964.

Kilmuir [David Maxwell-Fyfe]. *Political Adventure: The Memoirs of Lord Kilmuir.* London: Weidenfeld and Nicolson, 1964.

Kirchheimer, Otto. *Political Justice: The Use of Legal Procedure for Political Ends.* Princeton: Princeton University Press, 1961.

Knieriem, August von. *The Nuremberg Trials.* Chicago: Henry Regnery, 1959.

Kochavi, Arieh J. *Prelude to Nuremberg: Allied War Crimes Policy and the Question of Punishment.* Chapel Hill: University of North Carolina Press, 1998).

Larin, A. M. "The Trial of the Major War Criminals." In George Ginsburgs and V. N. Kudriavtsev, *The Nuremberg Trial and International Law,* 76–88. Dordrecht: Martinus Nijhoff Publishers, 1990.

———. "The Verdict of the International Military Tribunal." In George Ginsburgs and V. N. Kudriavtsev, *The Nuremberg Trial and International Law,* 88–98. Dordrecht: Martinus Nijhoff Publishers, 1990.

Lewis, Mark. *The Birth of the New Justice: The Internationalization of Crime and Punishment, 1919–1950.* Oxford: Oxford University Press, 2014.

Luban, David. *Legal Modernism.* Ann Arbor: University of Michigan Press, 1994.

Madajczyk, Czeslaw. "International Trials of War Criminals: Nuremberg and Tokyo, a Comparison and Estimation Half a Century Later." *Bulletin du comité international d'histoire de la deuxième guerre mondiale* 27/28 (1995): 231–43.

Marrus, Michael R. "A Jewish Lobby at Nuremberg: Jacob Robinson and the Institute of Jewish Affairs, 1945–46." *Cardozo Law Review,* Vol. 27 (February 2006), 1651–65.

———. "Three Jewish Emigrés at Nuremberg: Hersh Lauterpacht, Jacob Robinson, and Raphael Lemkin." In Ezra Mendelsohn, Steffani Hoffman, and Richard Cohen, eds., *Against the Grain: Jewish Intellectuals in Hard Times* (New York: Berghahn Books, 2014), 240–54.

Maser, Werner. *Nuremberg: A Nation on Trial.* Translated by Richard Barry. London: Allen Lane, 1979.

Mendelsohn, John. "Trial by Document: The Problem of Due Process for War Criminals at Nuernberg." *Prologue* 7 (Winter 1975): 227–34.

Mullins, Claud. *The Leipzig Trials: An Account of the War Criminals' Trials and a Study of the German Mentality.* London: H. F. & G. Witherby, 1921.

Murphy, John F. "Crimes against Peace at the Nuremberg Trial." In George Ginsburgs and V. N. Kudriavtsev, *The Nuremberg Trial and International Law,* 141–53. Dordrecht: Martinus Nijhoff Publishers, 1990.

———. "Norms of Criminal Procedure at the International Military Tribunal." In George Ginsburgs and V. N. Kudriavtsev, *The Nuremberg Trial and International Law,* 61–75. Dordrecht: Martinus Nijhoff Publishers, 1990.

Neave, Airey. *Nuremberg: A Personal Record of the Major Nazi War Criminals.* London: Hodder and Stoughton, 1978.

Niedhart, Gottfried. "From Total War to Total Peace? Reactions to World War II in Post-War Germany, 1945–1969/1970." *Bulletin du comité international d'histoire de la deuxième guerre mondiale* 27/28 (1995): 283–92.

Padfield, Peter. *Dönitz: The Last Führer.* London: Panther, 1985.

Pannenbecker, Otto. "The Nuremberg War Crimes Trial." *De Paul Law Review* 14 (1964–1965): 348–58.

Papen, Franz von. *Memoirs.* Translated by Brian Connell. London: Andre Deutsch, 1952.

Paul, Allen. *Katyn: The Untold Story of Stalin's Polish Massacre.* New York: Charles Scribner's Sons, 1991.

Persico, Joseph E. *Nuremberg: Infamy on Trial.* New York: Viking, 1994.

Poliakov, Léon. *Le Procès de Nuremberg.* Paris: Julliard, 1971.

Pomorski, Stanislaw. "Conspiracy and Criminal Organization." In George Ginsburgs and V. N. Kudriavtsev, *The Nuremberg Trial and International Law,* 213–48. Dordrecht: Martinus Nijhoff Publishers, 1990.

Priemel, Kim C., and Alexa Stiller, eds. *Reassessssing the Nuremberg Military Tribunals: Transnational Justrice, Trial Narratives, and Historiography.* New York: Berghahn Books, 2012.

Robinson, Jacob. "The International Military Tribunal and the Holocaust: Some Legal Reflections." *Israel Law Review* 7 (1972): 1–13.

Sack, Alexander N. "Punishment of War Criminals and the Defense of Superior Orders." *Law Quarterly Review* 60 (1944): 63–68.

Sands, Philippe. *East West Street: On the Origins of "Genocide" and "Crimes Against Humanity."* New York: Knopf, 2016.

Schabas, William. *Unimaginable Atrocities: Justice, Politics, and Rights at the War Crimes Tribunals.* Oxford: Oxford University Press, 2012.

Schacht, Hjalmar H. G. *Account Settled.* Translated by Edward Fitzgerald. London: Weidenfeld and Nicolson, 1949.

———. *Confessions of 'The Old Wizard': The Autobiography of Hjalmar Horace Greeley Schacht.* Translated by Diana Pyke. Boston: Houghton Mifflin, 1956.

Seidl, Alfred. *Der Fall Rudolf Hess: Dokementation des Verteidiges.* Munich: Universitas Verlag, 1984.

Sereny, Gitta. *Albert Speer: His Battle with Truth.* New York: Knopf, 1995.

Simmons, William B. "The Jurisdictional Bases of the International Military Tribunal at Nuremberg." In George Ginsburgs and V. N. Kudriavtsev, *The Nuremberg Trial and International Law,* 39–59. Dordrecht: Martinus Nijhoff Publishers, 1990.

Smith, Bradley F. *Reaching Judgment at Nuremberg.* New York: Basic Books, 1977.

———. *The Road to Nuremberg.* New York: Basic Books, 1981.

———. *The American Road to Nuremberg: The Documentary Record, 1944–1945.* Stanford, Calif.: Hoover Institution Press, 1982.

Speer, Albert. *Inside the Third Reich: Memoirs by Albert Speer.* Translated by Richard and Clara Winston. New York: Macmillan, 1970.

Taylor, Telford. *Nuremberg and Vietnam: An American Tragedy.* Chicago: Quadrangle Books, 1970.

———. *Anatomy of the Nuremberg Trials: A Personal Memoir.* Boston: Little, Brown, 1992.

Truche, Pierre. "La Notion de crime contre l'humanité: bilan et propositions." *Esprit* 181 (May 1992): 67–87.

Tusa, Ann, and John Tusa. *The Nuremberg Trial.* London: Macmillan, 1983.

Van Schaak, Beth. "The Definition of Crimes Against Humanity: Resolving the Incoherence." *Columbia Journal of Transnational Law,* 37 (1998–1999), 787-850.

Varaut, Jean-Marc. *Le procès de Nuremberg.* Paris: Perrin, 1992.

Watt, D. C. "Nuremberg Reconsidered." *Encounter* 50 (May 1978): 81–87.

Wheeler-Bennett, John, and Anthony Nicholls. *The Semblance of Peace: The Political Settlement after the Second World War.* New York: Norton, 1974.

Wieviorka, Annette. "Le procès de Nuremberg." *L'Histoire* 136 (September 1990): 50–64.

Willis, James F. *Prologue to Nuremberg: The Politics and Diplomacy of Punishing War Criminals of the First World War.* Westport, CT: Greenwood Press, 1981.

Woetzel, Robert K. *The Nuremberg Trials in International Law, with a Postlude on the Eichmann Case.* London: Stevens and Sons Limited, 1962.

Wolfe, Robert. "Putative Threat to National Security as a Nuremberg Defense for Genocide." *Annals of the American Academy for Political and Social Science* 450 (1980): 46–67.

Zoller, Elisabeth. "Grounds for Responsibility." In George Ginsburgs and V. N. Kudriavtsev, *The Nuremberg Trial and International Law,* 102–11. Dordrecht: Martinus Nijhoff Publishers, 1990.

———. "The Status of Individuals under International Law." In George Ginsburgs and V. N. Kudriavtsev, *The Nuremberg Trial and International Law,* 99–102. Dordrecht: Martinus Nijhoff Publishers, 1990.

Zorya, Yuri, and Natalia Lebedeva. "The Year 1939 in the Nuremberg Files." *International Affairs* 10 (October 1989): 117–29.

Acknowledgments (*continued from p. ii*)

Document 1: Reprinted by permission of FOREIGN AFFAIRS, Special Supplement, 1932. Copyright 1932 by the Council on Foreign Relations, Inc. www.ForeignAffairs.com "The Pact of Paris: Three Years of Development."

Document 7: Winston S. Churchill, excerpt from The Gatherine Storm. Copyright 1948 by Houghton Mifflin Company; © renewed 1976 by Lady Spencer Churchill, the Honourable Lady Sarah Audley, and the Honourable Lady Soames. Reprinted by permission of Houghton Mifflin Company. All rights reserved. Reproduced with permission of Curtis Brown, London on behalf of the Estate of Sir Winston Churchill. Copyright © Winston S. Churchill.

Document 8: Bradley F. Smith, The American Road to Nuremberg: The Documentary Record, 1944-1945 (Standford, Calif.: Hoover Institution Press, 1982), 28-29. Excerpt courtesy of the Hoover Institution Press, Stanford, CA.

Document 10: Bradley F. Smith, The American Road to Nuremberg: The Documentary Record, 1944-1945 (Stanford, Calif.: Hoover Institution Press, 1982), 42-44. Excerpt courtesy of the Hoover Institution Press, Stanford, CA.

Document 16: We thank World Peace Foundation for permission to republish an excerpt from Sidney Alderman, "Negotiating on War Crimes Prosecutions, 1945," in Raymond Dennett and Joseph E. Johnson, eds., Negotiating with the Russians (Boston: World Peace Foundation, 1951), 52-53.

Document 20: Excerpt from LETTERS FROM NUREMBERG, Senator Christopher J. Dodd with Lary Bloom, eds., copyright @2007 by Christopher J. Dodd. Used by permission of Three Rivers Press, an imprint of the Crown Publishing, a division of Random House LLC. All rights reserved. Any third party use of this material, outside of this publication, is prohibited. Interested parties must apply directly to Random House LLC for permission.

Document 22: Excerpts from IN BRIEF AUTHORITY by Francis Biddle, copyright @1962 by Francis Biddle. Used by permission of Doubleday, an imprint of the Knopf Doubleday Publishing Group, a division of Random House LLC. All rights reserved. Any third party use of this material, outside of this publication, is prohibited. Interested parties must apply directly to Random House LLC for permission.

Document 27: Excerpts from IN BRIEF AUTHORITY by Francis Biddle, copyright @1962 by Francis Biddle. Used by permission of Doubleday, an imprint of the Knopf Doubleday Publishing Group, a division of Random House LLC. All rights reserved. Any third party use of this material, outside of this publication, is prohibited. Interested parties must apply directly to Random House LLC for permission.

Document 72: Excerpts from IN BRIEF AUTHORITY by Francis Biddle, copyright @1962 by Francis Biddle. Used by permission of Doubleday, an imprint of the Knopf Doubleday Publishing Group, a division of Random House LLC. All rights reserved. Any third party use of this material, outside of this publication, is prohibited. Interested parties must apply directly to Random House LLC for permission.

Document 73: "Nuremberg Eighteen Years Afterward." Excerpt courtesy of De Paul Law Review, Chicago, IL.

Document 74: Reprinted by permission of FOREIGN AFFAIRS, 25, January 1947. Copyright 1947 by the Council on Foreign Relations, Inc. www.ForeignAffairs.com "The Nuremberg Trial: Landmark in Law."

Index